GW00342500

'An individual, unsettling and hilarious foray into the dangers of "doing it"' **JO BRAND**

'A bold and brilliant exploration of modern sexuality. Frank, fearless, and funny – just like Sofie. But I must admit, I was expecting a tad more tahini' **YOTAM OTTOLENGHI**

'This book had sex with my brain!' **SARA PASCOE**

'Sofie is my stand out favourite voice of our generation. Nobody has mastered the art of hilarity, vulnerability, relatability and razor-sharp precision of observation quite like them. This book is vital in its investigation into intimacy and I'm so pissed it wasn't released when I was younger. A must read at any age' **JAMEELA JAMIL**

'It's brilliant, refreshingly honest, and SO relatable. I'd choose this book over sex, any day!' **ROSIE JONES**

'Sofie Hagen is a joy in this world. Their work joyfully invites us into some of the most sensitive parts of our experience. In those tough and tender conversations, Sofie is exactly the guide you want: warm, curious, charming, thoughtful, informative, and funny as hell. What a gift of a person. What a gift of a book' **AUBREY GORDON**

ABOUT THE AUTHOR

So, you're reading the author's bio, are you? This must mean you're curious about the book.

How exciting. This pleases the author, **Sofie Hagen**, who is a multi-award winning (queer and nonbinary) comedian, author and podcaster. She published her first book *Happy Fat* in 2019 and when she realised that, following a messy break up, it had been six years since she last had sex, she decided it was time to write another one.

Sofie lives in London and likes her dog Hank, spreadsheets for everything and long walks on the beach (just kidding, they can fuck off).

Sofie has performed several sell-out shows and hates writing about herself in third person and wonders if her publishers will even notice if she just stops here. Yeah, I'll do that. Thank you for holding my book in your hands, I like you a lot already. I hope you'll like my book as much as I like you.

WILL
I EVER
HAVE
SEX
AGAIN?

SOFIE
HAGEN

BLINK

bringing you closer

First published in the UK by Blink Publishing
An imprint of The Zaffre Publishing Group
A Bonnier Books UK company
4th Floor, Victoria House
Bloomsbury Square,
London, WC1B 4DA
England

Owned by Bonnier Books
Sveavägen 56, Stockholm, Sweden

Hardback – 9781785120398
Trade Paperback – 9781785121302
Ebook – 9781785120404
Audio – 9781785120411

All rights reserved. No part of the publication may be reproduced, stored in
a retrieval system, transmitted or circulated in any form or by any means,
electronic, mechanical, photocopying, recording or otherwise, without prior
permission in writing of the publisher.

A CIP catalogue of this book is available from the British Library.

Designed by Envy Design Ltd
Printed and bound by Clays Ltd, Elcograf S.p.A

1 3 5 7 9 10 8 6 4 2

Copyright © by Sofie Hagen 2024

Sofie Hagen has asserted their moral right to be identified as the author of
this Work in accordance with the Copyright, Designs and Patents Act 1988.

Every reasonable effort has been made to trace copyright holders of material
reproduced in this book, but if any have been inadvertently overlooked the
publishers would be glad to hear from them.

Blink Publishing is an imprint of Bonnier Books UK
www.bonnierbooks.co.uk

For the next person I have sex with.

Please ignore the cobwebs.
And the crying.

CONTENTS

AUTHOR'S NOTE

A note to some of the people I have had sex with, who I mention in this book

IF YOU HAVE HAD sex with me, there is a good chance you will be in this book somewhere. I might even tell the *whole* story. Don't worry, you are anonymous. Or, in case that bums you out and you were hoping for a full-name shout-out, I guess I will say: I'm sorry, you are anonymous.

I need you to know that I have thought a *lot* about what happened between us. Memory is complicated, subjective and malleable. A lot of these encounters happened many years ago and many I have retold to friends (or on stage) so many times that there is a chance I will have changed details without being aware of it. I share what I remember to the best of my knowledge. You could remember differently and, fuck, we could both be wrong. I know what it's like to feel misrepresented by others – I have been doing stand-up for over a decade, in which time I have shared many experiences with fellow comedians (sexy and otherwise – the experiences, not the comedians, although, also the comedians) and I have seen those experiences fleshed out on stage, often with information I didn't recognise. I believe it comes down to the fact that we all experience and see the world differently.

I have had sexual encounters that shaped me and my sexuality for years. With one of you, after we'd had sex, I lay in your arms and looked out the window as the first snow fell that winter, and I felt so much love for you that I never wanted to leave your bed. I thought you were about to say something and I smiled, thinking I knew just what was about to come out of your mouth. Turns out, I didn't know. As you began vomiting, I threw myself off the bed, using your duvet as a shield. I could hear the vomit landing next to me on the floor as it slid off the duvet, like the newly fallen snow outside. Once it was over, I dropped my protective cover, got dressed and rushed into the living room where your five flatmates were still drinking.

'You need to change your sheets,' I told the guy whose bed we had had sex in. 'Because he threw up, not because . . . well,' I added quickly. And then I left.

I think about that sexual encounter probably once a month. Not the vomiting or awkward conversation with your housemates, but about the snow and the fact that you were super hot and I felt lucky that you wanted to sleep with me. And I don't think you ever, *ever* think about it. Or me. If I was to message you now and tell you that I'm writing a book in which I am going to tell people about the time we had sex, I believe you would simply reply, 'We had sex?'

And that is probably why I so willingly and honestly talk about my sex life – if you are one of the people with whom I have shared a bed (or a bush), I assume you have forgotten it. Or that it didn't matter to you. Or worse, that you regret it. Imagining that it *did* matter to you feels somehow self-centred and arrogant. I find it hard to consider myself to be a memorable fuck. Partly because I assume that everyone, other than me, has sex *all the time*. That for you, I was one of many.

Whereas for me, sex feels like a rarity, so when it happens, I will usually put the memory in a little box where it turns into an anecdote and proof that someone wanted to have sex with me. And the more times I show it to people, the more real it becomes. *Look! I did have sex once! It really happened!*

Because if you have forgotten and I never tell people, did the sex-tree really fall in the sex-forest?

All of this to say I am sorry if I tell the story of our sex in this book and you do not feel like it fairly represents you or the experience. And I am sorry if you read about our experience and realise that I felt differently about it to how you assumed I did. I am writing this book because I want to figure out *what's wrong with me* and step one is being honest about my past sexual experiences.

INTRODUCTION

AFTER I HAD SEX for the very first time, with a guy nicknamed Fingers, at the age of 16, I called my older brother and told him.

I was a bit surprised when he turned out to be less enthusiastic about it than me. He had been pushing me to get a social life, to get out there, to be like the other teenagers, ever since I first started obsessing over the boyband Westlife. When the posters covered every inch of my bedroom and I had to start using the ceiling, he begged me to go with him to one of his big club nights. He had enough social capital that he could bring his dorky younger sibling to one of the events he regularly organised in Copenhagen without losing too much street cred.

He insisted that most teenagers would be ecstatic to have an older brother who could get them into the best nightclubs and get them free drinks the whole night. I insisted that I didn't like loud music, unless it was Westlife.

At this point, everyone else my age in my town had already had sex years ago. I would hear stories about classmates having tried threesomes and anal, like it was standard behaviour. I had not even been kissed. My older brother just wanted me to fit in and not be such a weirdo. Which is why I was quite frankly offended that he didn't react better when I announced to him that I was now no longer a virgin. As a matter of fact, he instantly started humming loudly, to stop me from talking. But I had lots to say and I wanted him to hear it.

'What's the big deal?' I asked. 'I mean, *that's it*? This is what I've felt pressured to do for years? This is what the whole world seems to revolve around? *This*? I mean, it's *fine*. It's nice, even. But it was just simple and easy. The world didn't stop spinning and I'm still the same person as I was before.'

'La la la la la!' my brother responded and hung up.

When I think back, I don't remember if Fingers was still in the room, and therefore overhearing this conversation. I imagine if he had been, it would make his First Time Story a lot less fun. I'm not sure 'that's it?' is what a teenage boy wants to hear after his first time penetrating a vagina.[1] Yet I have heard enough horrifying First Time Stories to know that ours *was* probably above average. After school, we went back to his place, ate nachos and watched *Shrek 2*. Halfway through, we put down a towel because we had heard that sometimes you bleed. I laid down on my back, he put on a condom and we had sex in the missionary position while Shrek went on some adventure on the television. It lasted a while. It didn't hurt that much and I didn't bleed. Afterwards, he tied a knot on the condom and made sure to throw it in the bin outside so his mother wouldn't find it in the trash anywhere. I put my clothes back on and called my brother with the very genuinely felt question: that's it?

If I could go back and speak to 16-year-old me, I would tell her – well, a lot of things – to hold on to that feeling. That sex is simple and fun and something which doesn't have to change you. That it can be gentle and with someone who is safe. But I know that she wouldn't listen to the unhinged 35-year-old barging through the front door, ranting about how she should invent something called Instagram and not say no to going to that party in Manchester in 2014, because Prince is going to be there and she will regret not

---

1   Note that the vagina is the inside bit and the vulva is the outside bit. I know that we are saying 'vulva' now because it's often what we mean. We don't actually mean the inside tube. I just really hope that vagina ends up being one of those words which, after a while, we change the meaning of so it actually means the whole thing, because I really don't like the word 'vulva'. It makes me feel icky, like the words 'moist', 'journey', 'phlegm' or 'Tory'.

going forever. Instead, she would continue living her life and make exactly the same mistakes and learn the same lessons. And I would end up the same person that I am today: A person who is still trying to figure out what the big deal is about sex. But instead of wondering why *everyone else* keeps making a big deal out of it, I am now asking myself. Why has it become so complicated? It used to just be fun.

So, hello to you, reading this, and thank you for picking up my book. I will introduce myself.

I am a fat, queer, white, nondisabled, nonbinary person. I grew up in a small town in Denmark, in poverty,[2] raised by a single mother. I was born in 1988 and the first 13 years of my life were overshadowed by being partly raised by an abusive grandfather, so I am still living with mental health issues today. I did not go to university. After attending *gymnasiet*,[3] I worked briefly as a fundraiser in various charity organisations before discovering stand-up comedy. I performed on the Danish comedy scene in Copenhagen till 2012, when I moved to London, UK. I still live in London today, as I am writing this. I am also a quadruple Scorpio, a lover of musical theatre and nonfiction books about psychology and crime. I have a wonderfully stubborn dog named Hank and I rent my home.

---

2   But Danish poverty, which is slightly nicer than poverty in most other places in the world.

3   A Danish term for a mix between high school and college, where you voluntarily do three years of higher education, roughly between the ages of 16 and 19.

In this book, I want to explore how my body, mental health, queerness and gender plays into my (lack of) sex life. I want to look into how misogyny and the patriarchy affects our sex lives. And I want to re-learn what I thought I knew about sex.

This book is a documentation of my journey and the research I have done along the way to try to understand what makes having sex so difficult for me. It started as a diary – personal notes made just for me, as writing it down made me feel less alone. When a publisher showed an interest, I felt panic. *No one is going to care. No one is going to be able to relate.*

I created a questionnaire on Google that asked the question: If you are not having sex, but you wish you were, why do you think that is? It asked people to reflect over their lives – their good and bad sexual experiences – and tell me their stories. I sent it out to my 14,000 newsletter subscribers. I also posted it on all my other social media platforms. I knew I had to get it to a lot of people if I wanted any replies at all. I just knew it was going to be difficult, darn-right impossible, to find people who *also* weren't having sex as much as they wanted to.

Forty-eight hours after I published the questionnaire, I had to shut it down. I had 1,800 replies and they were coming in every minute. *So many* people were sexless. *So many*. Their reasons varied too. Anything from religious upbringings, physical disabilities and ailments, sexual trauma, gender confusion, cost of living crisis, being a new parent, being a closeted queer person, to having a partner they weren't attracted to. And hundreds more.

Since I was 16, I have had quite a few people inside of my body. Some were more welcome than others – like the surgeon who removed my inflamed appendix and that incredibly hot Dutch photographer in an Utrecht Airbnb, to whom I would have *given* my appendix, had he asked. Others have only been inside my vagina with their words or in my fantasies. Some of the experiences feel unreal, like fever dreams, like the guy who referred to himself as 'Big Mike' and claimed that he was moving to Finland the day after, despite there being no packed moving boxes or suitcases in his hoardery house. I wouldn't be able to pick him out of a line-up today.

I am torn between two different versions of that story. In one, I was 20-something, wild, confident and single. I met a hot guy in a bar and we went back to his place in Herne Hill. He read me some of his poems, I elegantly undressed and we had sex. Twice. The next day, when my hair was a sexy mess and I was deliciously hungover, I revelled in the fact that we didn't even exchange phone numbers, like I was in *Sex and the City. Oh God, I totally just fucked some stranger last night. Ha. He was so hot, too.*

Then there is the other version. The one in which I felt honoured that someone that conventionally attractive was interested. The one in which I was very aware that I was one of the only people left in the bar when he approached me and I ignored all the red flags – like the obvious lies about moving to Finland, clearly told for the simple reason that he wanted me to know that this would never become romantic. Just sex. The version in which I actually did leave him my number; he just never called. Though, a few days later, a friend of his got in touch and basically *requested* sex because he had heard I was 'willing to just do it with anyone'. In this version, while still at the bar, I desperately drank as much alcohol as I could afford because I needed to drown out the inner voice telling me that I didn't really want to do this. I wanted to feel wanted, I wanted to orgasm, I wanted to feel safe. Instead, I settled for what I thought would be better than nothing. *What if it never happens again? I'll regret saying no.*

Both versions feel true, at the same time. Part of me is adventurous. I do love sex. I am not looking for a relationship, I love my fat body and I don't particularly need to care about someone to have sex with them. But another part of me is shit-scared. Of intimacy and rejection. Of not being desirable to potential sexual partners.

And I wonder how soon after I slept with Fingers I stopped having sex with my full body and soul. I wonder when a part of me retracted and hid away, so I could have sex without panicking. And yes – I do wonder if I ever have.

Right now, as I write, I haven't had sex in **2,305 days**. And that seems to be quite taboo. In theory, I don't think it should be but, based on people's facial expressions when

I tell them and on my own automatic reluctance to do so, it is. The gasps. Oh, the gasps.

'What? HOW?' they ask, horrified, as if that's not exactly the same question I have for them when they tell me they recently had sex. *How? How did you do that?*

Let me stop here really quickly – I *do* know how sex works. Largely. I hate to brag, but I do know about the penis and the vagina. I also know, to an extent, of penises and other penises. I think I know almost nothing about vaginas engaging with other vaginas. Although, I feel fairly confident I know where the clitoris is – at least, my own. I don't think I've ever found my own G-spot, due to lack of trying, but I know exactly where to look for it: a couple of centimetres in and it should feel like a walnut. That's what all the magazines said.

I also know that you should be able to acquire some sex by either going out and speaking to people or by signing up for dating apps. I have a friend who had sex with her Uber driver last week. Another had sex with her boss. People seem to meet in all kinds of places and while I don't know what happens between 'hello, my name is' and 'shall we have sex now?' I know that it can apparently easily end with that.

I might even have one or two people in my phone who, if it was a life-or-death kind of sex-situation, I could ask to sleep with me and I think they would say yes. Well, first of all they would probably ask who was threatening to kill me if I didn't have sex and that's when I would hang up, realising that they'd seen through my ruse.

So when I want to ask 'HOW?' I mean – psychologically, how? Actually, how? In real life, how?

Particularly if you have been existing in the world as an outcast or a target. Girls are sexualised before they become women; trans bodies can often be made to feel like cages; Black bodies are subject to violence; the patriarchy rapes and we are all taught to hate our bodies for various reasons. Aside from this, most of us will have experienced heartbreak. Mistrust. Feeling unsafe. So many of us are suffering from depression, anxiety, PTSD, OCD and more. And while I grew up in Denmark, I have lived in the UK for long enough to know that you people, here, are mildly sexually repressed.[4]

So how do you just *do it*?

How did I just *do it?*

If I had known that the last time I had sex was going to be the last time I had sex, I would have looked at the penis a bit more. I would have given it a gentle, caring stroke and told it in a whisper, 'Take care.' I would have waved it goodbye like a woman saying goodbye to her lover in 1941 before he went off to war, never to be seen again.

Not to be dramatic about it but at this point, there is no more sex in sight. I'm 35. I was promised that this was

---

4   For anyone not British, when I say 'mildly sexually repressed' I mean 'super duper extremely sexually repressed' because you're not meant to say what you actually mean here. You say, 'I'm okay' when what you mean is, 'I suffer from severe depression', and the other person replies, 'Alright, cheers, mate', which means 'let's not actually discuss emotions now'.

my time. My sexual prime. Apparently, men have their sexual prime when they're 18. I am not quite sure who this refers to – definitely not any of the 18-year-olds I had sex with when I was also a teenager. Or, if *that* was their prime, I feel for whoever they're rabbit-sexing with right now. Should I message my first ever boyfriend and ask if he'd like to try again? It's only been 19 years . . . Don't you have some kind of right to have one more sex with your ex?

It's not that I don't *want to*. I have a sex drive. I like orgasms. They're quite nice. I like being touched. I would, in theory, like to have sex. By sex, I don't mean 'solo sex' – I have all the equipment needed for that sort of thing. I mean sex where someone else is present and also participating in the sex. You know, genitals, hands, kisses, that sort of thing.

I don't just mean sex with men. I am queer, as in 'I don't care which gender you are or aren't, I'm into it', but I've only ever slept with cis[5] penises. I'm a queer virgin.[6] At 35.

I sometimes try. I sign up for dating apps and swipe 'yes please' to anyone who feels safe, which is, let's be honest,

---

5   Cis meaning 'you were assigned a gender at birth and you still feel like that fits very well'. The opposite of trans, basically. There's a whole chapter on this later on, so strap in.

6   Look, I know virginity, historically, has meant 'woman vagina that has not yet been owned by a male penis' or 'pure and undamaged' or whatever else toxic patriarchal bullshit. When I say 'virgin' I simply mean 'has not yet had sex'.

not that many. But I can feel it – the desire. To have sex with this stranger holding a fish or petting a tiger. My sexuality is alive. I watch porn and masturbate and I can't wait to have sex with someone. I am very confident when it comes to sexting. And flirting with people who definitely aren't interested in me. Sometimes, I get a match on the dating apps. I will open strong. They reply and . . . A wave of discomfort overwhelms me. My abdomen feels tight, I start to sweat, my eyelids are heavy and I don't want to have sex anymore. I delete the app and get into bed, under my duvet, where it's safe. And I stay there. Unsexed and unfucked. And then it's suddenly been over half a decade and I wonder what is happening to me and why.

I have tried to read books to get some answers. I thought that maybe *Come As You Are* by Emily Nagoski would help me, as the thousands of reviews on GoodReads and every single person I have talked to about it ever said it would. Within the first couple of sentences, Emily tells me that this book will *transform* my sex life. Which is great – if I actually had a sex life. Don't get me wrong, it's an amazing and crucial book, but it is not what I need. Specifically. Right now.

I don't need a book to *trans*form my sex life, I need a book to *form* my sexlife. I need a book to help me make sense of everything that has already happened to my body and all of my conflicting desires.

The magazines don't help either. I don't need to know 416 different ways of pleasing my partner and I don't need to know anything about positions called things like the Thirsty Crane and the Backwards Bear Attack. I just need to know how to go from 'Oh, that person is kind of cute' to the naked bit. The fun bit.

Not that I am boring, sexually. I have desires. For example, I find the idea of fucking[7] a cis man in the butt with a strap-on wildly arousing and I have no doubt that there are loads of people out there who'd be more than willing to let me do this with them. Yet, the thought of having to research 'plus-size strap-ons' exhausts me and I can't get over the mental image of having to lift up my apron stomach and perhaps rest it on the man's back. *'Excuse me, sir, as I penetrate you from behind, may I use your lower back as a table for my fat?'* I don't want to get into the habit of using people's bodies as convenient surfaces. When I realised I could use my own stomach as a table for my can of Fanta, my housemates at the time had to have a very serious chat with me about 'using the table, like an adult' (my guess is that they were just jealous. #fatprivilege).

I try to explain it to my friends.

'It's been a while since I had sex,' I begin.

'I haven't had sex for *two months*,' my friend exclaims hopelessly with a sigh. I'm surprised she's even capable of breathing, let alone speaking, after suffering from such intense deprivation.

---

7   I think 'fucking' is too harsh here. I actually would just like to make love to a cis man's butt with a strap-on.

'Me neither,' I say. It's true. So many two months have gone by.

She shakes her head. 'It's *so* frustrating.'

She continues to swipe through her Tinder matches, unmatching with people if they wear the wrong shoes. She is wearing wool socks in bright pink Crocs because that is apparently *fashion* in Paris at the moment. It is *very* different from wearing cotton socks in sandals, though, which is a *faux pas* in Paris, and internationally. And enough of a reason to not fuck or love or know someone.

Meanwhile, I don't remember ever having *standards*. I have never known how to say no, so I have done some utterly appalling things. I once fucked a man in a bush who had a pregnant fiancé at home because he pointed at the bush and said, 'Wanna fuck in that bush?' and I simply nodded because what else do you say? Hindsight is beautiful, isn't it? 'No, thank you' is what you say. You say, 'No, thank you, I will not be having sex with a drunk, engaged, mediocre comedian in a bush – which will later turn out to have been not much more than a lone ficus – in Central Copenhagen on a Tuesday.'

What I am saying is: What shoes people are wearing is clearly *not* going to be what keeps me from them.

Once, when I was 17 and working in a sex shop (after having lied and said I was 18), I met up with an older guy I had met online, in a forum just for discussing sex. I was an avid poster. I was the youngest person on there and I would regularly ask about things that I was wondering about. How do you shave down there? Does the first time hurt? Why do I only get wet sometimes? Do fat people have sex? A guy is asking me to get naked on my webcam – is that normal? I have written erotic fanfiction featuring Westlife – would anyone read it and tell me if it sounds like I know what I'm talking about?

Despite what you might be thinking about an online sex forum, this was the most supportive community I could have asked for, as a chubby teenager with questions. The other people on the message board treated me like a younger sibling and were all incredibly protective of me. They would kindly and patiently explain to me anything I needed to know. I made online friends with a 40-year-old sex worker who talked frankly about her job and her experiences. When at one point I said I wanted to do sex work myself, she took the time to tell me all the pros and cons and explain that she didn't think I should do it yet. And if I still wanted to do it when I was older and my frontal lobe had finished developing, and I was ready to deal with the occasional shitty customer, the stigma and the battles against a sex worker-hating government, I was welcome to contact her. She just wanted me to be safe and certain.

The man from the forum who I met up with worked at my local train station, making sure the trains were on the platforms they were meant to be on. He took me into the cockpit[8] of an empty train and closed the door behind

---

8   I'm pretty sure it's not called a cockpit.

us. He had kind brown eyes and dark hair. When you're 16, anyone older than you is ancient. I just knew he was old. In retrospect, he was probably my age now, possibly younger. I was so turned on and I just knew that he knew. I'd read enough erotic fiction to know that when you are turned on, your eyes turn blank and people can tell. To be honest with you, I have never considered double-checking if that is actually true – instead, I have lived my life terrified of the doorbell ringing while I am watching porn in case the delivery person takes one look at me and thinks, 'Red cheeks, blank eyes, yeah, she's watching step-sibling porn.'

I have other tells that I am turned on. If I am speaking English, the occasional Danish word slips in. As if there is not enough blood in my brain to adequately differentiate between the two languages. (It's important to just remind you here that I am from Denmark and Danish is my first language. It is not an odd brain injury that causes me to be fluent in foreign languages whenever I am horny.)

The Train Guy let me push some buttons and sit in the driver's chair of the train. Fortunately, this all took place in Denmark, so speaking fluent Danish was to be expected of me in that situation. But not only could the Train Guy see my eyes (which were, at this point, so blank that they functioned like two mirrors. I imagine I looked exactly like those choir boys in Bonnie Tyler's 'Total Eclipse of the Heart' music video), but he also knew me from an online message board, on which I had announced that my newfound fetish and obsession was to have sex in public. And there we were – on an empty train, on a secluded platform, where the train had to wait for days to be serviced. No one else was around, just me and a handsome man in a bright orange uniform. When he moved slightly closer to me, my vagina fluttered and my mouth turned dry. I could not believe I was about to have sex in a train cockpit.[9] Unfortunately (or so I felt at the time), I was right to be unbelieving. He asked me a bit about my home life and how I was feeling. He talked about the forum as a safe place where he had met many people he came to know as friends.

Maybe he invited me there fully intending to have sex with me, but then saw that behind the probably teen-obnoxious online profile, I was just a 17-year-old. And my eyes most likely didn't look horny, rather they just looked innocent. Or lost. Maybe he never had any intention of sleeping with me – he might just want to keep an eye on me and make sure I was okay. I can appreciate that now, as an adult, of course. Am I still sexually frustrated on behalf of my ignorant teen self? Of course I am. Need I repeat that he was wearing a uniform? Though admittedly not one of the sexy ones: military,[10] fireman, Burger King. Bright orange is officially the least sexy colour. But nevertheless: uniform. But as an adult, after having consumed hundreds of hours of true crime since, am I also painfully aware that

---

9 Yeah, that's definitely not the word.

10 If you ignore, you know, all the murder.

I could have been one hundred per cent dead because of my horny trust in online acquaintances? Oh, absolutely.

What now strikes me as odd is how I never took this as a rejection. Despite having fairly low self-esteem, I was incredibly confident that I was at least sexually wanted, even if I was not attractive. I just *assumed* that Train Guy had wanted desperately to have sex with me but maybe he was scared of getting caught by his boss or it was too cold in the cockpit.[11] That it could be because he wasn't attracted to me never even crossed my mind.

I cannot quite grasp how I could be so sexually free as a teenager – only to, with time, shut down. I have gone from seriously looking into the possibility of being a 17-year-old sex worker, specialising in fetishes and kink, openly discussing this with a whole group of strangers, confident that the entire world wanted to fuck me – to being a 35-year-old who panics if someone swipes left on my dating app profile.

I last had sex on 19 November 2015. When you google 'days since 19 November 2015', Google suggests you click on a site that tells you All The Things That Happened In History On This Date. It tells me that Barack Obama was the president of the US and David Cameron was the prime minister of the UK. 'Hello' by Adele was on everyone's radios. The sixteenth annual Latin Grammys took place in Paradise, Nevada; it was Jodie Foster's

---

11 At this point, it'd be a shame to google it.

birthday and, of course, the whole world was celebrating World Toilet Day.[12]

I could attempt to forget about it. (Sex, that is, not World Toilet Day.) Strangle the realisation that I am a horny adult who wants a sex life, with Netflix,[13] food, social media, a book, work, by focusing on all my other issues, other people or whatever else I can use to *not feel*. There is nothing wrong with this approach; it's called a defence mechanism for a reason. Sometimes you are just not strong enough to face what feels very dangerous.

But I think I am. Now. Right now.

And I can decide to look my vagina in the eye(s) and say, 'Hey, you often let me know that you would like for me to share my bed with someone who can make you feel good. And while I know I have the tools, the skill, the practice and a subscription to the sexiest porn star on OnlyFans to make you happy, you want to start seeing other people. *I get that*. So. Let's do this.'

A study I found identified 237 reasons why people have sex and it feels fair to assume there are probably just as many reasons why people *don't* have sex.

---

12 According to UN Water, 4.2 billion people live without 'safely managed sanitation' and around 673 million people practise 'open defecation'. It's a serious issue and you would know this if you had bothered to look into World Toilet Day.

13 The comma in this sentence is quite important. I want a sex life. I don't want a sex life with Netflix, food and social media.

In this book, I have not been able to cover all of them. It's also important to say that while I talk about asexuality in the sexuality chapter, this book generally does not discuss not *wanting* to have sex. I have had to stick to the issue of not having sex when you do want it. I am also very aware that there is a whole group of people who *want* to have sex but cannot, due to illness or disabilities. I do not feel equipped to talk about this, while I completely respect that it deserves all the attention it can get. Parenting is another topic I have found it hard to cover. So I cannot promise you will be able to find your exact experience in this book, but hopefully you will still be able to learn from others, as I have included some of the stories kindly shared with me by the 1,800 people who got in touch.

You'll see that there are two types of chapters in the book. There are the main chapters, which cover some key areas that affect how we feel about sex and whether we have it or not, like body image, sexuality and gender. In writing these, I spoke to Smart People Who Know Stuff – such as sex educator Justin Hancock, sex and relationship therapist Chantal Gautier, trans author Juno Roche, former sex worker, artist and podcaster Miranda Kane, Drag King Jodie Mitchell and flirtologist Jean Smith. In between these chapters there are some Diary Entries – my thoughts and past sexual experiences that I wrote throughout writing this book, as I tried to process what I was learning and what that meant for me. I jump around in time, remembering things from my past, as I try to make sense of the present.

I am going to be excruciatingly honest – as honest as I can be, whilst avoiding legal repercussions – even when it doesn't make me look good. I know I am flawed and I doubt I can move forward and get the sex life that I want (or even figure out exactly what that would be) without putting my cards on the table.

One of the things I have struggled with in writing this book is that I am a comedian – not a psychologist, a medical professional, a scientist, a sex therapist, sex educator or sociologist, or any other professional who you might traditionally expect to write about a subject as potentially high stakes as this. The last thing I want to do is contribute to a world that is already full of misinformation and celebrities taking wild guesses about health-related issues and presenting them as fact. I do not want to be part of this discourse. Though this is not completely possible, of course. In my research for this book, I have found contradictory claims made by actual professionals, as even within science and between experts opinions differ.

There are issues about which I am unmovably convinced that I am right – such as, for example, in the case of gender. I believe that trans women are women; trans men are men; nonbinary people exist and gender is a spectrum and can be as fluid as you experience it to be. There are people who disagree and I consider these people to be wrong. I will never present their transphobic argument as in any way valid or as 'their side of the story'. The transphobic discourse around gender is severely harmful to trans people (and cis people, actually) and allowing it any space in any media only contributes to the harm. Trans people have existed forever and we will always continue to exist and denying this is ridiculous. I am unrelenting in this stance.

With other standpoints throughout this book, I am less certain. When it comes to the sciences like psychology and sociology, I am still learning, still understanding, and I do not think I will ever reach a point where I don't need to keep learning. I can present what I have learned *so far* and what I believe to be true *right now*, to the best of my ability. I have tried to write in a way that is accessible to my fellow non-academics or multi-linguals. And I have tried not to make broad statements that I am unsure of.

This is why I need to make it clear, up front, that this book is a collection of my experiences, thoughts, feelings, memories, speculations *and* of the information and knowledge I have accumulated – not only on this journey to figure out my sexual problems but also in general, in life. You are reading one person's recollection, one person's point of view, and it is up to you to take on board however much of it you feel is relevant to you. It is not a book full of facts – and actually, I reckon there are very few books like that in existence. Even the ones written by scholars, academics and professionals are ripe with bias, personal interpretations and false claims, either because the author intentionally placed them there or because time has a tendency to prove us wrong.

When I started writing the book, I felt like I was not

educated enough to take this on. Or perhaps, smart enough. Call it imposter syndrome or, perhaps, call it true. Either way, you are reading this now because I decided to do it, despite my concerns. One of the reasons why I went ahead is that on the desk in front of me is a stack consisting of 23 books about sex, all of which I have read (or, at the very least, skimmed carefully). There are more in my bag and on my shelves and on their way. And I have now had many conversations with actual experts and professionals. Yet, nothing made me feel as radically different as when I started reading the 1,800 submissions that came from strangers, that detailed 1,800 different people's perceptions of their own sexual issues. I felt less alone, instantly. In their stories, I learned more about myself. I felt a sense of community, of support, of being part of something bigger than myself. This was when I started feeling confident in writing the book. Not because I necessarily have all the answers, but because I am in a unique position of having these many stories and being privileged enough to write a book, to have the opportunity to bring you an exciting and important sample of the experiences of others that will hopefully make you feel less alone, too.

I am not standing on a podium in front of you, lecturing you on what is the right answer. I am your friend, sitting next to you on the sofa, walking you through what *I* have learned and what *I* (think I) know. I am also simply telling you *my story*. What I have experienced. Some of which I have most likely not fully processed yet, to be honest.

Some of which I only processed as I was writing it. It is safe to say that I write this book from a place of wondering. Of not knowing but wanting desperately to know.

When you read this book, you will undoubtedly start to wonder about your own story – your life story in general or all the little stories from your life that cumulatively make you, you. That can feel quite overwhelming at times. My therapist has a very beautiful way of framing this, which I would like to share.

> Think of yourself as text. You write your own text. And others can – and they will – read your text and interpret it in different ways; that's always going to happen. You can't control how they interpret you. There will be people writing your biography, writing their own text about you, and you can't do anything about that, other than kill them. Not actually kill them, but metaphorically speaking.

I only took slight offence that she felt like she needed to deter me from actual murder. She continued:

> And we do live in a world where the emphasis is on the observer rather than the subject of the observation, unfortunately, but that's only more reason why you need to hold on to your text. Your text wasn't written in your childhood and it can be rewritten. We're ever changing. It's part of the story,

but not all of it. So you sit down with your quill and you write the parts of yourself that you want to be. You go, 'who did I want to be again?' and then you write it. You don't let others write it. And sometimes you'll find someone has written in your text and you can go, 'hang on! That's not me!' and then you delete it and insert whatever you want instead.

As you read this book, I hope you can do the same thing. Take whatever you can use to rewrite your story – and leave the rest.

The Break-Up

(And what I've been doing for the last eight years instead of having sex.)

January 2022

I will later learn that my agent is right – the title I desperately want for my new show is shit. But I am annoyed; I think 'Dead Baby Frog' is an excellent and far superior show title to 'The Parable of the Boiled Frog'. Time will reveal that neither of the titles are that spectacular – and actually, neither is the show itself. I do not know any of this yet. In December 2016, all I know is that my agent is pissing me off by suggesting that my instincts are wrong. I take to Twitter and send a frustrated, late-night direct message to a *more famous,* older, more experienced comedian. 'Hey,' I start, 'Can I ask your advice about a show title?'

'Go on,' he replies instantly. I explain the situation. I tell him which title I prefer and which title my agent prefers. He is on my side and not just that – he is on my side in a very *alpha* way. He is infinitely confident that *we* are right and my agent is wrong. I swoon. And I will continue to swoon all throughout Christmas, as we do not stop messaging each other. In the beginning, these messages are all about stand-up show titles and posters and tours. I feel warm inside each time he tells me that he agrees with me and that, when it comes to the comedy industry, *we* are so much smarter than others. When his name pops up on my phone, I feel giddy.

One night, the messages take a turn. 'I'm so sorry,' he begins, 'I am in a very stressful situation right now. I can't explain it, but I'm having a panic attack. Will you talk to me?'

My heart jumps into my throat and I frantically begin to talk him through it. 'Take five big, deep breaths. Name five things you can see, four things you can touch, three things you can taste, two things you can smell… Just breathe, notice your feet on the floor, talk to me, tell me what is happening.'

A few minutes later, he is fine again. He thanks me and apologises for being so vulnerable. Not a problem. *NOT A PROBLEM AT ALL.* Quite the opposite: I am grateful for the opportunity. This famous, handsome, confident man *needed* me. He needed help and I provided it. I am special. Useful.

Seven years later, I tell a therapist how it all started and in doing so, it occurs to me: 'He was more than a decade older than me. I was in my twenties. He had resources, friends, family... He didn't *need* me. Why would a 40-something man need the help of a 20-something younger comedian? We'd just met.' and my therapist says the word 'grooming'. *But I'm an adult,* I think. *It shouldn't be possible for someone to 'groom' me at this age.* I want to tell her she is overreacting but it also feels right. I thought I had been falling in love with him but that is not how love is meant to feel. I was just falling under his control.

In January 2017, I learn that he has a girlfriend. I feel silly for thinking that the constant texting, the trauma bonding, the fact that I get to see sides of him he tells me 'no one else sees' means we are more than just friends. I think to myself, *I am just misreading signals.* Why would someone *like him* want someone *like me*?

At the end of January, we are still texting daily. I wake up and check my phone and there will be a message from him saying, 'Why are you not awake yet?' and I feel warm inside. *Just friends.* It's a normal *friend*-thing to do. One day, I send him a photo of my view from a beach holiday I am on. My feet are in the photo so I joke, 'I guess if you have a foot fetish, I just gave you some free content.' He gets weird and won't tell me why. Like trying to extract water from a rock, over the course of the next 24 hours, I manage to get a partial truth out of him: he does have a fetish. He is immensely ashamed. Only very few people know about it. It isn't feet. It's worse. I would *simply be disgusted* if I knew.

Desperate to know what it is – and desperate to be included in this secret – I promise that I will not be disgusted. That I am super open-minded.

In 2022, my therapist will say about this, 'So you promised him you would have no boundaries at all?' The word *'grooming'* comes up again.

He finally, and seemingly reluctantly, tells me the secret, after I have been begging for over a day, and not before I have raised genuine concerns that it is something illegal. It isn't. Yes, it is unusual and yes, some people would squirm at the thought. But not *me*. I'm cool. I am now his confidante. I tell him that I think it is super great and fine and that I would love to ask him questions about it.

I do. I ask how it started and he tells me. In great detail. He shares stories about the fetish. He tells me the stories as if they were short stories. He paints the characters involved with so much detail that I know exactly how they look, the way they smirk, the smell of their hair and how the tension between them feels. I am transported back to 1994, 1998, 2002 and whenever else he partook in his fetish with people. It is not a simple fetish – he cannot just look at a photo of it – he needs the entire situation to be right. It cannot be *any* person, it has to be specific people. And they have to feel a certain way about it, too.

I begin to envy the people in the stories. I want to be

described with as much attention to detail. I want him to remember how I smell in 20 years' time. He describes the women as goddesses with an intoxicating hold on him. He never uses sexual words. He never says 'pussy' or 'dick'. At most, he will say that he was 'affected' by the situation and I am left to just imagine a bulge in his jeans. Which I do. And it 'affects' me.

His fetish does not involve touch or sex. You could walk in on him doing it and never know that he was turned on by the situation. In the same way as you could watch someone do the dishes and not know that person is incredibly turned on by doing the dishes. But I will know, now. He is intelligent, interesting, sexy – and most importantly, he is *letting me in*. I am one of the few that knows this huge secret. He seems vulnerable. His vulnerability feels like a fragile piece of porcelain and it is my job not to drop it or smash it. I have to constantly hold it carefully in my hands – not be too loud, not push it, not ever let it go. I see him on television, knowing that tens of thousands of other people are watching too, but no one knows him *like me*.

Sometimes, he will disappear for days. We will have sent hundreds of texts back and forth each day for months and then suddenly, nothing. For days. I will begin to panic. What if I fucked up? What if I did something wrong? I will cry for hours. Cancel work. I begin to worry for his safety. I check all of his social media. Seeing a sign of life is almost worse – it means he is *fine*, but just ignoring me.

Eventually, he will text me back. If I mention that I was in any way upset or concerned, he will make me feel guilty for making him feel guilty. 'I was working,' he will say, exasperated. 'Everyone wants me to be there for them, 24/7, and I'm just doing my best.'

I end up apologising – 'I'm sorry, I should not be pushing you this hard. I know I am just lucky to know you.' I refuse to be like these *other* people in his life, demanding that he is available to me 24/7. I am cool. I am *chill*. I stop hounding him when he disappears and I never tell him that I panic and cry. That would not be *chill*.

One day, while we are both still pretending that we are *just friends*, I ask him if I am the type of person he would find attractive. If he has ever imagined me doing this fetish thing with him. He admits that yes, of course he has. I feel lucky. I am on a bus going through Elephant and Castle when I ask him about his girlfriend. His reply lights up my phone and face: 'Oh, she knows about us. She loves that we talk about sexy stuff together. She knows that I need this.'

I start to cry as I tell him, 'I have been kept a secret so many times in relationships and I never want to be that again. This means the world to me. I'm so happy.' He promises me that he will never keep me a secret.

A year has passed but a year with him feels like less than that. While the texting is intense and daily, he is busy being famous. I have seen him maybe five times in real life and each time is brief and in public. The conversations about his fetish have evolved – they are now fantasies that we take turns sharing. I have learned everything about his fetish, enough to be able to construct scenarios that will turn him on to the point he has to excuse himself from meetings and go to the bathroom to 'give himself a hand'. We insert people we both know into these fantasies. I learn which adjectives he finds particularly hot. When it is his turn to share a fantasy, I often have to google the words I don't know, which I love. *It is sexy to be smart*, I think. And he is smart.

It is so different from any sexting I have ever participated in before. With my ex, I would get a late-night text that just said 'my dick is in your mouth' and I would feel nothing. While new Celebrity Boyfriend simply begins by describing a room, an outfit or a character's complex state of mind, and I feel more turned on than ever before.

We say, 'I love you' quite quickly, within a few months, and shortly thereafter, we admit to being *in love*. We announce that we miss each other and long for each other, in between the fetish stories we share.

When we do see each other, we hold hands across a table or our legs touch. He will come to my room in a shared flat and we might not touch at all. It feels like torture.

More than a year passes before we do the fetish together. It is, to this day, one of the most sexually exhilarating things I have ever experienced. Even before I meet up with him, I felt like I have horniness coming out of both eyes. My knees are weak and I forget how to speak English.

You could have walked in on us and you would not have known that this was extremely sexual and intimate because this is the nature of the fetish. But we know. At no point do we touch. We are fully dressed. In one sense, we do an incredibly mundane thing together, but if you knew what we knew, you would have seen a sexual act that had a year of foreplay leading up to it. My face is red for three hours afterwards and my eyes glazed over. His hands shake and I can *see* that it 'affects' his penis too.

Still, no kissing. I am painfully aware that from the outside, it does not look how it feels. We rarely see each other in real life, we text about scenarios that are not inherently sexual, we do not touch and he has a girlfriend. But he will text me that I am the love of his life. That he cannot believe how perfect I am. That he tracks my flights so he will know exactly when I land, so he can text me again. That he would love for us to have the same sleep schedule because waking up or falling asleep without hearing from me is too painful. He tells me he loves me. I tell him that I love him too.

And we do not kiss. We also don't do any of these things in front of his girlfriend. 'She knows about us,' he reassures me, 'but that doesn't mean she wants to *see* it or *hear* about it.'

I understand.

Almost a year to the day after he first messaged me, I am at a small gathering with him, his girlfriend and a few mutual friends. His girlfriend makes a small comment that makes it feel like the room is spinning because it is suddenly clear to me: she does not know about us. He lied. I *am* a secret. I feel incredibly stupid. I blame myself. I *should have known.*

The next day, I confront him. I demand to see him in person. I say, 'She doesn't know about me, does she?'

He shakes his head. His face is white and somehow wrinklier than normal. He looks like he has been awake for weeks. Is he shivering?

'Are you okay?' I ask. I am not.

'Everyone is just so upset with me all the time and I am just doing my best,' he says in a deep, husky voice. 'I don't know what to do. I won't harm myself, I think...'

It feels as if the floor disappears beneath me and I put my hand on his. 'It's okay, you'll be fine. I'm here.'

And that is the extent of the confrontation. Over the next four years, he subtly threatens suicide whenever he is held accountable for any kind of behaviour. Over the next five years, I stay his secret partner. I befriend his girlfriend and suppress the guilt because he wants me to. 'It will make it easier for us to hang out.'

Kissing me is something he *really, really* wants to do, but it would make him feel too guilty and also, if he kissed me, he would not be able to stop. I accept that as a reply. I let him know – calmly, so as to not upset him – that I would not be comfortable doing anything else physical *before* we kiss. I explain that my awful ex refused to kiss me during sex because he liked that I did not get that intimacy. It made me feel cheap and taken advantage of. I tell him that I will not touch his penis before he kisses me.

A couple of weeks later, in a cab, he places my hand on his crotch. I want to move it but I don't want him to be upset. Besides, it is *touch*, something I crave. And yes, I set my boundary but maybe I shouldn't be so strict. Of *course* he can't kiss me. It would be mad. But this is just my hand resting on his hard penis, in a cab. I feel *lucky*.

In 2022, my therapist will say: 'So you actually managed to set a boundary and he then crossed that boundary deliberately, to test you.'

A year and a half into our relationship, we go out, all of us. His girlfriend, him, me and a mutual friend of ours. She is beautiful and I know she is on his list of People He Is Attracted To. The morning after our night out, she tells me with a giggle that he was texting her in a flirty and sexual way the night before. I laugh and say, 'Oh my god, really?' and go to the bathroom and cry. I sob violently for over an hour and text her that I have food poisoning and she should leave.

I text him. He tells me he made a mistake, that he doesn't know what to do, that he is suicidal now. 'I can't believe I hurt you, when you mean the most to me in the entire world,' he says. He is crying, he says. I end it. He shows up at my home and apologises. It feels like a huge gesture; we so rarely see each other. I feel lucky.

I tell him that I am not opposed to him seeing other

people. I am technically other people. But I need to know if he is. 'Just tell me – if you want to do something with her, just let me know. And it's fine.'

He shakes his head and starts to cry. 'No, I only want you. I am not interested in her. I was drunk. I was stupid. I will never speak to her again.'

I sigh. 'I would never ask you to do that. Of course you can speak to her. Just tell me if it gets sexual or romantic?'

'It won't. Ever. You're all I want.'

I trust him. Four months later, I catch them texting. She had sent him a sexy photo of herself. He explains that she might have a crush on him but he keeps rejecting her. I suggest that we could just *tell her* about us, but he says no. He will not explain why.

At her Christmas party, I see her grabbing his knee. I leave the party without my coat because I am crying so much, I just need to get out of there. He tells me, when he shows up at mine later, that she was just holding him for balance. That I am *crazy* if I think he would risk what we have.

At his birthday party, she has her hand resting on his penis for over an hour, even though his girlfriend is in the room. She doesn't see it, but I do. I take a photo of it so he won't be able to lie to me (or rather, so he won't be able to convince me that I was making it up). I am shaking and weeping in the cab, all the way home. The next morning, he tells me that it didn't happen. I show him the photo I took. Their faces are close together and her hand is fully covering his entire crotch. He says it must have happened for just a second because he didn't notice it *at all*.

'I spent my entire birthday looking after you, making sure you were alright, and I thought it would be okay if I took a little time for myself, to catch up with friends.'

'Her hand was on your dick,' I cry. 'Sorry for ruining your birthday with my drama,' I also say.

He promises me that we will tell her about us, so she will stop molesting him in public. But we need to figure out how. He makes me promise not to tell her anything without his consent. I promise. The next two years, he refuses to talk about it again.

On his girlfriend's birthday, he gives me a peck on the mouth. We are four years into our relationship and this is the closest thing we will ever get to kissing. All we have ever done at this point is lie naked next to each other in a hotel in Brighton while his girlfriend is on holiday. I don't sleep. I cry so hard while he snores because he still doesn't touch me. We have a view of the ocean, we have had wine. We undressed and he fell asleep. I feel so unwanted. I never tell him this. I do not want to upset him.

The pandemic saves me. I get a dog, which irrationally infuriates him. 'Now we can't see each other as much! It's pretty much impossible!' he says. I am confused. We have seen each other three times in a year. I made myself available whenever he had a brief window, during which he was on his phone, tweeting to fans. When I asked him to please be present in the room, he informed me, annoyed, 'These people need me!'

'It's impossible to lie in bed together when you have the dog,' he says. No, it isn't. And we do lie in bed together. He half-heartedly holds me and my dog is excited to say hi to him. But he hates my dog, so I send Hank to the floor instead. The first time they meet, my dog pisses on the floor. He has not done that with anyone else. Trust your dogs, they know.

Our relationship feels strained, so we meet up to talk. I begin to cry and his phone rings. He picks it up and conducts an interview with BBC Leeds while I weep silently, so as to not disturb him. Afterwards, he has to go. We will find another time to chat, he says.

We never do.

Five years into this, in January 2022, I open my phone to buy train tickets for a trip next month. I type in the wrong letter at the beginning of my email address and his email address comes up, along with tiny stars that together make his password. I don't even think – I hurry to Gmail and put his details in. He must have accidentally saved them to my iCloud when he used my computer once. Then, I'm in. His entire life appears before me and I feel a five-year-long sigh of relief from finally seeing it, rather than the tiny glimpses he would sometimes allow me.

There are so many women. I find a fetish fantasy in his drafts, written for someone else. It starts with the words 'this is not how we usually do this', so I know there is a 'usual' way they do this.

I break up with him over text. 'Let me explain,' he says and then I don't hear from him for another twenty-four hours. I text him again: 'I'm still waiting?'

'People are just demanding so much from me at the moment,' he says. 'I will reply before Tuesday.'

It's Saturday. I wait till Tuesday. On Tuesday evening, I message him again. Wait till Thursday, he lets me know.

'I am breaking up with you,' I text him. 'I am not waiting a week for you to let me.'

He sends a long letter over email. It explains that I have got it all wrong. Everything has caveats. Yes, he is madly in love with me, but also things are complicated and he is just under so much pressure at the moment and he actually blames me for ruining us because I got that dog and he is just in a tricky situation and the pandemic was really hard for him and he just doesn't know what he wants and other I'll Take 'Things Emotionally Immature Men Say Instead Of Just Getting Fucking Therapy' for £500, please.

I keep looking through the screenshots I took of all his emails. The receipts. I feel a bit like a superhero for outsmarting him and looking in all the right places, for discovering the secrets he had tried to hide. It's a lot of admin to have lies and secrets, and sometimes, apparently, you forget about the drafts folder. I never tell him exactly what I found in his emails, I just tell him that I 'know everything'.

His letter tells me that whatever I found, I am misinterpreting. He mentions the dog again, as if the dog I got in 2020 made him sext with someone else in 2019. If that is the case, then my dog is magical and I am glad I got him. He writes an entire paragraph about how he needs to stop beating himself up. That he has suffered enough. That he needs to stop self-blaming. The letter is full of excuses, lies, manipulation, deflection and self-pity. There is no accountability, no honesty and, most importantly, no apology.

I write a reply which is arguably a lot more tempered than it should be. I tell him that he needs therapy. I write:

The world likes you. We all just walk around loving you unconditionally. You keep saying that you're being treated unfairly by people, but the call is coming from inside the house. You are the only person who is uncomfortable with your truth. Maybe that is why you lie so much, to everyone. You don't think you deserve to be loved, so you fuck it all up. You make sure we hate you, the way you think we should. I don't think you're a bad person, I think you're a deeply broken person. I think you're shit-scared to look yourself in the mirror. You're not keeping the truth from us. You're keeping it from yourself. You hurt other people because you are trying to protect yourself from your own self-hatred. You wish I would just call you a piece of shit, because then you can be the victim. I'm not going to do that. I forgive you and now I'm moving on.

I send it and I never receive a reply.

So now it's a week into January 2022 and I'm trying to tidy up this cesspool that is my home, filled with stuff I shamefully bought on Amazon in a desperate attempt to fill the void with same-day delivery. Instead of picking up and moving a suitcase full of tour props, I kick it, so it flies into the living room, hitting my sofa table, which causes a can of half-empty lukewarm Coke to drop onto my rug. I sigh with the drama of someone shaking their fists against the sky and pick it up. Half-arsed, I throw a dirty t-shirt on top of the spill. That must be enough.

All the feelings are coming to the surface. I wasn't enough. I wasn't good enough. He told me I was crazy. He told me he could trust me. That he loved me. I really thought I was loved. Why didn't he ever touch me? Did he also give her the same excuses, that he wasn't ready, that he needed to wait, or did he only need to wait with me? I am so fucking rejected and unlovable.

After putting chamomile teabags into the fridge to cool off so they can eventually make my eyes look less puffy and red, I go on the hunt for literature that will help me feel alive again. I google 'books to make me feel whole'. I come across a *New York Times* bestseller with a quote by Adele on the cover. (Incidentally, I always go to Adele for my advice on literature, just like I go to Stephen King for all my music recommendations and to Bob the Builder for advice on cooking.) Adele will know. She's been through a break-up or two and she's stopped crying for long enough to record a couple of albums about it.

I download the audiobook version of Adele's favourite book and start to listen. Soon, I am hurling various objects across the room in a fit of rage. The book is supposed to be about a woman whose husband has been cheating on her throughout their marriage and how she leaves him and is all fine alone. But within a couple of chapters, she meets someone new. Not only does she see this person across the room and instantly fall in love, but the woman in question also falls back in love with her. Immediately. People can just tell from across the room that these two are meant to be together forever.

Aw, isn't that just swell? I'm so freaking fucking happy for them. I instantly start to weep.

Just two beautiful women simultaneously falling in love, having hot lesbian sex, moving in together and getting married. Great. Well done. What a struggle it must be to be a super hot, newly 'out' lesbian who now has to move her husband's leather armchair out of the living room and replace it with a beautiful coffee table from Anthropologie. Oh, I'm so glad to be in the pits of rejection-depression (rejession?) and hear about these two lovebirds finding each other. It must be so hard to just be hot and attracted to someone else hot. Is this what you wanted, Adele? To read about two people getting together, all hot and easily?

Really? I thought you were on my side, Adele. You used to be fat too. You used to feel rejected too.

I furiously fold cardboard boxes that have Amazon tape holding them together and shove them into a recycling bag. I'm furious at the beautiful lesbians and I see myself as the contrast to them: all fat and floppy, my stomach full of scars because apparently, I have something called dermatillomania, which means I pick my skin all the time without noticing it. And I've only just noticed. My stomach looks like a battleground, scabs, wounds and the like all around. My boobs too. Then there are the stretchmarks, which I'm fine with, I'm fine. But then there is also the fairly big lump on my scalp. I think it's growing and Google doesn't even have the common decency to tell me it's cancer. Instead, it's just some fucking massive zit that grows UNDER THE SKIN and I'll have to pay to have it drained 'if it bothers me'. Of course it bothers me. It was never part of my dream growing up that one day I would have to write down 'drain scalp lump' in my personal planner. I never thought I'd hope I had scalp cancer just because I'd rather die than look like a cartoon character that's been whacked on the head by a sledgehammer. I angrily kick my (IKEA) coffee table into place because somewhere, a while ago, a beautiful woman fell in love with another beautiful woman.

I realise that I don't actually know if the author and her soon-to-be-wife are hot. There is an ever so tiny chance that I might be projecting, I think, before kicking a chair into place.

By hot, of course I mean thin. Which is society's most accepted definition of 'hot'. When I say hot, I mean conventionally attractive. Some people might be into scalp lumps, stretchmarks and stomachs big enough to be used as tables, but this isn't the norm. It isn't what we see on TV. I am not conventionally attractive. But I do think I am attractive. I guess I just don't think many people agree.

I google the author of the *New York Times* bestseller that I am reading to see if she looks like Shrek's wife or Cate Blanchett.

Of course she looks like Cate Blanchett. She is tall, thin and blonde, and her now-wife (I knew it) is also tall, thin and blonde. But with short hair. In another shameful moment, I google 'Adele weight loss' and the publishing date of the book. Just like I thought. Adele read and recommended this book after she, herself, lost weight. Of course. Thin people sticking together. Adele sees herself as a thin woman, now also able to find love. How will she even write her next album? Will it just be called *33 (People I fuck every day because now I'm thin)*? With tracks like 'River Lea (and other places I've fucked)', 'Hello (person I fucked last night whose name I completely forgot already)' and 'All I Ask (is for you to stop calling me, I'm too busy fucking)'.

I know that my thoughts are ugly and deeply rooted in low self-esteem. I don't remember having low self-esteem before I met The Comedian, five years ago. But now it's right under the surface of my skin, making me hate women I have never met.

I look up the woman from his drafts folder on Instagram. I click 'Message'. She follows me, of course she does. She probably didn't know about me either. But she must have been suspicious, like I was. I don't want to see her or meet her. I don't want to talk to her. I never really liked her. But I still want her to be safe and happy. I message her, rather vaguely, that I hacked into his emails and that I know one thing: she needs to be careful with her heart.

An hour later, she unfollows me. I understand. I would have unfollowed me, too.

I go back to hating Adele and the happy lesbians. It has been five hours since I sent the break-up text and I am lashing out and I feel like a very bad feminist. I do love Adele. I'm also a bad therapy client. I should be conducting myself with grace and self-composition. I try to remind myself of the many lessons I have learned in therapy that I always, conveniently, tend to forget as soon as the session ends.

'Anger doesn't exist – anger is always a feeling that hides something else, usually fear or sadness,' I do remember my therapist saying last week. I wonder if she will let me talk about Adele for an hour in our next session or if she will ask me to instead sit with my feelings and figure out what this is really about.

I know what it's about. I'm sad and scared. Regardless of how toxic a relationship is, it feels safe because it's familiar.

I have sent so many 'Why are you ignoring me?' texts

that my autocorrect fills in 'hy are you ignoring me' automatically when I type 'W'. But just because my autocorrect has adjusted to this way of living, doesn't mean I have to.

'But what are you not saying?' my therapist kept asking in our last session, pre-break-up, as I was talking about how understanding I was of his situation.

'He's struggling too, you know? He's been socialised as a man, taught that his feelings are not to be felt and he's super stressed; he has so many things to do and so many people want something from him all the time, and he's not used to me setting boundaries so—'

'But what are you not saying?'

I shrugged. My brain felt empty. I had nothing. Okay, maybe I had a tiny bit.

'I guess, I am a bit... annoyed, I guess... that he doesn't really listen to me,' I said.

She was quiet then. I don't like it when she's quiet because that makes my brain fill up with words and my heart fill up with feelings that I was planning on keeping deep inside.

'Like, you know, fuck him, actually. I'm also struggling. But I take care of it. I have two therapists, I've read all the self-help books, I have friends I talk to about my feelings, I keep a diary, I work through it. I've been so fucking patient with him. I told him four years ago to go to fucking therapy – and you know what? I told him it was because I just wanted him to be able to be happy. And I do. I do want him to be happy. For him. Because I love him. But... it's also fucking for me. Because his inability to deal with his fucking feelings is hurting me. I don't want you to fucking go to fucking therapy for your own sake, it's for fucking me. FUCK YOU.'

My eyes filled with tears though I was stubbornly holding them back. I knew my therapist wanted me to cry, to express my feelings, but that's why I couldn't do it. I couldn't have her win that round. I managed to swallow the feelings and take a deep breath. The tears disappeared. *Ha!* I thought. *You didn't get me this time. Therapy vs Sofie Hagen: 0-1.* The feelings were safely back in the box. Though my therapist was still quiet.

'What are you not saying?' she asked.

'I think that's it – that's all the stuff I'm not saying.'

I knew it was the wrong answer as it came out of my mouth. My therapist knew it too, so she remained quiet. This time I couldn't hold back the tears, as the feelings flew out of the box and hit me smack in the face.

'I just thought I was done with this,' I wept quietly. 'Before The Comedian, I tried so hard to make Johnson love me and it didn't work. I tried so hard to make my ex before that love me and he couldn't. I've been doing the same thing since I was a teenager.'

My therapist continued to sit there quietly, letting her silence be the puppetmaster in her evil plan to win therapy. Fuck.

'Well... since I was a child. I couldn't get my dad to love me either.'

The magic words. Dad. And childhood. I cried silently while she just looked at me with care. She nodded understandingly. How was she keeping herself from celebrating the win? Maybe she would punch the air the second the Zoom call ended. Maybe she would message a colleague and say, 'I just broke a client completely,' and her colleague would say, 'Congratulations! Let's go for drinks!' while I cried myself to sleep.

Though admittedly, I couldn't see any of this in her facial expression. She just looked like someone who really cared. It felt uncomfortable. She just wants me to feel. I will start analysing something my mother said and she will just smile and nod and follow up with 'And how does that make you feel? Where do you feel it in your body?'

And after a long time of just trying to connect with myself, I will say, 'My chest.' We then focus on my breathing, where my feet touch the floor and me being in the present. And when I try to go back into my head, where I am safely detached from my body, she will bring me back down. 'Sofie, as you're telling me this, right now, where do you feel it?'

She will also notice my breathing. She will suddenly burst into a huge grin and say, 'Oh that was a good one!' and I won't even have noticed that I just sighed so deeply that I almost breathed out a lung. When you train as a Somatic Experiencing therapist, you learn the difference between people's breaths. Apparently, I sometimes breathe really good.

That is going to be crucial, I think. That I know how to breathe. Because now, in the immediate aftermath of this break-up, there is not a lot of it happening. My chest feels tight, my eyes are sore, I feel like I am drowning.

I have already decided, at this point, that I want to embark on a sex-journey and that I might want to write about it too. In fact, I have wanted to write a book about sex for years, but since I was in a (physically) sexless situationship – which I assumed was a (physically) sexless pretty-much monogamous relationship – it didn't feel relevant.

But in the bright light of day that makes my eyes sting. It is now obvious to me that a sexless situationship with a person I am emotionally more or less co-dependent on is incredibly relevant to my sexual liberation journey. And it only makes sense that I am here, with my heart torn out of my chest, but somewhat emotionally liberated. It makes sense that my journey of sexual liberation starts with emotional liberation.

Perhaps that is the first lesson learned: maybe emotions and sex are not counter-opposites. Perhaps they are more connected than I'd like to think.

1.

SEXUAL

MISEDUCATION

I AM STARTING MY sexual *voyage* at the very beginning and I would like to take you back there with me. Back to Adam and Eve, back to our collective (probably horrendous) sexual education, back to the messages we all received before we embarked on sex ourselves. There is no doubt that everything I learned from magazines, porn and my school moulded the attitude I have towards sex today. Not to mention the attitude of the people I have slept with.

One of my first boyfriends liked to pin me to the bed when I said no to having sex with him. I would ask him to stop and he would smirk, as if it was all a sexy game. I would end up reluctantly 'letting him' have sex with me because I did not know how to say 'no' more clearly than actually saying the word 'no' repeatedly. Eventually, I kicked him in the dick. The smirk disappeared from his face in an instant and he said, 'What the fuck was that?'

'I said no?' I replied, confused about his confusion.

'But... The men's magazines. They say that women like to be pinned down. That... they don't mean "no",' he stuttered.

We will discuss sexual assault later on in the book, where this anecdote also belongs, but when it comes to sexual education, it feels particularly poignant. My boyfriend at the time and I were the same age, had gone to some of the same schools and had probably received the same sex education. Which I don't recall, at all. Maybe I skipped school that day or maybe it was just so insignificant that it slipped my mind. I know there was no mention of consent. I know there was no mention of pleasure. There was definitely no mention of queer sex. I vaguely remember a banana having a condom rolled onto it while kids were laughing, but that could just as well be someone else's anecdote.

I have no recollection of my mother talking to me about sex either. Again, perhaps she did 'have the talk' with me and I just blocked it out completely. But the truth is, I learned about sex from the internet, television, books and magazines.

My first memory of being turned on is from my eleventh birthday. I had been allowed to drink Coca-Cola all night – so when I headed for bed, I was wide awake.

Around 1am, I was trying to find something to watch on the TV in my room. This was in 1999, so imagine one of those heavy cube TVs – small in screen but big in circumference. I was flicking through channels until suddenly, naked people appeared. My heart stopped. I do not remember if I ended up masturbating that evening but the next day, when my mother had left for work, I called the Danish version of Childline. A man answered the phone and I told him that I had just learned that I was a pervert. A sex-obsessed child pervert. I had watched porn and enjoyed it. I was addicted to it, I told him. I somehow knew I wasn't meant to watch *or* like it. I assumed that watching and liking it meant something was wrong with me.

'Okay, first of all, you need to know this: what you saw wasn't real. That's not how sex is in real life,' he told me, 'And it's natural to like sex. You're not a pervert.'

I hung up, feeling a bit confused. What I had seen was a man and a woman kissing and slowly undressing each other. When they were fully naked, a curtain flowed in front of the camera and they both turned blurry as the camera panned away. If 'sex in real life' was not two people kissing each other and undressing, what was *it?*

It took me a few years before I realised what kind of porn this Childline worker assumed I had watched. We got the internet in 1999 and I spent New Year's Eve fearfully watching the clock on the computer count down to the year 2000, hoping it would not cause the world to explode, while listening to Will Smith's *Willennium* on repeat.

The clock turned to 00:00:01 and the world was fine and I found some more erotic stories to read. *Watching* porn, back then, was a difficult task. It took five minutes for a simple photo to load and I was only allowed to be online for an hour a day, so I would *read* my porn.

I wonder how much that affected the way I experience sex today, compared to those whose porn was visual. In the written stories, the focus would be on the circumstances and the emotions of the characters, with vivid descriptions of sensations and details. When *watching* porn, you often have to fill in the narrative blanks yourself. Seeing two people having sex does nothing for me. I need a back story. I need to know *why* they are having sex. If the answer is 'because they are both hot', then I am not interested. Besides, as a Childline worker told me, that is not real sex.

I grew up atheist, in an atheist family, in an atheist culture. But of course, there is no denying the general impact religion (specifically Christianity) undoubtedly has had on (specifically Western) society, regardless of how atheist one's home might be. I say this to make my background clear. When I read through the 1,800 submissions to my online form for this book, I realised just how different my upbringing was to a lot of people's.

Take N, a late-diagnosed autistic 21-year-old nonbinary person from Scotland, who uses she/her pronouns. N grew up in a small Scottish community and whilst neither she nor her parents were religious, in primary school she would have to say a prayer each morning and regularly attend church and read stories from the bible.

'I didn't really think this affected me much until I realised that I think every action I do is leading up to some judgement day where I'll be deemed good or evil; so, I've obviously still got religion on me somewhere,' she says.

Growing up, no one around N talked about sex and there was no sex education, apart from when a lady came into N's school and gave her and her classmates leaflets letting them know they were about to get hairy armpits.

'At home, if we were unlucky enough to be watching a film with our parents and sex happened, we were all told to cover our eyes.'

N, who says she grew up thinking she was straight, had a lot of boyfriends in primary school: 'I was teased a lot for it. I guess it's kind of funny for adults seeing little kids be boyfriend and girlfriend, like an inside joke, or a go-to conversation starter for adult clout. But I definitely felt embarrassed and kind of ashamed of having a boyfriend from such a young age. People would ask my dad why he "let" me have a boyfriend, as if he had a say. This culture of men owning women or trying to collect them like trophies is such a big problem where I'm from. That translated into high school-teenage boys being really misogynistic and constantly trying to have sex with pretty girls to show off. I didn't realise it at the time, because I didn't have the words for it, but definitely a lot of my first sexual experiences were coerced because all the boys wanted me for was to have sex so they could celebrate it together and get their numbers up. For me, sex was something you do for a guy, like a favour. Deep down, you didn't really want to. You weren't excited for it. You just sort of owed it to the people who had asked enough times. Now, that is obviously pretty fucked up, but everywhere I saw sex it looked like it was something a man does to a women if he manages to convince her. It wasn't until probably the third year of university that I realised that I was supposed to enjoy sex and be excited to have it with someone, and that it's so messed up to want to have sex with someone who isn't really into it. I still don't really understand why someone would ever want to trick someone else into sex or why someone would want to have sex with someone who is not giving enthusiastic consent.'

After these revelations and a bunch of one-night stands, N promised herself that she would only have sex with people who she wanted to have sex with. When she got in touch with me, N hadn't had sex in two years: 'It's not that I don't want to have sex with someone, it's just that I want to feel really comfortable with them first and I really don't like it if I feel pressured into anything or if I get the feeling that they're expecting sex from me within a certain time frame. I think the way that modern dating is so centred around sex means I don't really fit into that scene anymore. Tinder, Hinge, all of that. I don't think my standards are incredibly high but I'm quite apprehensive about meeting new people because of the culture I grew up in.'

When Eve realised she was naked, after chomping down on that apple, she was aware of her own sexuality. And that was it. She and her freeloading boyfriend, Adam, were out, ejected from paradise for being dirty little horndogs. And now, *some* years after that (allegedly) happened, I consider my awareness of my own sexuality as slightly wrong, slightly dirty, slightly shameful. I was never directly told that the bible was a guidebook, nor was I specifically told that wanting sex made me filthy. But it has undoubtedly trickled down.

I was growing up when Britney Spears transitioned from schoolgirl (acceptable) to catsuit-girl (big slut), when Christina Aguilera sung 'Dirrrty' and when a girl from my class had 'whore' spraypainted on her front door because she had, it was said, given a boy a handjob at a party. The boy had nothing spray painted on his door, by the way. I learned that wanting sex was whoreish and that you did not want to be whoreish. Meanwhile, women's magazines taught me '13 Ways To Give Your Man A Blowjob' and 'How To Keep Your Boyfriend Interested'. I was instructed not to be nagging, not to create drama – and not to deny a man sex.

Because a man's sexuality was uncontrollable, in a sort of natural, sexy, funny way. You could see a dick walking home from school if *that man* decided to flash near the playground again. Once a kid told our teacher about this happening and the teacher laughed and said, 'Just tell him it's smaller than your dad's, that'll embarrass him.' It was not considered assault or as something that could be very traumatic for the *child* who witnessed this. A man forcing a young girl to see his penis was *funny*.

I am eager to re-learn everything I thought I knew about sex, so I pick up the book *A Practical Guide to Sex: Finally, Helpful Sex Advice!* by Meg-John Barker and Justin Hancock. It is written so that school children will be able to understand it and part of me feels silly for reading it. *I surely know all of this already*. There is a paragraph about 'diverse bodies' that says:

> There are whole books and chapters on how disabled people, older people, pregnant people, fat people or trans people have sex – as if sex were a different issue for them because of their 'different' bodies. We think it's more useful – and more enjoyable – to adopt this approach for everybody rather than just for these specific groups. We don't only have to learn what is different about a new person's body if they come from one of these groups, we have to learn what's different about any new person's body because every body is different.

I do know this. Of course, I know this. It's *obvious*. Yet, it does something to me. I highlight it with a purple highlighter and stick a Post-it note on the page, so I can go back to it later. But if it is so obvious and I already know this, why does it feel so radical and life-changing to read it on paper? It feels comforting to have someone *tell me* these things. I can't even imagine how it would have felt if someone had told me this back in 2005, before I first slept with Fingers.

The reason I have the book is because during a very brief stint on a dating app, I matched with Justin and told him I was writing this book. He told me he had written a book on sex education and I was intrigued. Not long after I bought the book, I deleted my dating profile – the panic flooding through my body at the very mention of meeting up with someone told me that I was not ready for that to happen yet. So I felt slightly weird reaching (back) out to Justin to ask him if I can talk to him about the book and sex education in general. But it feels important to talk to someone about what we *actually* need to know about sex, before getting (back) into it.

Justin Hancock, who is a sex and relationships educator and author of the books *A Practical Guide To Sex: Finally, Helpful Sex Advice!* (co-written with Meg-John Barker) and *Can We Talk About Consent? A Book about Freedom, Choices and Agreement,* is sitting right in front of me, on a chaise longue at the Barbican in London, whilst tiny children run around right next to us. When we first sat down, no children were present, but just as we started to talk about sex, the prams appeared. Justin does not mention the children so neither do I. I keep telling myself that *it's fine*. First of all, Justin speaks at a low volume, and second of all, the children are too young to understand what Justin is saying. And to be completely honest, I barely understand what Justin is saying and I'm in my mid-thirties.

'I think one of many useful ways of understanding what sex is, is to think about it as a kind of assemblage of different factors. There is a great paper written by Nick J. Fox and Pam Alldred called "The Sexuality-Assemblage". "Assemblage" is a philosophical term coined by Gilles Deleuze and Félix Guattari. They would say that things don't exist in and of themselves. A thing is always existing in relation to other things. And that "in relation to" is a crucial way of understanding how things emerge from a complex assemblage of various factors, relations and affects,' Justin says, when I ask him, 'What is sex?'

'Sorry, PhD talk,' he says and continues, 'The way I have been explaining this to young people lately is to talk about the "Kissing Assemblage". When we talk about kissing, we would say it's when one person's set of lips meet another person's set of lips and those lips meeting is a kiss.'

I nod. Yes. That is my definition of a kiss.

'But there are kisses that are not sexual and there are kisses that are very sexual. I asked my students to look at iconic movie kisses. They often pick the Spiderman upside-down kiss, *The Notebook* kiss, *The Lady and the Tramp* kiss. And I ask them: "what makes these kisses romantic or sexual?"'

'The spaghetti?' I ask.

'The fact that they were prevented from doing it, or the rain, or pretending it's another person. The build-up to the moment, the nature of their relationship, how old they are, the immediate environment.'

'And the fact that it's Spiderman,' I mumble to myself.

'So if we think about sex as being an assemblage of different factors, we can understand how some things are sexual and some or not.'

My favourite movie kiss is between Meryl Streep and Clint Eastwood in *The Bridges of Madison County*. Meryl Streep is a lonely housewife who feels trapped in a comfortable marriage, with her two children and husband gone for a few weeks. Clint Eastwood, a photographer travelling the world, comes to town and she helps him out. Meryl Streep struggles with her conscience, her love for her family and loyalty towards her husband, which contrasts with her deep, burning desire for the handsome Clint Eastwood, who's appropriately sweaty and rough-looking. She buys a new dress and feels silly for doing so. She puts her hand on his shoulder and pulls it away immediately. Meanwhile, Clint wants her but also wants to respect her boundaries. Besides, he is a free bird and will not be tied down by love. An hour and 15 minutes into the movie, they begin to dance in her kitchen, to 'I See Your Face Before Me' by Johnny Hartman. We see them dancing for an entire minute before he kisses her forehead. Another 40 seconds go by before his lips touch hers. She pulls away a bit and then hesitantly kisses him. She pulls away a bit, not as long as before. He is now insistently kissing her and she gives in and kisses him back. It is the point of no return and the hottest movie kiss in the history of cinema.[14]

'Foucault would say: look, we're surrounded by discourse that makes it harder for us to figure out what and who we are.' Justin – who is not unsexy but sexy in a different way to Clint Eastwood, more *'if Clint Eastwood went to Cambridge, lived in East London and kept referencing Foucault'* – interrupts my horny thoughts. 'All the should-stories, all the stories we have about how we *should* do things, make it really, really hard for us to figure ourselves out . He says that we should imagine that we are standing beside a sculpture of ourselves and we are constantly sculpting and re-sculpting that sculpture. We are kind of constantly figuring out who we are and figuring out our own sexual subjectivity in that way. So my job is to give people resources to figure out what sex is for them. Is it not to provide more discourse, which just makes figuring out your own sexuality that much harder.'

'I'm kind of annoyed,' I say, deciding to be fully honest.

---

14 Opinion: author's own.

'What I learned about sex growing up was incredibly toxic and often wrong, but at least there was a script. This whole *it is whatever you decide it is* thing is confusing. I quite liked that there were rules, even if the rules sucked. It made it easier.'

Justin Hancock brings up the patriarchy and how what we have learned about sex will often uphold it. *The Power of Dads*. How do we get more dads? By getting women pregnant. What matters in upholding traditional male-dominated structures is focusing on men getting horny and women being available for the men's horniness; everything else is irrelevant – including but not limited to consent, queer sex, female pleasure, foreplay, conversation. What we learn about sex is that men have penises, they go into the vaginas of women and then the penises ejaculate and that is it. That is sex. Then more men will be born to stick more penises into vaginas.

'So that is the scripture of "how to have sex". Some people enjoy that kind of sex, which is, you know, great for them. But most people don't. A lot of people don't have bodies that can enjoy that kind of sex. And if we are paying attention to the script rather than to each other, we are reducing the capacity for joy. And we are increasing the capacity for non-consensual sex.'

In Justin and Meg-John Barker's book, they present a list of 'differences between enjoyable and not-so-enjoyable sex', as suggested by the students they have taught in the past. The potential reasons for why the sex was enjoyable or not-so-enjoyable are things like how 'in the moment' they felt, whether they compared themselves to other people, how focused they were on achieving a certain goal, whether they were seeing sex as a performance, how consensual it felt, how aware they were of their sensations and how connected they felt to themselves or anyone else involved.

If what makes sex not-so-good, bad or problematic is to do with following certain rules or scriptures, being too much in your own head, making needless comparisons, performing sex or being unaware of sensations and consent, it seems like the answer to good sex is to do with being in the moment. Being present, noticing sensations, being aware of your own internal world and the messages (verbal or otherwise) you receive from your partner. Essentially: *not thinking, but being. Existing. Noticing.*

Justin explains, 'We have to see it as a process of emergence from an entanglement. There are possibilities for connection happening all day, every day, as soon as we leave the house. Or even when we're in our house. And it's not about those connections leading to you finding a person to marry and buy a house with – it's about noticing connections and what psychologist Barbara Fredrickson calls "micro-moments of positivity resonance". I experienced it today – I went out to get a coffee earlier and the woman behind the counter made eye contact with me. We had a little interaction when I was getting my card out to pay. A micro-moment of positivity resonance.

Our pupils dilate, to take in more of the other person, our hearing adjusts to the frequency of the other person, our vagal tone [the activity of our vagus nerve, a crucial part of our nervous system] kicks in to regulate our heartbeat and our breathing, and our neural pathways map on to the other person in this mimetic way. And we feel, in that moment, just a little bit connected to that other human. The more we get used to experiencing those connections, the more our body slightly adjusts. And we emerge, just a little bit more, into the world around us.'

I make a note in my notebook that says, 'I am not having sex with the bad guys every time I have sex'. I need to remember the feeling I am sitting with, which is an unfamiliar feeling of *being present*. I am definitely in my own head when I have sex, as I am trying to control a negative outcome based on my past experiences. In other words, if one guy in 2005 pinned me down during sex, I need to make sure the guy in 2015 does not do the same. I carry my past experiences with me in a suitcase that I unpack whenever I have sex again. And this stops me from being present, from noticing, in the way Justin is talking about. I remember a Danish print advert from 2006 from the Board of Health Authority, stating 'Only with a condom, are you alone in bed' which was written across a photo of twenty or so (arguably) hot people getting undressed in bed.

Likewise, when you have sex with me, you're embodying all the people I have already had sex with, and some of them were not respectful. So instead of noticing your movements, your signals, your body, I am anxiously anticipating that something bad will happen. That does not for joyful sex make.

'I'm surprised you haven't mentioned safety yet,' I say to Justin, as a child runs past us screaming at the top of its lungs, like a live-action condom advert. 'Because in order to be present, you *have to* feel safe.'

'We *need* safety. And how we get to safety, how we get to trust, is by paying attention to those moments of connection. It's why we have dates with people. To have a – as the kids say – vibe check. Which is: what are the tiny ways that are almost imperceptible, that the other person makes us feel safe, that lets us know that sex with them would be pleasurable and enjoyable? Are you able to have moments of joy with that person? Are you able to, you know, have eye contact, smile together, share a moment of observation? Are you able to shut out other people's noise and not be distracted—'

A child screams and throws a toy into his mother's eye, so I miss the next sentence out of Justin's mouth.

'Trust is like a collection of lots and lots of micro moments that happen between you. Now, this is difficult for a lot of people, due to their past experiences. So they'd find it harder to trust someone.'

I nod, thinking about my autistic friends and my friends with ADHD, for whom something like eye contact and being able to focus in loud environments can be a struggle.

And myself – living with the effects of a pretty traumatic childhood (more on that later) means that my nervous system is in a constant state of fight/flight. It is constantly stressed. And stress is the opposite of safety. Your body is warning you that something bad is about to happen. How do you surrender to the moment, how do you notice the little things that make you feel safe with another person if your body is convinced you're about to get chased by a sabertooth tiger all the time?

I feel like there must be answers to this. I will find answers to this.

When I read Justin and Meg-John's book, one thing stood out to me in particular. A small thing, something that should not have altered something in my brain chemistry but, alas, it did. The chapter called 'Communication and Consent', under 'Active Consent', refers to kinks specifically, and how within kink communities, it is normal to have a check-in moment during sex, when you check how the other person is feeling. Sometimes it can be a '1 to 10' system, where 1 is 'This is not at all okay with me' and 10 is 'Oh my god, this is amazing keep going'. Other times it can be a traffic light system – green for go, amber for 'not sure', red for stop.

I underlined *and* highlighted 'not sure' several times, as I stared at it. At no point had it occurred to me that it was okay to not always know. In the past, if I have felt uncertain during sex, I have not wanted to say anything because even though I wasn't sure how I felt, I didn't want it to *end*. I never considered that I could have said, 'Hey, can I have a moment?' or 'I'm actually not sure how I feel about this.'

I also wonder if perhaps I *did* sometimes express feeling uncertain but the person I was having sex with did not notice it. Either because they never learned to pay attention to the nonverbal signals or because they had not learned to care.

'I came up with a theory,' I tell Justin proudly, looking at my notebook where I scribbled down my theory earlier that day in a café in Soho. 'Or, maybe it's not a theory, but more a, just... a way of looking at something?'

Justin looks at me, waiting patiently for me to make sense.

'So,' I continue, 'I call it The Four Stages of No.'

'Of *know*?' he asks.

'No, of *no*. As in... No, thank you. The Four Stages of No, Thank You.'[15]

He nods slowly.

'Okay, so, I think in order to feel safe during sex, we have to go through the Four Stages of No... N-O. First of all, you have to be able to trust your own ability to feel if you *want to* have sex or not. Does your body want to? Or is your body saying no? Then, you have to be able to trust your ability to say no. I have often known that I did not want to have sex but I didn't want to upset the other

---

15 Aren't you glad you didn't buy the audiobook instead?

person, for example. The third stage is that you have to be able to trust that your partner can hear or interpret your no. Maybe you have said no with your body language or maybe you have been a bit vague or careful; so you have to trust that they are capable of seeing that. And lastly, you have to be able to trust that the other person, if they hear and understand your no, will stop doing or pursuing the sex. Right? I think if you are able to have trust in all four stages, you can feel safe during sex.'

'I like it,' Justin says, clearly super threatened by how effortlessly academically smart I am, just off the cuff. 'And what you are talking about is consent. Because of the discourse around sex, people tend to see consent as being this thing you have to get over, in order to do *the thing*. You *have to* get consent. It depicts consent as being an event, a singular event, instead of seeing it as this unfolding process which is part of everything, which should always be present. Consent is what we do in order to enable us to have a really great time and it is there to prevent us from having a really bad time.'

The children seem to be getting closer to us, and both Justin and I lower our voices. The last words out of Justin's mouth are almost whispered: 'Bad times happen when people pay attention to the scripts rather than each other. It happens when we stop treating people as humans. The way we think about masculinity is all about how men are supposed to be rational and strong and, you know, the mind is superior to the body and the mind controls the body. And you have to just be... hard. It's both men and anyone doing masculinity who is at risk of producing violence, if you leave it unchecked.'

On my way home, I try to note down everything I learned from my conversation with Justin. Besides feeling justified in my decision to never have children, I leave with a curious and exciting feeling in my body. There is hope for future generations – even if these things are not being taught extensively in all schools all over the world, at least the information is readily available in books and online. Consent was never a word we discussed when I was young. Consent was taught to cis men through men's magazines, which told them to ignore any sign of it. Because, as previously discussed, it is for the greater good of the patriarchy if penises go into vaginas a lot. But consent in the context of it being an exciting thing, a door to deeper connection and better sex, is mindblowing. Similarly, having realised that I can just say 'maybe' is potentially life changing. In my head, it used to be either 'yes, I will go all the way with you, no matter what' or 'no, never, get away from me'. The fact that I will, from now on, be able to say, 'hmm, not right now but maybe later' or 'I am not sure – would you be willing to explore this feeling with me?' during or before sex makes me feel... well, a lot safer.

All of that being said, though, I am also left with a feeling of hesitation. I love the 'maybe' because that is where I exist right now. Somewhere between 'no' and 'maybe'. I fear that over a decade of toxic sex with toxic men has left me too damaged. Then again, surely it can't be too late to fix this? Just because I didn't grow up with healthy, fun, exciting sexual education, I can now never have sex again? That does not seem right and I am eager to figure this out.

My Porn Star Friend

July 2022

'At this point, she was moaning and she was so wet. I could tell she wanted me. I turned her around and said: I'm going to fuck you now. And then I did. It was great.'

He has the biggest smile on his face as he tells me, in great detail, about his night.

'My bed still smells of her,' he had texted me before I arrived, all sweaty and out of breath from having to walk up to his hotel room on the third floor. When he opens the door, he is naked, apart from a small white towel wrapped around his waist. He apologises for the nudity, which I found to be a strange thing to do, since I have not just seen him naked a lot, I've seen him masturbate and have sex with multiple women.

'How can you tell when someone wants you?' I ask him.

I'm scared that I want him and that if I do want him, he can tell. My eyes must look shiny right now. I try to look as neutral as possible and I make sure my tone is as relaxed as if I'm just asking him what he had for breakfast. (I know what he had for breakfast because there are McDonald's and Pizza Hut paper bags and boxes everywhere, because they were starving after all the ravenous lovemaking.)

'You can just tell,' he says, his French accent making everything sound a lot deeper than it necessarily is. 'You can tell how she reacts when I touch her. Her breathing becomes, uh, what's the word—'

He mimics someone breathing little gasps out of horniness. I swallow hard. 'Irregular breathing, yes,' I say, barely being able to catch my own breath.

'So how does this work?' I ask him. 'Our friendship.'

'What do you mean?' he asks as he starts recharging the batteries for his camera. The sex he had with the Halle Berry lookalike last night was all filmed, of course. He is yet to ask her if he can put it online but he is certain that once she sees how sexy they look together, she will say yes.

'Well, I haven't seen my other friends masturbate. It's not normal for me to watch my friends have sex. And like, I don't m—' I rephrase instantly. 'And none of my friends have ever masturbated to a video of me having sex. I think I would feel... weird? Maybe?'

'Masturbating is not their job, though,' he shrugs. 'My best friend watches me. I'm sure he wants to fuck me.'

Is he saying that I want to fuck him? Do I?

'And also, yesterday, you got a bit pouty when I told you I hadn't watched *all* of your videos.'

'Pouty!' he laughs, and sighs. His eyes dart around the room for a moment and land on my legs. 'You have nice calves, by the way.'

'Are these the calves?' I say, grabbing my calves, knowing full well that, yes, those are my calves. That is how I feel most comfortable reacting to compliments. By instantly changing the topic to be about anatomy. If someone told me I had pretty eyes, I'd probably start talking about how I only recently realised that I had dark brown eyes and not just 'brown eyes'. Anything but a 'thank you'.

'I need to tell you the rest of my date!' he says excitedly, 'So we fuck in the shower for a long time. Then someone knocks on the door and I think, *Oh, of course, other people in the hotel probably don't appreciate hearing us moaning and fucking to The Weeknd at 3am.* I open the door and this man tells me that there is water dripping from the ceiling. We must have been in the shower for too long. And he is very awkward; I'm just wearing a towel and I have clearly just been fucking hard. I apologise, of course.'

'Of course,' I say, as if this has all just been a story about hotel etiquette and politeness. But Brutus is already back to the story.

'I go to fuck her up against the mirror because I want her to look at herself as she is being fucked by me.'

I swallow. My head is spinning, trying to figure out

the context of this. We're friends. *Mates.* This is just a friend telling me about a lovely little experience he had. A friend whose dick I could definitely describe very well to the police if it one day robbed me and ran away. *Officer, it was surprisingly nice looking, you know, for a penis. Quite round around the top, actually. I don't really know how to measure stuff like that, but like... Almost the size of two male palms? Reddish. It ran that way. No, I've never seen it flaccid, actually.*

'I fuck her on the sofa after that.'

He smiles, which makes his little, dark and very French moustache spread all over his face. My other friends don't turn me on. Not even accidentally. But that is what's happening right now. I am definitely turned on. And he is a professional at sex, so he must know that that is what is happening. Is it on purpose? Is he trying to make me flustered? Or is this just so normal to him that he doesn't even realise that people outside the porn industry don't have these conversations?

'We order so much food. And I just look at her and I get hard again. I ask her if we should do it again and she says, "We have to do something while we wait for the pizzas." And then we fuck again, just primal and quick. It was over in minutes.'

'She called me a sex god,' he says. 'I am so fucking confident today. I feel amazing.'

I nod. 'Yeah, once I gave a guy a blowjob and halfway through he stopped me and said: "Let's just be coworkers."

Before this, we were friends. I wasn't even friend-zoned, I was demoted all the way down to coworker.'

There is a beat in the dense air of the hotel room, which smells like someone else's sex. He hasn't opened the windows yet. He looks at me like I have just told him about the time I lost my entire family in an earthquake. His smile is gone in an instant.

'Wow. When was this?' he asks, his voice full of worry.

'Oh, forever ago.' I chuckle nervously. 'Like... 2012?'

He sighs with relief. 'Oh, okay, because I thought if it was recent, it could be the reason why you're not having sex. Like it could be a trauma.'

People usually laugh at my coworker-blowjob story. But then again, most people don't know that I haven't had sex in seven years. And most people aren't French sex workers. Honestly, most of my friends' go-to response is always humour and laughter and sarcasm. Brutus's is compassion and care. And now he cares about my feelings that were hurt by this coworker in 2012.

That makes me care about my hurt feelings. And since feeling feelings is terrifying, I try to joke about it.

'Oh, I have so many stories like this! So much sexual trauma! Don't worry, you haven't even heard the worst bits!' I laugh, realising that there wasn't really a joke in those little high-pitched exclamations, I just delivered it as a punchline.

Brutus smiles. 'I want to hear all of them. I will help you have sex again.'

'Yeah, that'd be nice,' I say, when what I mean is: thank you.

As I walk down Denmark Street in Soho, London, I am smiling behind my mask. My knees are slightly wobbly. Since I first met Brutus, only two days ago, I guess I have been... constantly turned on. It makes me feel slightly dirty, even acknowledging it. We became friends almost instantly. We're eerily similar, whilst also being completely and utterly different.

'The virgin and the whore', he had named us. I had sarcastically laughed at it but also had to realise that yeah, I do sort of feel like a virgin. And at this point, I think, I kind of want to be the whore. He has made it look so fun. So easy. He said the word 'primal' a lot and talked about how, when he had sex, his head was mostly empty and he was fully in his body. I can't even imagine not being in my head. During our conversation, I was so flustered and excited that my mind was exploding with thoughts.

Where do you even find people to make vid—

Oh! I watched some last night and you need better audio, have you consid—

What's your family like?

No, first, we should get something to e—

This is, by the way, such a cool hotel, you hav—

You can actually connect your camera to the power supply, you just nee—

Do you have a lot of friends who aren't—
. . . Why am I so turned on right now?

My voice felt shrill and I kept being hyper-aware of my body language. It went from tense to defensive to masculine and unbothered. At no point was I just relaxed and myself. It was like my entire body and nervous system knew that I am about to go on some kind of journey that is going to be uncomfortable. Because I am going to have to face some truths. I am going to have to unlearn and let go and confront. I probably have to be able to say stuff like, 'Fuck me up against that mirror because I want to look at myself', and learn to shut off my brain and just *go primal*. Instead of quickly entering fight/flight mode and saying things like, 'Are these calves or ankles? Isn't it funny how body parts have names?' to get out of emotionally intimate situations.

It is four days after the hottest day ever in the UK. Forty degrees. It is still hot outside and I hurry into TK Maxx to take advantage of their air conditioning. There is a full-size mirror and I look at myself. *This,* today, feels like the beginning. The real beginning. There is no going back from here. Brutus has already texted me again, promising that he will help me to have sex again. He is like me – loves a project and cannot let things go. He will not rest till I have sex.

I text back and remind him of the goal: it can't just be sex that is the goal. *Good* sex, is the goal. A whole sex *life*.

'I'm so ready to help you,' he replies and sends me a

photo of his hands, on which there are new, large masculine silver rings. 'Bought two more rings!' he adds.

He is wearing pale pink, shiny nail polish. *God,* can this man get sexier?

Yes, this is the beginning.

Everything since the break-up has just been the prologue. The break-up in January launched it. That is when it hit me that I had spent the past five years focusing on a man who made a lot of promises and told a whole lot of lies and never once even kissed me. Lots of sexy texts but no touching. And I told myself it was enough. And then sometimes, I would break down. I would sob violently into a pillow while the words *why doesn't he want to touch me?* roared in my head. *I feel so unwanted.* I would eventually manage to re-repress those sentences and replace them with good ol' fashioned self-gaslighting: *Of course he wants to touch you, there are just reasons. You're just being silly. You're an independent person; you've just got mental health issues. You don't* need *your situationship-kind-of-boyfriend to actually touch you, you just need to deal with your daddy issues.*

In my early twenties, I texted a friend whilst drunk. 'This isn't an actual request or anything, I'm just really, really sad and pathetic right now. I just wanted to ask: if you didn't know me personally and all the lights were off and no one would ever find out and you were drunk, would you have sex with me?'

He was one of the coolest people I knew; I felt

incredibly *less than* compared to him. He had almost died twice: first he survived cancer and then he survived a car driving off a bridge and into the ocean. He had a large tattoo of a skeleton drinking whisky on his chest that he got spontaneously, just because he wanted it. He was also in med school and had very beautiful blue eyes.

'I would fuck you in broad daylight, in front of everyone,' he replied. I started crying and texted back, 'Thank you.'

I felt incredibly lucky that I had such a hot, cool friend who was willing to lie, just to make me feel better.

I know. Saying it out loud, telling other people, changes this from a nice memory about a nice friend to an incredibly sad memory that points to something being very deeply wrong with my self-esteem. Like when I told Brutus about the coworker who stopped me mid-blowjob, thinking it would be funny, when actually, it was just the airing of trauma that probably, maybe, should make you feel... bad for me.

Around the corner from Brutus's hotel on Denmark Street is the Phoenix Theatre, where, currently, the musical *Come from Away* is playing. Underneath the Phoenix Theatre, down some stairs, off a side street, is the Phoenix Arts Club. A cabaret-venue-slash-bar with old musical posters on the walls, a red carpet and red curtains in front of the small stage at the back. I love this place so much.

It's where I met Johnson, the last person I had sex with. It's where he first told me he liked me. It's where we would get drunk and hold hands. I held my 20-something birthday party here. I have done countless shows on the small stage and, before the makeover, in the small back room where half of the seats were really old aeroplane seats from god knows when.

I descend into the venue, immediately embracing the aircon. It's closed – a man is building a huge display for the venue's window, a Drag Queen is rehearsing an upcoming show in the back of the room and in the corner sits Peter, the manager and one of my closest friends.

'So you had a meeting nearby, or?' Peter asks, as he hands me a Coke from behind the bar. I nod.

'Well, it was more just... hanging out. With... Okay, google this name: "French Brutus",' I say excitedly. Peter sits down at his computer and types it in. I see his facial expression go from inquisitive to what can best be described as 'oh wow'.

'Okaay,' he says and smiles. 'And why were you seeing a porn star?'

I tell him about my new friendship. Peter's eyes are so kind. Dark brown, like mine. He is incredibly handsome and intelligent. If he is standing in a group and someone comes to stand close by, he will automatically open the circle to let the new person in. He will say, 'Sorry, you were saying?' to you after someone cuts you off, reassuring you with his eyes that you have been seen and heard, at least by one person there. He gets visibly angry when he hears of people being treated badly. He is husband material.[16]

And now, he is letting me interrupt his work to talk nonstop about this sexy French porn star I just hung out with and about how I'm soon going to enter into some kind of sexual liberation period of my life. I appreciate him.

We are joined by the Drag Queen and a guy called Travis, a piano player. Travis is wearing a white linen shirt that is half open, revealing a hairy chest. He has a full beard, brown eyes and he is slightly balding. His trousers are also loose and linen with faint reddish stripes. I am leaning my elbow on a chair next to mine and he leans his elbow on the same chair. I feel like he quickly looks down at my boobs, but I can't be sure. Maybe I'm now just seeing sex everywhere. I think about Brutus fucking that woman last night. I look at Travis and think, *How would we even get to that place?*

It's easy when you're a porn star. It's pre-decided that you are going to have sex. It's just like a very sexy business meeting. If I was to do a musical project with Travis, I would have no doubt how to do it.

Oh hey, Travis, you're an excellent piano player and I am actually writing a show where I need some piano

---

16 And if this was a romcom, this would be me setting the scene for a friendship that will blossom into a relationship at the end, when Peter shows up at my wedding and says, 'Stop! He doesn't know you like I do! I know that when it rains, your left ear itches. I know that you like honey in your bolognese. I know that you cried when you watched *Titanic* because tiny boats next to a big ship really scare you. And I didn't see this before, but I see it now. I love you.' ... But just to nip this in the bud, spoiler alert, that is not happening.

playing. Could I send you an email with a pitch and then if you're interested, we could meet up and you could run me through some ideas?

Easy. I'd know exactly how to do every single step of that journey.

But sex.

Oh hey, Travis, I think you're incredibly sexy and I would like to have sex with you. So, uh... I don't know if you live nearby or...? I don't know if we can go to mine; you see, my dog sleeps in my bed and I don't know how he'd react. And also, it's real messy and I'd be nervous that you'd judge me. And I'm a bit sweaty, because I had to walk up three flights of stairs earlier. Oh, wait, condoms! Fuck. I guess we need that? I mean. Do we... kiss now? Or later? What if there's awkward silence? What if I'm bad? What if you stop me midway through and say, 'Let's just be acquaintances'?

How do I even know if I do want to have sex with him? Did I want to have sex with him before I caught him maybe-looking at my boobs?

Travis and the Drag Queen go back to rehearsals. I look at Peter, raise my eyebrows and say, 'Gay?'

Peter smiles, 'Straight, actually.'

'But in a relationsh—'

'An open relationship,' Peter says.

'Hm,' I squint. 'With...'

'She's incredibly beautiful.'

'Oh,' I say, defeated.

'What?' Peter asks.

'Well, if his type is incredibly beautiful…'

'No, he's not like that, actually. He's attracted to people for their personalities.'

'Oh,' I say, defeated again, but this time for comic effect. Is my personality attractive?

'I think he likes you,' Peter says with an encouraging smile. I nod and squint again. *What's the catch?*

I text Brutus that I've just met someone who is really, really hot and sexy, just as Travis walks back to our table, as if summoned.

This time I stare at him, trying to figure out how I actually feel. I become self-aware again, noticing how I sit, how I talk. At one point, Travis says that he's enjoying the quiet and I instantly lower my voice. Bad sign. Co-dependency 101.

Later, outside, I joke with Peter about him. I make crass, overtly sexual comments, in a proper Lads in the Locker Room way. Peter recognises it for what it is: a defence against my own insecurity. I hate myself slightly for having done that, as I get on the Tube home.

2.

SEXUAL TRAUMA

I REMEMBER PASSING THE bottle of rum to my friend Sally, who would slug it and pass it to Erik. He would take a sip and pass it to me. It wasn't till the next day I realised that I only *assumed* they drank from the bottle, too. In fact, they hadn't. They had just passed it between them and back to me. That is how I ended up drinking an entire bottle of rum, while Erik and Sally remained in control of their minds and bodies. I was *drunk*. Being in my early twenties, fat and quite hardened by the Danish drinking culture meant that I still had some of my consciousness left. It's not like today when I can have one beer and still be hungover a week later.

Sally left the flat, winking at me and Erik, as if this

whole thing had been a set-up for us to hook up. I remember lying down on his bed and grabbing my phone. I sent a text that said, 'He has LPs on the shelf, a blanket from IKEA and you are very drunk.' A few seconds later, I received that text. *Good,* I thought, *I've informed myself of what's happening here.*

I remember gathering all my strength to focus on saying one sentence, and on saying it with as much force as possible: 'Whatever happens, I do not want to have sex.'

Erik, who was now lying next to me on the bed, started sulking. 'Come on!' he said. Did he pout or am I just imagining that now, in retrospect?

I do know that he would not stop pleading. *Come on. Please. I just want to go down on you. I love going down on women. I love licking pussy. I just love it so much, I just want to do it. Come on, please let me.*

I said no and I qualified my no: I don't want to. Besides, Sally and I have been on a two-day drinking tour of Copenhagen – I haven't slept and I certainly haven't showered.

I already felt self-conscious about my vagina. I became a hairy teenager in the early noughties, when all vaginas needed to be shaved, waxed or have a little landing strip on them. No one taught me to shave my vagina, so I would do it using whatever I found in the bathroom. Which just so happened to be an old, dull razor. My mother has a very specific kind of privilege where she shaved her legs once as a teenager and no more hair ever grew. So the razor had been in the bathroom for years. And its first job out of retirement was my vulva. I was 17 and was about to go on my first ever holiday with my first ever serious boyfriend. I had to walk like a crab from the plane to the airport shuttle. Once we got to the hotel, I pulled off my pants, revealing a bumpy, bloody mess. I spent the entire weekend in Berlin in the hotel room, legs apart – and not in the sexy way but because the pain was so bad. My boyfriend had to go and fetch ice cubes that I could calm the irritated area with.

Since then, I struggled with the idea of shaving *down there*. Instead, it was just hairy, and I knew, in the back of my mind, that men hated that. That it was probably *dirty* and *gross*.

Erik kept pushing me, 'Come on, I really, really want to, I promise it's fine, I don't care how it looks or smells or tastes, I just love it.'

Fine. My resistance seemed to be bothering him and I felt guilty. I stumbled into the bathroom, where I tried to wash my vagina over the sink as well as I could. Just to appease him. To make him stop. I walked back into his room and lay down on the bed. He placed himself between my legs and began doing what I had specifically asked him not to do only a few minutes earlier. Then, he quickly stopped and pulled away.

'Ew, that tastes disgusting. Oh god,' he said and lay down next to me. It felt like a punch in the gut. My entire body recoiled in shame. The room that had been spinning around me came to a sobering halt. I wanted to leave my body, just float out of the room and never return.

He then proceeded to have sex with me. I don't remember anything about it, other than that it happened. I woke up the next day and grabbed my bag and my clothes. I didn't dare to get dressed in there in case he woke up. Instead, I got dressed on a snowy Copenhagen street in late December. I was too hungover and potentially still too drunk to care who saw me half-naked. I'd rather the whole world saw me naked than him waking up and saying or doing whatever he would have said or done.

I met up with Sally to go over what happened. We talked about it as if it was a consensual, pleasant hook-up. We giggled and discussed whether or not Erik like-liked me. If I had a chance at a romantic relationship with him. I didn't tell her about his comment about my vagina. I didn't tell anyone for over a decade, nor did I let anyone's face near my vagina. I either didn't tell her that I'd said no to the sex, or I did tell her and we laughed at how funny it was to make such a comment.

It would be years before I realised that it had most likely been planned. That Sally had brought me to her friend's place, that they had decided to get me drunk enough that she could leave me with him. So he could have sex with me. I learned much later that Sally was psychologically *slightly unwell* – which is my attempt at *not* pocket diagnosing someone. Of course, I can't know for sure. Perhaps it was just Erik's doing. Perhaps there was no *plan* at all. Erik probably didn't plan on raping anyone that night and perhaps he still doesn't think he *has* raped anyone.

A couple of months later, Erik texted me and asked if I wanted to go on a date. We hadn't spoken since that night. I said yes and he told me where to meet him. I got showered, got ready, did my hair, makeup, the whole thing. I went from my flat in West Copenhagen to a street corner in South Copenhagen to wait for him. And wait I did. I don't recall how long I stood there before I realised it was a prank. He didn't reply to my messages after that and I never saw him again.

I felt stupid for falling for the prank. It wasn't till much, much later, when I began to reframe the night in question as 'rape' instead of 'drunken sex', that I began to feel stupid for even agreeing to a date with my rapist.

It's challenging to write about rape that occurred in 2008. The way we discuss sexual assault, rape and consent as a society has changed dramatically, and so has my own definition of it. When I was ten years old, I remember being told that rapists hid in bushes and would jump out and rape you if you walked past said bush. My grandfather told me this in his garden and he told me, in no uncertain terms, that if ever someone tried to rape me, I should kick the rapist in the dick or bite it off. I remember nodding and saying, 'okay!' and, at the age of ten, immediately internalising the idea that if I get raped and I don't end up with a bloody penis in my mouth, I probably should have fought harder and it's my fault.

Rapists were scary men, violent men, hiding in parks or other miscellaneous greenery, ready to jump you in the middle of the night. And you would then scream and kick and only if they were physically stronger than you would you be raped.

I did not consider what happened with Erik rape at the time. And even now, I struggle to refer to it as such. And yet, if a friend had told me the same story, that is exactly what I would have called it, firmly and without any doubt. I would have shouted it at my friend repeatedly until she stopped making excuses for him. *You said you didn't want to. Even if you hadn't, you were too drunk to consent.* I would have worn a t-shirt that said: 'Shut up, you were raped, you didn't do this to yourself, he is a bad man' until she accepted it. But it's not someone else, it's me. And I have this deep, lurking feeling that *people would get mad at me if I called it rape.* That I should take responsibility for drinking so much, for 'giving in', for not fighting him physically. I changed his name and there is no way for anyone to trace this story back to the real person behind it and yet I feel guilty for telling you about it. *What if it makes him sad?*

I am endlessly more protective of the men who have assaulted me, attempted to assault me or emotionally abused me than I ever have been of myself in situations with men. I have reluctantly said yes to sex, even though I did not want to, because the guy wanted to and I did not want to make him sad. I didn't want to be a prude or a tease.

Besides, I knew that a no would be up for debate. 'But,', they'd start, 'you said you would. You were flirting with me. You went with me home. You slept with my friend. You're fat, you can't play hard to get. I came all this way. I really, really want to.' All of which are sentences I have genuinely heard after saying no to sex. My boundaries became a hurdle to leap. A battle of wits. Who can best make the point for or against sex. They would always win.

When reading through the many emails I received from people in response to my questionnaire, I saw that a lot of people refer to this particular kind of assault as 'politeness rape', 'grey area rape' or 'favour rape'. As in, we do it because it feels impolite to say no. Or we do them a favour. Or we didn't scream and kick, but we also never actually consented. Not with our words or our body language. It's the kind of assault that makes it difficult to feel like you can blame your rapist for not 'picking up on' your subtle signs that you don't want to do it. Because a lot of us have still not learned that anything other than full, enthusiastic consent is problematic at best.

In between kicking-and-screaming rape and 'oh my god, I would LOVE to have sex with you!!' sex, there is a myriad of complex, diverse and complicated variations of sex and assault. And we tend to favour the man's side. We tend to be more concerned about men potentially losing their jobs and/or reputations over an alleged allegation than we are about the victims.

In fact, men are way more likely to be raped themselves

than they are to be falsely accused of rape. According to Gov.uk, in the UK, 20 per cent of women and 4 per cent of men have experienced sexual assault since the age of 16. Eighty-three per cent of those did not report their experiences to the police.

Reading through all those responses I received, I saw sexual trauma in almost every single story. In my own history – sexual or otherwise – trauma is incredibly prevalent. I spend a lot of time thinking about trauma. I have regular therapy trying to deal with my childhood trauma. I can't talk about sex without talking about sexual trauma – and I can't talk about sexual trauma without talking about trauma.

So I need to talk about *what* trauma is. Recently, there has been a lot of criticism aimed at young people, specifically on social media, for overusing the word 'trauma'. The critique is that 'running into your ex in the street isn't *traumatising*' or 'you don't get PTSD from having to go to work', and that using these serious terms diminishes the reality of them. The reality being that PTSD, or Post-Traumatic Stress Disorder, is something severe and not-to-be-talked-about casually. I find it hard to agree with this. Trauma isn't something that just happens to a few unlucky people, who are then gifted permission to be the only ones to talk about it. We all experience variations of trauma. A break-up can be traumatic. Falling down the stairs can be traumatic. The people who gatekeep the word 'trauma' are also the same people who are quick to say 'toughen up' when people bring up bad experiences. I believe it is good to talk about trauma, as long as we also *understand* what it actually means.

Firstly, I need to make it clear that my knowledge surrounding trauma comes from personal experiences and the wisdom I have picked up from people, literature and medical professionals around me.

I suffer from C-PTSD. Complex Post-Traumatic Stress Disorder. The difference between PTSD and C-PTSD is subtle but important. Post-Traumatic Stress Disorder usually follows a *specific event* that was traumatic. Say, a car crash, an assault or a significant loss. You went through life just fine and then bam, a Big Thing happened and now you struggle to sleep, you get flashbacks and have nightmares. You feel constantly on edge and certain triggers emerge. If you were in a car crash, maybe the thought of getting into your car again is overwhelming and you decide to walk instead. The sound of a car horn makes you jump. Maybe the song you were listening to as the crash happened comes on the radio and you start to sweat, shiver and feel numb. This would be PTSD.

While PTSD is something that happens to you along your life journey, C-PTSD – Complex Post-Traumatic Stress Disorder – *is* the journey. C-PTSD happens when you experience chronic trauma for a long period of time. Like when you have a 'bad childhood' or you were in an abusive relationship. When the trauma is not one big event but rather a constant happening. For me, this was growing up with a narcissistic adult, who was also sadistic in his ways. He was emotionally abusive and controlling of everyone in his life, including his wife, his step-daughter – my mother – and me. But since I was a child, I was easier to control, so he latched onto me like a leech.

When I was ten years old, my mother moved to another part of Denmark to get away from him. Even then, it took years before I managed to stop talking to him or visiting him. His ghost continued to haunt my everyday life. If I turned on the TV and the volume was above average, I would freeze with fear, because if that had happened around my grandfather, he would have berated me and forced me to watch the TV on the highest possible level until he felt like I had been punished enough. I developed an eating disorder because I was repeatedly told that if I did not eat all my food I would be hurting my grandfather's feelings and I would be a bad, evil child for doing so. He would deliberately serve me more food than was possible for a child to eat, force me to eat it all and then mock and humiliate me for being chubby later. My food issues lasted long into my adulthood and they can still reappear in moments of stress or pressure.

The tricky thing about having C-PTSD and about attempting to explain your childhood to people is that it doesn't always sound as bad as it was. *Oh, he told you to eat all your food and then he turned up the volume on the TV? Big whoop.* But therein lies the terror – you are gradually, slowly traumatised and torn apart, and when it's over, you find it hard to point to the actual problem. But the biological truth is that I grew up in an environment in which my nervous system was constantly set to HIGH DANGER.

C-PTSD often means that your very foundation is unstable. If you grow up in a safe environment in which you develop a healthy sense of self-esteem and boundaries, where you are taught to listen to your instincts and trust yourself, you are more likely to be able to deal with whatever life throws at you later on. If you live with C-PTSD, however, it is quite possible that your whole being is built on fear.

Imagine you are walking along a corridor. In the distance, the corridor turns a corner. As you approach it, suddenly, someone jumps out from around the corner and screams. Maybe you scream too, maybe you instinctively punch the person, maybe you freeze. The person starts to laugh and you realise that oh, it is just your friend Brian playing a prank on you. You take a deep breath and shake it off and maybe you even laugh too.

Our bodies are equipped with a nervous system that controls our every move. The nervous system picks up on relevant cues and it lets you know what is happening. Your feet are cold, so your nervous system sends a message to your brain, so you can decide to go put on shoes. Sometimes it will completely circumvent your conscious brain because it knows you take *ages* making decisions. Like if you touch a hot stove, it will not have time to first send a message to your brain and have you *decide* to move your hand, it will just move your hand for you, so you are safe.

That is all the nervous system wants for you. For you to be safe and for you to stay alive. This is super important to know and internalise. Everything we do, however irrational it may seem or however actually damaging it might be, is just our nervous system trying to keep us alive and well.

It is important that your nervous system is quicker than your brain. If you had to rely on your wisdom for survival, you would most likely be dead. If you step out on a road and a car is about to hit you, you do not have time to look at the car and think, 'Oh, will you look at that. There is a car headed towards me. I should really move out of the—' Bam, you are dead. Instead, your nervous system has got your back. It will hear the screeching of the car wheels, notice the fast moving object in your peripheral vision, sense other people moving back, and it will lunge you backwards before you're even aware of the existence of the car. To keep you safe.

These micro-indicators of threat are picked up by your amygdala – that little almond-shaped structure inside your brain which, together with your limbic system, is what keeps you safe. It detects danger and makes your body act accordingly.

So – you are walking down the corridor and a person jumps out in front of you. Your amygdala reacts instinctively to *something out of the ordinary* happening. At this point, it does not know if you are in danger or not, so better safe than sorry – it launches your defence.

You may have heard of The Four Fs before. Fight, Flight, Freeze, Fawn. These are most commonly referred to as the Four Trauma Responses. You will notice that not a single one of them is 'have a think about your situation and then determine what is the best approach'. That is because it is an integral part of being a living being – this part of our anatomy developed way before our clever, smart brains did. Back when we were monkeys and fish, we had these trauma reactions. You will see it in nature documentaries. Besides, if you are suddenly attacked by a lion, you do not have time to figure out if perhaps talking some sense into the lion would work out well for you or not. Bam, you are dead.

The amygdala does, however, go through a decision-making process to determine which of the four Fs will garner the highest chance of survival. If a car is fast approaching you, fighting it will not help you. In that case, you will most likely step out of the way – or, as it really is: flee. If you are attacked by someone, it is natural to freeze. In nature, this is the equivalent of 'playing dead' in the hope that the predator only wants to chase a live prey.

That is essentially what those three Fs do – fight is fight, flight is 'run away', freeze is 'play dead'. Fawn, however, is a bit more advanced and the latest addition to our bodies' nervous systems. It is where you negotiate. It is

Stockholm syndrome. It is where you comply in order to keep yourself safe. In a domestic violence situation, where fighting and fleeing are both too dangerous and freezing is not an option, you have no choice but to 'fawn'. You comply, you do as you're told, you go with whatever the dangerous person wants. *That* is what will keep you safe in this particular situation. Children will sacrifice their authentic selves and repress anger and rage, to preserve the attachment to their primary care giver because without it, they will die. We are neuro-biologically primed to respond in ways that preserve bonds and avoid rejection.

But our go-to reaction, when possible, is fight. That is why when your friend Brian jumps out in the corridor, before you have a chance to think, you punch him. What happens next is important. Your consciousness catches up with the situation and you realise: *Oh, it is Brian.* This is your hippocampus getting involved – the part of your brain that learns new information. It then sends this information on to your prefrontal cortex, which is where you make your decisions. You decide that this is not an actual danger. It's. Just. Brian.

Your prefrontal cortex then sends this information to your amygdala, which tells your entire body and nervous system to call off the danger alert. You are safe. Brian is safe. The corridor is safe.

Usually, you will then have a small physical reaction. You will sigh deeply, shake your body a bit, make a sound. Maybe you say, 'For fuck's sake, Brian!' or you kick something or shake Brian. When your amygdala sensed danger, it sent adrenaline rushing through your body, as you needed to be ready to fight or flee. Adrenaline is this wonderful thing that makes you capable of running away from danger, even if you are in pain. It is why people have been known to run on broken legs or not realise they are missing a limb, because the adrenaline helps to override all other body signals to get them away, so they can survive. Then, once you are safe, you no longer need this adrenaline, so your body wants to get rid of it. So you shake it off or breathe it out. You *move*. In nature, you will see lizards shake their entire bodies as they finally escape the snake that has been chasing them.

For a moment, you thought you were in danger. But you were not and the moment passed. This is not a trauma, so it will not give you PTSD.

Now let us rewind – you are walking down the corridor and someone jumps out and screams. Your amygdala senses the danger, sends the adrenaline, norepinephrine and cortisol into your body and calls for the possible trauma reactions to happen. But you cannot fight or flee. And it is not your friend Brian. It is someone who wants to cause you pain. And he does.

The signal that 'you are safe, it is just your friend Brian' never reaches your hippocampus or your prefrontal cortex. They, in turn, do not inform your amygdala that everything is fine, because it is not fine. The adrenaline stays in your body for a while. Even weeks after the event, you are on high alert. Any corner, any corridor. The danger alert is stuck in your body like when you have tried to print something that is never printed. It stays in the printer queue trying to detect your printer, so it can finish the job it was asked to do.

That is trauma and *that* is what causes PTSD. When you are treated for PTSD, it is often the case that you are trying to 'move the trauma' through your body. You are trying to print the document so your queue is empty again. Sometimes you might be asked to imagine a scenario where you punch the guy in the corridor and get away. Our brain is so primitive that it often cannot tell imagination apart from real life. I have, in the past, been asked by my actual therapist (who, I swear, is a professional) to imagine physically fighting people who have caused me trauma. Or I have been asked to imagine that I ran away. I had to imagine all the details – I turn around, open the door, I'm wearing running shoes, it is raining, then I am running through the street, I turn a corner... And I have to imagine running until I feel my heart rate going down. In those moments, I experience the feeling of the trauma *leaving* my body.

In my case, of C-PTSD, we are talking about numerous experiences of trauma, some intertwined with each other. When you are a child and you experience danger, you are inherently aware that you do not have many options. You are dependent on your parents in order to survive. You cannot feed yourself. Without your parents, in nature, you would die. So you cannot fight or run away. You can only comply, to the best of your ability. You live in a constant state of 'danger is imminent'. If a parent is violent, you will spend your every waking moment trying to learn the triggers that make them act violently. You will know exactly which floorboards creak because if you step on those, your father will be enraged. You are careful with every word you say because if you say some of them with the wrong intonation, you may set him off. Or perhaps your mother often leaves and you never know when she will return. So you keep an eye on the door at all times and try to ration the little food you have. What is true for all of these examples is that your amygdala is constantly detecting potential danger.

Your parents' job is to make you feel safe. If you have a bad experience at school, you go home to your parents (or parent figure) in distress and they comfort you. Your parents hold you close to help you regulate your emotions and make you feel physically safe. In a perfect world, in a perfect childhood, you would then learn how to soothe yourself when things are rough. You would learn that bad things happen and you can get through them. Your body would feel like a safe place to exist.

It is important to note that trauma does not always just stem from parental neglect or violence. Systemic oppression, such as racism, poverty, ableism, Islamophobia, antisemitism, fatphobia, transphobia, homophobia, misogyny and so on, can all contribute to C-PTSD.

A 2012 study from the *American Journal of Public Health* examined the correlations between experiencing racism and the feeling of stress in the body. Latinx participants had conversations with white people who either had egalitarian or racist attitudes and during this, the participants reported their emotional and psychological states whilst their cardiovascular responses were measured. The conclusion showed that not only does experiencing racism lead to psychological and cardiovascular stress responses, but so does *anticipating* racism. Even when the racist person was not present in the room, simply knowing that they were about to meet them raised the participants' cortisol levels, which is what causes stress. The amygdala knows that danger is coming so it is preparing the body for fight or flight.

This means that even if you grow up in a loving, emotionally stable and caring environment, if you belong to a marginalised group, when you leave the house, you are likely to be on alert, in some capacity or other. You just have to be a woman walking home alone at night to know the feeling of anticipating danger. In that situation, you are stressed. Your body is ready to pump out the adrenaline so you can run or fight. Often, nothing will happen. And you make it home and you take a deep breath and *shake it off*. Your brain tells your body that it's okay, you are safe now, you made it.

But sometimes you do not make it. It may not even be a full-on assault. Maybe you were followed, approached, threatened, shouted at. Something that arguably happens way more to people belonging to marginalised groups than those who do not. Do these events *always* cause PTSD or contribute to C-PTSD? Not necessarily, no. But they could. And sometimes they do.

Those of us who have felt unsafe during sex or in sexual situations, and those of us who have survived rape and assault, need to be aware of the ways our bodies can react to these traumas.

As I was about halfway through writing this book, I got scared. I was afraid that I would discover that the only reason I struggle to have sex is that I've experienced *oh so much* trauma. And that I am very specifically broken, in a very specific way, which would prove to be both unfixable and unrelatable to anyone else. I nearly let this thought stop me from finishing the book. That was the point at which I received the 1,800 responses from people of all ages, genders and backgrounds from all over the world and realised that even though none of us had the exact same experiences, trauma plays a big part in *everyone's* stories. Out of the 1,800 submissions, a total of 30 did *not* include a sexual assault of some kind. From being flashed by a stranger on a bus to being repeatedly and systemically raped, they showed me that almost all of us have experienced *something* that overstepped their personal boundaries.

I realised I needed to speak to someone who works with sexual trauma. And fortunately, I know just the person.

'What are the consequences of sexual assault?' I ask Chantal Gautier over a Zoom call.

Chantal is a sex and relationship therapist, psychologist and a senior lecturer, and today she is wearing a soft-looking navy sweater to accompany her high-fashion bob. She exudes an incredibly calm and considered energy. It helps that I already feel like I know her a bit – my friend Peter said her name when I told him about the book. 'You would love Chantal,' he said, and I did. I initially emailed her asking her to be my therapist. I thought it would be smart to have my *main* therapist to fix the childhood trauma stuff and then have a *sex therapist* on the side to fix all of the sexual trauma I have. I saw Chantal twice as a client before I realised that I was doing the same type of work with both her and my main therapist. Trauma is all connected and you cannot easily separate it into different areas, I now know.

I am excited to speak to Chantal again, just a few months after I saw her last as a client. But this time I am trying to leave my own personal stuff at the door and instead put on the journalist hat. And so my first question: what is the aftermath of sexual assault? Not in terms of what happens to the assailant – we know that 99 per cent of rapes reported to police in England and Wales in the year ending March 2020 ended in no legal proceedings. But instead, what happens in the body and in the mind of someone when they have been assaulted?

'Sexual assault can really have profound and lasting

effects on the survivor. Of course, there are physical effects, like the physical injuries you might sustain as a result of the assault. You might also be at risk of STIs or pregnancy. There can be other physical consequences like insomnia. But there are also emotional and psychological effects, like PTSD, which is a big one.'

Chantal lists just some of the symptoms of PTSD. Flashbacks, nightmares, feeling tense, having difficulty concentrating, insomnia, feelings of isolation, negative thoughts about oneself or the world alongside physical signs of stress.

'A lot of survivors might not even be aware that they have PTSD types of symptoms.'

I nod because I can relate. I have friends who have gone through big, traumatic break-ups only to be completely baffled as to why they have no appetite, a headache or a sudden rash. Together, we will blame everything else in their life, from what they've eaten to what they've watched on TV, before we settle on it just being 'one of life's big mysteries' or – a popular one – 'probably a menstrual cycle thing'.

'These symptoms can develop into situational depression, or if you already have clinical depression, it can exacerbate it. Some survivors might struggle with anxiety disorders or suicidal ideation. Survivors often grapple with feelings of guilt, shame and self blame. It might also include issues around intimacy. Some survivors might struggle to maintain an intimate relationship with their current partner. Or when forming new connections, they might experience issues around trust, so they might not trust people enough to get close to them.'

I nod so hard my glasses almost fall off, alongside my journalist hat.

'Why does it affect people differently?' I ask. 'As in, two people could in theory experience exactly the same sexual assault but react differently. Why is that?'

'What is important to recognise is that people's lived experiences are inherently unique. People's reactions to trauma are shaped by a combination of biological, psychological and sociocultural factors. And all these factors interact with one another and determine how you recover. It's not about the thing that happened, it's more about how it messes with you afterwards, because of what happened to you. Which is why factors like culture, personality traits, temperament, coping mechanisms – denial, avoidant behaviour, and of course the support network we have around us, all come into play.

When I was 18, I went to a nightclub in Copenhagen for 20 minutes before realising I do not like nightclubs. I took a cab home. Instantly, the cab driver started commenting on my body. He told me that many female clients would pay him with sex and that he actually preferred that to money. At this point, he was driving slowly, despite being on the motorway. I knew we were headed for a forest road, where we would be surrounded by nothing but trees and fields. I was clutching my phone which had no battery power left while I stared at his cab licence, trying to remember his full name and number. The cab driver mentioned in passing that he was from Iraq.

At the time, my best friend was from Iraq and that same morning, we had talked about mental health. She had told me that some older men in her family thought mental health issues were contagious and we had laughed about it. I hoped that my cab driver belonged to this small group of the Iraqi population in our area and started listing all the mental illnesses I knew. 'I am bipolar, I have depression, I am absolutely certified insane, I hallucinate, I am schizophrenic, I have anxiety,' I blurted out, without knowing what most of the words even meant. He might not have believed that it was contagious – he could have just been very turned off by how weird I was being – but nevertheless, he sped up and dropped me off outside my mother's flat and let me pay. As soon as I entered the building, I started shaking and crying as I realised how frightened I had been. Nothing happened and there is no way of knowing if anything *would* have happened if I had not started acting incredibly weirdly (and slightly offensively?).

A couple of years after I moved to the UK to do comedy, I got invited to perform at a comedy festival in another Nordic country[17] than Denmark. Some other comedians

17 It is a testament to how unsafe it is to talk about predatory men in comedy that I am not even comfortable revealing which country this took place in, just in case it gets back to the person responsible.

and I flew to a tiny airport where we were picked up by the comedy promoter. He then drove us five hours till we came to a tiny town, where the comedy festival was taking place. That is where, after a show, he gave me a very long and intense hug that made my blood run cold. I laughed it off and tried to get him off me, saying, 'Ha ha, alright then, that's enough.' I noticed that he had made sure he hugged me far away from the other comedians, out of sight of most people. But when I pulled away, he would not let go. 'Please don't touch me,' I said, with a polite and anxious smile. 'I will touch you, if I want to touch you,' he snarled into my ear, in a threatening tone. We were interrupted by a comedian coming over to ask a question.

What strikes me about both situations is the feeling of being stuck and not being able to get away. Despite my cool looks,[18] I am not one to jump out of a moving car on a motorway and I am not willing to hitchhike to the airport from a small Finnish[19] town. Both times, I had to stay in the vicinity of men who were acting in a threatening manner. I wonder if I would even remember these instances if they had happened in places from which I could easily escape.

'Almost everyone who replied to my form had experienced some kind of sexual assault, ranging from having someone expose themselves to them or send an unsolicited dick pic to violent rape,' I say to Chantal.

---

18 Shut up.

19 Whoopsie.

'Yes, in England and Wales, 1 in 4 women have been raped or sexually assaulted as an adult, 1 in 6 children and 1 in 18 men. Five in 6 women who are raped don't report it to the police – and the same is true for 4 in 5 men,' Chantal replies. Her data was from Rape Crisis England & Wales, she explains. All these numbers feel too low to me. Perhaps it is because I have been researching sexual assault so much or maybe it is because of my own experiences that I am biased, but I feel like the numbers must be higher. I present this thought to Chantal.

'Probably that's because we don't have a universally agreed understanding of what sexual assault means. If we have no access to the information that tells us what rape is, then we might not even know that that rape is what we are experiencing. For example, take rape within a marriage. There are still people who do not believe that you can be raped by your partner, if you are married.'

According to a 2018 YouGov study, more than a third of people over the age of 65 and 16 per cent of people aged 16 to 24 do not consider forced marital sex to be rape. A third of people in Britain think it is not usually rape if a woman is pressured into sex but there is no physical violence. A third of men believe that a woman can't change her mind during sex. Forty per cent think it's never or usually not rape to remove a condom without a partner's consent. Which, just to be clear, it is.

'Which is why it's so great that we're now learning more about enthusiastic consent,' I say. 'But a lot of people in my survey mentioned this thing they called 'self-rape' or 'politeness rape', which is when you *don't* actually want to have sex, but you say yes and show a 'yes' and do it anyway. And I definitely recognise this from my own life. It feels like you then enter into this... grey area.'

'The shadow side of the Wheel of Consent.'

'Sorry?' I say, taken aback.

'Remember when we talked about the Wheel of Consent?'

And I recall. The Wheel of Consent is a model created by Dr Betty Martin, who also wrote a book on the topic called *The Art of Receiving and Giving* and came up with 'the three minute game'. The game goes like this: you touch your partner how they want to be touched for three minutes. You then let them touch you the way they want to touch you, while you make your boundaries clear. It is meant to be more sensual than sexual – we are talking gentle stroking of your skin, not full-on anal play. You then switch and it is *your* turn to touch your partner the way you want to touch them, whilst listening to and respecting their boundaries. And finally, you touch them the way they want to be touched.

If that is complicated, you need to take a look at the Wheel of Consent. Imagine a nice, pizza-shaped wheel. You can also imagine a pie-shaped wheel. Or a flat basketball.

Divide it into four quadrants. Each quadrant is based on an exchange between people – this can be sexual touching or something as innocent as a handshake or making someone a cup of tea. Let us, for the sake of the theme of this book, make it sexual.

According to the Wheel of Consent, there are four different approaches to an exchange or activity between people. Giving, taking, receiving and allowing.[20]

If I touch you the way *you* want to be touched, I am *giving*. (And you are **receiving**.)

If I touch you the way *I* want to touch you, I am *taking*. (And you are **allowing**.)

If you touch me the way *I* want to *be touched*, I am *receiving*. (And you are **giving**.)

If you touch me the way *you* want to touch me, I am *allowing*. (And you are **taking**.)

Everything within this circle is consensual. Lovely, lovely sex can be had within the wheel.

But outside of the circle, consent is removed and this is what we call 'the shadow side'.

If I *give* without agreement, I may be a people-pleaser, a martyr, a 'rescuer' or a do-gooder.

If I *take* without agreement, I am a perpetrator or a thief.

If I *receive* without agreement, I may be exploiting or leeching off someone.

If I *allow* without agreement, I may be a victim or a doormat. I tolerate and endure. I am passive.

---

20 The original Wheel of Consent names these serving, taking, accepting and allowing, but I changed 'serving' and 'accepting' to 'giving' and 'receiving', as that made the theory much easier for me to understand when I was learning about it.

That last one – tolerating, enduring victim – is a mode we step into when we allow someone to have sex with us, even though we do not want to. When we technically say yes when our heart is not in it. The martyr/do-gooding rescuer is a mode I recognise. The 'if I give you this sex, will you then like me? Why will you not take my sex?' mode.

'How does it affect you, when you do this? When you allow someone to have sex with you, even though you don't want to? I know it isn't technically rape but it still doesn't feel good,' I ask Chantal, who seems concerned with the terms 'self-rape' and 'politeness rape'.

'It is your responsibility to say that you don't want sex,' she says. 'But yes, it does not feel great. I think part of the problem is that we struggle to articulate our desires. And to say no to things. Instead, we end up being all about that 'people-pleasing' vibe, mostly because we are scared of letting our partners down. But also, when we dig into the whole desire and arousal thing, it can get a bit tricky. Your brain might be yelling one thing, but your body another, like you might not even realise that you're not really up for the whole sex thing, and if you end up doing it, you could end up feeling disconnected or dissociate during the sex because you're not really into it. Or in extreme cases, your body might shut down altogether, making penetrative sex impossible, a condition referred to as vaginismus.'

The word 'vaginismus' showed up in my survey 76 times. The whole idea of the survey was to hear about the experiences I am not familiar with myself, so I read them all with curiousity. One of these stories came from W. W grew up in an evangelical and repressive household in Texas, where sex was only talked about in a shameful way and virginity was emphasised. When W was just ten years old, her parents got her a promise ring and told her that it was so that she would stay a virgin till marriage.

'I was ten years old!' W wrote. 'I think about that all the time now. What a weird thing to do.'

Around puberty, W developed vaginismus. 'It's supposedly rare, although I've come to find out that it might not be as rare as doctors think, since most of us with the condition don't tell anyone and don't go to the gyno.'

Vaginismus is a psychological and physical condition where you experience pain when you try to insert anything into your vagina.

'Tampon, speculum, fingers, penis... You get the picture. It really wasn't so bad when I was younger but I think it started because of the whole "fear of God's wrath" messaging. Also because I suffered an injury when I fell off a diving board and had to have about 20 stitches on my vulva when I was 11 years old.'

In W's sophomore year of college, she was raped at a party.

'It was very violent and painful. After that, the vaginismus got so bad I couldn't even tolerate a Q-tip being inserted. I thought I was a total freak, so I didn't really pursue sexual relationships much until I discovered that I could sort of tolerate non-penetrative forms of sex if I was very drunk. So I just kind of hooked up with people when I was out partying throughout my twenties, but I always felt really sad about it.'

W, who is 36 years old today, was into her thirties before she figured out her official diagnosis was vaginismus. 'I had been kicked out of gynaecologists' offices before for not being able to submit to an exam and no one had *ever* mentioned that it could possibly be a legitimate medical problem rather than just female hysteria. I swear to God, we are in the 1950s when it comes to this issue. I didn't really do any research. I'm not sure why but I think it's because I was feeling shame. Or maybe, subconsciously, I thought I deserved to feel pain on insertion because it's somehow immoral to use a tampon?'

Then W found a Facebook group full of people with the same problem and learned how to advocate for what she wants. 'It was one of the most enlightening experiences of my life. I have now tried to deal with the pain through physical therapy and have had some success. I use these things called dilators, which are basically a set of graduated dildos. You just lay there in bed and insert them slowly and then allow the muscles to relax around them. It has helped but not solved the problem.'

W finds that when she opens up about all of this to potential partners, they tend to get scared. 'At this point, sex basically just isn't part of my life, even though I want to be able to connect with someone at that level. I did have one boyfriend a couple of years ago who I could have sex with because he was understanding about all the things that had happened to me. He was responsive to my needs. We never had penetrative sex and he never guilted me about it or tried to push me to do stuff I didn't want to. That had never happened before, so I felt very hopeful. Usually, men – never women – try to push me. It makes me feel so unsafe and so unseen. It's like this overwhelming feeling of obliteration. Like I don't exist for myself anymore but for the feelings and desires of another.'

Vaginismus affects up to 1 per cent of the population and it is considered a psychological issue. It's believed to be related to either traumatic sexual experiences, sexual abuse, strict religious and/or strict sexual upbringing or fear and/or anxiety issues. However, not everyone with vaginismus reports having had these experiences, and the research seems to be lacking, to say the least. W's comment about us being in the 1950s when it comes to information on vaginismus seems accurate. I am never surprised when the medical industry's research into conditions that primarily affect women is just that emoji where a man shrugs.

'Vaginismus, it's not because there is something wrong with a woman's vagina, it's because of the pelvic floor muscles that contract around the vagina, making it impossible for any form of penetration,' Chantal says.

When I was still doing stand-up in Denmark, I was at an open mic one night. One of the male comedians went on stage and tried a new joke he was working on. He told a story about the time he went to a house party because he fancied a girl who was going to be there. When her friend started flirting with him, he said no – he did not want his crush to see him with someone else. He kept rejecting the friend, who was very persistent. At the end of the night, he could no longer see his crush and since he was staying the night, he went upstairs and climbed into bed. He woke up to the feeling of the friend inserting his penis into her vagina. She started riding him as he was trying to come to his senses.

The audience did not laugh and neither did the group of comedians watching from the side of the stage. The comedian walked off to a scattered applause and looked confused. With a huge grin on his face, he said, 'That was so weird. That didn't work at all.'

We all stared at him.

'You were raped,' one of the guys exclaimed. 'Dude, you were raped. She raped you.'

We all watched his face as he realised that his anecdote was not a *funny story*, but him experiencing sexual assault as a teenager. Though seemingly a bit shocked, he laughed it off and the night continued as if nothing had happened. When I shared this with a male housemate, he told me that he had experienced the same thing more than once. It affected his sex life and he found it hard to get, well, hard, in the aftermath. I tell this to Chantal who nods.

'I call it "erection on demand". So, no surprise then, that persons with penises feel similar pressure, like people with vulvas, when it comes to sex. I counsel many male clients who struggle with erection or ejaculation problems, low desire, performance anxiety, body confidence issues and trauma.'

'I do forget the men sometimes,' I admit. Men are told that they are supposed to want sex all the time and we are told that men want sex all the time. So if a man doesn't want to have sex with you, it feels personal. We are told that he *should* want to have sex with us. Or else, we are just super ugly. And if we don't want to have sex with men, we are prudes or damaged somehow. Either way, we take it incredibly personally. And that can't be easy for men to deal with either – you know, if they don't want to hurt our feelings.

'We tend to blame ourselves for sexual assault, right?' I ask Chantal.

'We internalise the myths,' she explains, 'which is also brought into the courtroom. You know, *oh she is promiscuous, she wore a short skirt, she was drunk. She has to take some responsibility for her own self respect. Why was she drinking to oblivion?* And so on. It is typical for survivors to internalise that. Let's be honest, if we saw a male-bodied person standing at a bus stop looking pretty damn hot, maybe with his shirt half open, are we going to say the same thing about him? So, we must ask ourselves where these damaging myths come from. Of course, the mainstream, non-ethical, unhealthy porn doesn't help. Yet, we have generations that are being brought up believing this is the norm. Sadly, most of the time, non-ethical porn doesn't show how things go down in real bedroom situations. And this can mess with relationships and our sex life, especially when someone's banking on what they see in adult content and then realises it's not exactly what their partner is into or expects in real life. This can be a total let down.'

As we are nearing the end of our conversation, I decide to share my little new model with Chantal. 'Can I tell you about The Four Stages of No?'

She laughs, 'Of course, go on.'

'It's a four-step process. First, you have to trust your own ability to feel if you do not want to have sex. You then have to trust that you can express that "no". Then you have to trust that your partner can interpret that "no" and understand it. And finally, you have to trust that your partner has the ability or willingness to stop when they understand the "no".'

'The last one,' Chantal says carefully, 'the other person's willingness... or ability to stop. I would actually say it is whether they are willing or not, period. It is always a choice that they make, Sofie. If you choose to ignore a no, then that is a choice you have made.'

'Yes. That's... That's very...' I find myself speechless. 'I had not spotted that. Why did I say "ability"? Everyone has the ability to stop.'

'Yes,' Chantal says, and I realise that it feels good to be told that.

'And I'm thinking about the first one. Your own ability to feel if you want to have sex or not.'

I nod.

'If you think about the people who are thinkers and might not have the capacity to feel or who are not in touch with their bodily sensations, what happens to that group? Those people who primarily exist in their brains.'

I blink a few times. It feels like a test I am about to fail.

'I would be tempted to say that if you are unable to know if you want to have sex or not, then you... shouldn't have it?'

'Thinking about wanting sex, is that different to feeling like you want sex?' Chantal asks.

I feel slightly faint. 'When I try to find the answer in my body, I think "Do I want this?" and then I look for signals that show me that yes, I do. And if nothing comes up, I have to make a brain-decision. But if I am not in touch with my body, should I be having sex?'

'You might not feel a desire. You might not be aroused. You might be aroused but that doesn't necessarily mean you have a desire for sex. You might have a desire, but you might not feel aroused. It's complicated, but really, tapping into our pleasures comes down to how open and willing we are and letting our bodies do their thing naturally.'

There is a long pause. I realise I am not cut out for the academic life. My little Four Stages of No did not stand up to a nuanced critique and I feel deflated. I wish it was all a lot more simple.

'This is probably really crucial,' I admit, 'and it makes me think of self-protection because that is what trauma reactions are. The reason I find it so hard to communicate with my body is that I exist mainly in hyper-vigilance, so I don't feel safe enough to do so.'

'Remember when we talked about the Window of Tolerance?'

The Window of Tolerance is something we all have. It is the state we are in when we are calm and at ease. When we have a sense of safety. We can access reason *and* emotion. We are present. This is what we might call the 'ideal state' or the 'optimal state'. But, as we know, there are other states. We can also go into 'hyper-arousal' mode, also called sympathetic mode (because this is the sympathetic nervous system that is activated), also called – fight or flight mode. We are on high alert. Our heart is racing, we are irritated, panicking and we are more likely to act impulsively. Then there is the opposite of that – the hypo-arousal state, also called the parasympathetic mode or freeze mode. This is when we go numb. We dissociate and shut down. We play dead. We are fatigued. We want to stay in bed all day and stare at a wall or a screen.

Trauma tends to minimise your Window of Tolerance. You could exist in hyper- or hypo-arousal mode most of the time, only briefly visiting your own Window of Tolerance. For those of us with quite severe trauma, the Window of Tolerance might not even feel that comfortable in the beginning, because it is so unfamiliar. Part of the therapeutic work is getting used to feeling safe. And then, slowly, your Window of Tolerance increases. Five years ago, if I'd had to have an uncomfortable confrontation with a neighbour, it would have been so overwhelming that I would have shot straight into freeze mode and I would have spent a week in bed, staring at a wall. The tiniest thing could throw me completely off course. Today, while I am still needing to do a lot of work, a confrontation would only send me into a state slightly outside of my Window of Tolerance – and I know to go all-in with self-care, self-soothing techniques and whatever else I need in order to calm down my nervous system again. My Window of Tolerance is a lot bigger than it used to be.

'Yes, I remember the Window of Tolerance,' I answer Chantal.

'Knowing when you are stepping out of this Window of Tolerance and why is important. Let me give you an example. A lot of survivors deal with this heavy shame thinking they should have fought back or done things differently. Truth is, when our brains sense danger, our survival instincts kick in. We might fight, flee or even freeze up temporarily. Freezing is a common reaction to rape or sexual violence, and it's crucial for survivors to know that freezing doesn't mean giving consent. Instead, it's just the body's automatic survival mode, reacting to a threat. So, when we freeze, it's not a choice we are making, there is nothing we can do. So, learning about the body's stress responses is a good start, and so being able to identify when you do go into the fight, flight or freeze mode, and what external threat, negative thought or past trauma is triggering this response mode. And most importantly, except for life-threatening scenarios, do you have the ability to self-regulate these.'

'And how do we do that?' I ask.

'We do that by practising mindfulness. And how do we know that? By tuning in to what our bodies and thoughts are up to, the ones that make us either fight, run away or freeze up. But we also need to think about what our triggers are. Could there be a fear of rejection? Could there be a fear of abandonment? A fear of losing control? A fear of feeling unsafe? If we can identify what the potential triggers are before we step out of the Window of Tolerance, and learn to sit with the feelings, even when these are uneasy, this helps us enormously. Once we know what is going on or what we are feeling, then we can begin to self-regulate because it puts us in the present moment. When we're in the here and now, we can be present, and we do mindfulness, deep, slow breathing or grounding exercises, or anything that helps us get deeper into our bodies.'

I realise that this is the second time that 'being in the moment' has come up: Justin Hancock said it as well. It is all beginning to make so much sense. There is something about sex and intimacy that feels threatening to me, or unsafe, or dangerous. So my nervous system gets dysregulated and I go into shut-down mode. This has happened so many times before and there is something oddly calming about knowing what went on in my body in these situations. I feel privileged that I have been able to get help with this in therapy.

A lot of people shared with me that they were in relationships and marriages in which they didn't have sex either because they have a low sex drive or their partner does. I ask Chantal about this. She explains that we will all have different levels of libido, and that libido can fluctuate depending on which life stage or developmental stage we are in. Sometimes it will be higher, sometimes lower.

'When you are in a relationship with someone, there can be what we refer to as a "mismatch of desires". What that means is that yes, in the beginning of a relationship, usually for about a year and a half or two years, couples are having sex like rabbits. Because of the limerence stage, when all the hormones are all over the place and people are in their bubble and just want to be with that one person all the time. After a while, that settles, otherwise we'd never get any work done. That is when the cracks sometimes emerge. Because after some time, as people get more familiar with one another, the sex wears off.'

F is 33 years old and describes herself as 75 per cent straight, 90 per cent of the time and as a 'plus size goth' who feels like a 'born again virgin'. F went to Catholic school in outer London in the 1990s and 2000s, where it was considered okay to bully each other for body hair, for 'being virgins' and if you looked even the slightest bit different. F looked different. She called herself an 'alt girl' with pictures of emo boys in her art folder and her thumbs poking through holes in the sleeves of her navy school cardigan.

'This mean schoolgirl environment created a deep anxiety in me which meant I always wore black t-shirts under my school shirts so no one could ever see my naked body or sports bra. This humiliation carried out into my relationships with men. I was convinced they had the same outlook on my body as the girls at school did. I would always want the lights off, never walk naked in front of anyone. I avoided swimming on holiday with people, for fear of them seeing me in a bathing suit.'

F began engaging with kink, allowing partners to perform humiliating acts on her in a sexually degrading way because the only way she knew how to feel accepted was to please people, regardless of how much it hurt her.

'This need for approval was also why I never exposed or went to the police about any of the partners who sexually assaulted me. I would just accept it, grieve it and move on. Until the final one.'

One night at a party, F caught a man attempting to sexually assault her friend in her sleep. He grabbed F, slammed her against a wall and threw her across the room. As he was about to punish her for catching him, people came rushing in and he had to stop.

'I remember feeling really shell shocked and I couldn't speak. He was the only one I ever confronted and that was just because this time it wasn't only me he hurt, it was my friend. People around me just carried on partying. I tried to drink through what I had just witnessed. My friend woke up, oblivious, and started partying with the guy and everyone else. It was a wake-up call. I eventually confronted him, as the party was ending. I found my voice, despite how terrified I was of him. Then he disappeared and I never saw him again. Well, I do see him. But only in the faces of strangers sometimes.'

Standing up to the abuser was a liberating experience for F and it gave her the strength to grow in her that she never knew she had. When she turned 30, she realised that feeling shame was holding her back.

'It is only now I know that if someone wants to sleep with you, they have already imagined what you look like under your clothes and they are gagging to see it in all its natural glory.'

F is now in a long-term relationship with someone she loves very deeply. In the beginning, they were very sexually active, but as the years went by, F began to feel like she does not have a working libido. He wants to have more sex, more regularly, and F holds back. Weeks and months go by without sex.

'Those experiences in my past changed my sexuality forever. Being manhandled by sexually deviant teenage and 20-something boys has really damaged my sexual ideologies. The idea that I have to fuck like a porn star because straight men think that's normal sex. My idea of normality is warped and it is so hard to undo it. My partner is so amazing, loving, supportive and kind. And I don't know how to explain to him why my sex drive isn't where either of us want it to be and I don't know if it will ever come back – and maybe that's okay? I am still aroused by lots of things, I still find him very attractive, but there is a part of me that just can't find the 'sexy' me anymore. Is it just because I am fat, happy and content and I just prefer sleep now?'

F's story is not just a story about a dwindling desire for sex, since F is a multifaceted person with a complex background – as we all are. While I am a big fan of Blaming It All On Trauma,[21] I ask Chantal if there could be other stuff at play here.

'Well, what I would usually ask a couple is: are you a sexy-body or a sexy-brain?' Chantal offers.

'Excuse me?'

A simplified explanation is as follows: in this framework, which was coined by Dr Patricia Love, you can either be a sexy-body or a sexy-mind. A sexy-body is a person who walks around ready for love-making. They are easily aroused or when stressed, they may use sex to unwind. A sexy-mind is someone who needs a sexual context in order to become fully aroused. They need to feel calm and be free from stress. The circumstances need to be right for them to feel desire.

---

21 An alternative title for this book.

It makes a lot of sense. In TV and movies, when someone swipes all the office supplies and documents off a desk so they can have sex on it, my head always begins to hurt. How can you have sex when all those documents are now scattered all over the floor? What if someone comes in? It is why I am stressed out by those porn scenarios where the pizza delivery guy brings the pizza but then ends up fucking the bored housewife. He is at work. Someone will be angry with him. How can he have sex when his boss is probably calling him wondering where he is? And how can she have sex knowing that the pizza is getting cold?

Yes, according to the sexy-body/sexy-mind framework, I think I might be a sexy-mind.

In *Come As You Are,* Emily Nagoski[22] explains further, using the Dual Control Model of Sexual Response theory developed at the Kinsey Institute by Erick Janssen and John Bancroft. According to this, our sexual response system has two parts: the Sexual Excitation System and the Sexual Inhibition System. The Excitation System is like a gas pedal in your subconscious that is looking for reasons to be turned on. If you are out buying groceries on a grey, boring Monday and suddenly, a hot person holds eye contact with you and smiles, your Excitation System sends a signal to your genitals to 'turn on'. The dusty fax machine in your pelvis receives the fax: sex might be incoming! Tidy up and get ready.

---

22 Which, by the way, is the bible when it comes to sex education and I highly recommend it.

The Inhibition System does the opposite. It is constantly looking for reasons to *not* be horny. Whilst it sounds like a real buzzkill, you are actually grateful that it exists. It is the reason you are not suddenly turned on at your great-aunt's funeral or at the dentist's.[23] It looks out for threat. That threat could be to your social status (your family will never let you forget the funeral where you started humping the casket[24]) or to your relationship (your partner will never forgive you if you sleep with the dentist again) or perhaps it could be the threat of STIs. The brakes are set in motion if your Inhibition System decides that the threat is likely to happen.

This means that becoming horny is a two-part system. You need to stimulate your Excitation System whilst removing threats to the Inhibition System. You can be listening to Marvin Gaye, while your butt-naked, sexy partner is doing a sexy dance in front of you, but if the fact that the dishes are still in the sink is something that stresses you out, your Inhibition System will throw ice-cold water into your veins.

Women tend to have more sensitive Inhibition Systems and men tend to have more sensitive Excitation Systems. In other words, women tend to be sexy-minds, while men tend to be sexy-bodies. I mean, go figure.

Sexy-mind is also often referred to as 'having a

---

23 Although, am I wrong, or is there something quite sensual about the dentist? Someone so close to your mouth. I don't know. I just don't know.

24 I swear, I wrote this before I watched *Saltburn*.

responsive desire' and sexy-body as 'having a spontaneous desire', again popularised by author Emily Nagoski, who points out in her book that responsive desire is healthy and normal. We need to stop considering it a dysfunction to need stimulation in order to become turned on. A lot of us tend to feel like there is something wrong with us if we can't just be ready to go as soon as the pizza delivery guy rings the doorbell.

Understandably, if you are a sexy-body – a person with a spontaneous desire – and you are in a relationship with a sexy-mind – someone who needs sexy circumstances – you can feel rejected quite easily.[25]And likewise, if you need stimuli to get horny, you might easily feel pressured by your partner if they are ready to go whenever. Therefore, it is important to understand both sides.

Chantal explains, 'A sexy-brain can get easily distracted because they are always in their heads. Outside stress can mess with how open they are to getting frisky. That's why certain things matter, like having everything sorted, the perfect setup with the right sheets, lighting or a tidy bedroom. A sexy-body can get close even if they are stressed and don't have all their ducks in a row. If couples understand these differences, the sexy body will get that while it's usually the sexy-brain that decides whether or not sex happens, it's not about rejection, rather it's because of how their partner and

---

25 Of course, I wonder if you can be both sexy-body and sexy-brain or if you can be fluid? This is a very helpful model to a lot of people but we should probably not just accept that we are all one of two things.

they are wired. But if you know what needs to happen for a sexy-brain to be in the mood for sex, then you can prepare for it. This understanding can really help couples move forward and strengthen their connection.'

I remember being in a long-term relationship when I was a lot younger. As soon as the sex stopped, I felt immense amounts of pressure to 'get back into it'. Not even necessarily because of my partner at the time, who was as patient as he could be, but because I felt like I *should* be having sex. I share this with Chantal.

'The pressure to have a certain type of sex can be a stressor as well. If we believe sex is all about penetration or that we need to have orgasms (preferably simultaneously), that can put a stop to intimacy quickly. Our perceptions about sex come from all the messages we picked up while growing up. Like, society has taught us that if a woman can't have an orgasm through penetrative sex, there's something wrong with her. In reality, only 4 per cent of women actually can orgasm through penetration alone, without any form of clitoral stimulation.'

'Whereas if you remove all the pressure from sex,' I say, 'it can just be a pleasurable and fun experience, and sexy-brains might not be so stressed out by the prospect of it? It feels like we're coming full circle because we are back to debunking myths and learning what healthy sex feels like.'

Chantal nods and sighs. 'There are so many young people in their twenties and beyond who come to see me with anxieties they have developed around sex... It's heartbreaking. And it's not always because it's trauma related. It's because of how they think sex needs to be. So we have to break that chain of thinking.'

I try to imagine what a future sexual encounter might look like if I take on board everything I have learned so far. I can already immediately rule out picking up a stranger in a bar – I am a sexy-brain and I would be way too stressed out about the logistics of it all. I have a dog and a morning routine I am very fond of. My Sexual Inhibition System would step on the brakes immediately. No, it would have to be with someone I already knew a bit. Pre-planned, at least a little. I would make sure to check in with myself. *Do I want to have sex?* And if I don't feel present enough in my body to know the answer, it is a no. And I will be brave enough to say that no to whomever I am with. Because I no longer suffer fools, this particular person will be very cool with it. They will say something like, 'That's okay, I am happy enough just stroking your arm for hours, I swear on my name, which is Lea DeLaria.'[26]

I suspect I will eventually feel quite safe with Lea. Safe enough that I can exist in my body without feeling scared. Then, I might feel turned on and ready to have sex. I will communicate this, like a grown-up adult would. And, as we go, I will continue to stay present. And communicate. And listen out for signs from myself or from them. Body language, eye contact. And hey, if I no longer want to

---

26 It's my fantasy, shut up.

have sex, I just say that. I will simply say, 'Hey, can we take a break?' And Lea will say, 'Of course. I want you to be comfortable.' And we will spoon instead. All the while, I am listening to my body and my desires, I set my boundaries and I stay in the moment.

This sounds like what sex is *meant to be*. I have never had *that* sex before. But if I am ever to have sex again, it is the kind of sex I want. It may not be with Lea DeLaria present, but it damn sure will be with *me* present.

The Very Last Time
I Had Sex

June 2022

(But I Am Also Thinking About January, April and November in 2015.)

It is 2015 and I am preparing to have sex with the guy I am going to spend the rest of my life with. This means frantically googling 'how to have sex' because I am so nervous that I'm sure I've forgotten how to do it. I am also swinging a razor – my body has to be naked and smooth. I do not want a single hair between me and him when we make love for the first time. The plan is to have a few drinks in a pub in Camden and then go back to his place, where we are going to spend the whole weekend.

This will be in stark contrast to the past two years,

133

when I have longed to be alone with him and not have to share him with coworkers – or his girlfriend. The closest thing I ever got to getting him alone was when we would be the last two people left in the pub at closing time and we would wander down to Trafalgar Square, sit on the steps and just talk. Even then, I had to share him with passersby, drunken tourists and, of course, the absent but still very existing girlfriend. She might as well have been sitting between us, creating a physical barrier. But still, nothing could stop my heart from beating out of control when he looked at me. It still can't.

I exfoliate, rinse, repeat, cut my toenails, pluck my eyebrows, spend ages picking out the perfect outfit for him to remove later. An oversized long black t-shirt with a belt in the waist. And tights. I feel sexy. I am sexy. I am also terrified. Two years of wanting this and now it is happening. Two years of people telling me, 'He will never leave her. They never leave their girlfriends.' Eventually, I believed it. 'That's okay,' I'd assure them, 'But it doesn't change how I feel about him. I wouldn't know how to change that.'

Then, one day, as I was in the middle of packing for a two-week long trip, I got a text from him. At this point, we hadn't spoken for months. It had been too painful to be around him, so I had told him not to message me again. He had respected that. Until now. The words seemed to jump out of the screen and poke me in my heart. 'I broke up with her.'

Still holding the phone and staring at the words, I slowly sank from my bed to the floor. I folded my body into an anxiety-pretzel and blinked a few times. My brain tried to solve the text like a puzzle. Maybe I misunderstood it? Maybe 'I broke up with her' could mean different things in the UK; like, it could be slang for... I married her. Maybe it was autocorrect. And he meant to write 'I bought up with her'. Like, he bought a flat with her. It *couldn't* mean that he was single. *They never leave their girlfriends.* Then the next text came. 'I would love to see you.'

My heart stopped. I felt the unvacuumed, scratchy carpet on my cheek as I inhaled months of dust. My vision blurred. So this is a panic attack, I thought. Neat.

We met up as soon as I was back. Our first kiss happened up against a closed Subway sandwich restaurant. It felt familiar. Still hesitant to fully believe that this whole thing was real, I said, 'Just so you know, there is a real chance that I might fall for you at some point,' and without skipping a beat he said, 'I'm already there.'

When I see him at the pub on the night of Our First Sex, I cannot believe my luck. That he is there, in front of me. All my nerves disappear. It is not possible for me to feel scared or nervous when I am with him. We are talking about a guy who is so kind, so pure, so understanding. He would never judge. And he looks at me like there was no one else in the room.

A week before Our First Sex night, I had asked him, 'Do you ever see us, you know... maybe being like, proper...

together? Like, maybe one day in the future... we'd be a couple? Maybe?'

And he looked at me with wide eyes and said, 'I've imagined us living together. Travelling... I'd love to go to Thailand with you. Do you want kids?'

I had to pinch myself hard to keep myself from turning into an anxiety-pretzel again. Instead, I just stopped fighting the disbelief and I accepted it. We were actually in love. And we were actually going to have sex, get married and holiday in Thailand, apparently.

We pick up some beers on the way back to his. He lives in a small studio flat that looks exactly like I would expect. It smells of him. We take a seat on the sofa and start talking. He goes quiet. *GREAT,* I think, *what is it? My breath? Did I forget to shave my occasional moustache?*

'What?' I ask, with a smile that has been on my face for months at this point. He looks at the floor. When he finally looks back up at me, his face is crumbling.

'I –' he starts with a croaky voice. He clears his throat and says clearly and concisely, 'Last Monday, I fell in love with someone else.'

If this was a movie, this is the point at which the screen fades to black. Then my face pops up again, but this time, you can tell that I'm seven years older because I now no longer have a fringe (and at the bottom of the screen it says 2022). I am sitting in front of my computer, in my one-bedroom flat in London, where I live alone with my dog. I'm sharing this story with Brutus. He wants to know the details of The Last Time I Had Sex, thinking it's a great place to start. It has been a few months since we first met and he is still adamant that he will help me get a sex life. I am surprised that I still feel sad when I say the words 'Last Monday, I fell in love with someone else.' It was *so long ago*.

'God, you really need to get over this guy,' he says.

I roll my eyes. 'I am! This was ages ago!'

'If you don't get over him, I'm going to round-kick you in the face.'

I laugh. You really can say anything in a French accent and still be charming.

He smiles,

'You still haven't had sex with him. In the story.'

I had collapsed onto his floor, bawling my eyes out. I found it hard to breathe, so I loosened my black t-shirt dress which I pulled over my knees, making myself into a pretzel of grief. In between sobs, I asked him what had happened.

He was also crying as he explained. 'We've been friends forever. She came over just to hang out and then... it just happened. We haven't done anything. She doesn't know that I'm in love with her. But I am. I'm so sorry.'

I gasped dramatically, 'On a M*onday*.' And went back to crying.

When I tell you that he eventually just went to bed, leaving me on the floor, it might sound like he is a heartless monster. It certainly felt like that at the time. But looking back, realistically, I had been crying on his floor all night and it was getting light outside and there was no end in sight. He was just sitting on the sofa, watching me be broken on his floor, for hours. There was nothing he could say.

Once I was alone, I found some paper and a pen. I started writing a goodbye letter that I was going to leave for him to wake up to. But each time I tried, I started crying again. Eventually, I just crawled into bed with him and lay awake, staring at the wall, crying silently.

The next day, we finally had Our First Sex. After both crying for hours, we ordered pizza and watched a movie. With mascara all over my face, swollen eyes, a red nose and pizza breath, we suddenly kissed hard. We stumbled into the bedroom and had sex. It felt familiar, vulnerable and *just right*.

When it was over, we were lying next to each other, sweating and catching our breath. 'I do have feelings for her,' he said. 'I am *also* in love with you. Oh God... have I made a mistake?'

I turned my head and looked at him. 'It doesn't matter. The damage is done. I'm no longer a choice.'

I started crying again and ordered a cab. I asked him not to contact me ever again. I divided up the pubs we would usually go to together with our mutual friends and let him know which ones he could go to and which ones I would go to. Just for a while. My legs were shaking as I descended the steps of his building. The cab was waiting. Right before I closed the door, I heard him shout, 'Wait!' and my heart stopped. *OKAY, okay, fine, I lied, I'm still a choice, of course I'm still a choice, I will always be a choice you can make, it's okay, I'm here, I love you, let's go to Thaila—*

'You forgot your wallet,' he said as he caught up with me and the cab.

'And that was the last time you had sex,' Brutus says, back in 2022. He nods, ready to start analysing. I press my lips together and squint, not wanting to tell him that actually… no.

He lifts his eyebrows, 'You went *back* to him?'

I nod. 'But it was different.'

'So this wasn't even the story?'

'No, but it's important for you to know the background. I'm sorry that it's not about you for two seconds!'

He laughs in disbelief. 'Okay, okay, tell me the story then, love.'

Six months later, I was a different person. I had emotionally armoured up. I had briefly had a boyfriend with whom I ended things over text, him begging me tearfully to reconsider while I felt nothing. It was so easy to not care. My career sort of exploded around this time. I was suddenly being offered shows that had previously seemed impossible to get. I stopped being broke at the end of every month. This only added to my feeling of invincibility. I flew to Los Angeles and New York to suck up to executive producers and US agents, two weeks before I had to be in London to film my first stand-up special for the BBC. At some point, in the middle of it all, I texted Johnson, casually asking if we shouldn't go ahead and meet up. Just for old times' sake. 'I'm fine,' I promised him. 'I'm so good. I've never been better.'

I went to his new place – an even smaller studio flat in Finsbury Park. We drank vodka and orange juice and talked about the past six months. I asked him what had happened between him and the woman he left me for. He said, 'Nothing. She didn't like me back.'

I tried not to smile. We ended up drunkenly dancing to the soundtrack of *Little Shop of Horrors* until we collapsed onto his bed, where we had sex again. I pushed him against me, as if I wanted him to fully melt into me. He was shivering and couldn't stop kissing me, my face and my neck. It was so simple. And easy. And fun. Yes, he had fallen in love with someone else and he had broken my heart, but he had been honest about it. I trusted him. He saw me and liked me. I felt safe in his arms.

The next morning, as the sunlight hit us through the blinds, he smiled at me and my thick layer of emotional

THE VERY LAST TIME I HAD SEX

protection cracked. I knew in that instant that I couldn't stop the words from coming out, like when you're hungover and you know you're about to throw up.

'Are you sure we shouldn't try again? Can we at least just have sex again? This was fun, wasn't it? I still like you, you know? I'm not sure I'll ever stop. Do you want to try being us again? We can just meet up every once in a while and do this, right? We can't just go back to nothing again. Right?'

Johnson never lied and neither did his face. He didn't even have to say anything; I understood. The Walk of Shame to the Tube station was more like a Walk of How The Fuck Did I End Up Back Here Again? It had taken me those exact six months to stop crying over him. I had bragged to friends about how fine I was with everything and how I 'just wanted to fuck him'. That I wasn't interested in more, anymore. That I was too confident to go back to someone who hurt me so much. That I was a different person now.

I met up with my friend Larry in Soho. We took a selfie together – my hair is messy and I'm wearing a yellow cardigan. That's how I remember the date of the Last Time I Had Sex. If I ever forget, I just have to scroll back through my Instagram profile and find that photo. I look happy in it. Hungover, but electrified. I had that Post-Sex Glow. The previous day's makeup was still on my face. I hadn't yet been home, so I had not yet been emotionally crushed by reality, by the door slamming behind me and

141

finding myself left alone, in my empty room. That's when it will all occur to me: he didn't want me then and he doesn't want me now.

'You felt safe with him and then he broke your heart. Then you thought you were safe enough in yourself to just have sex with him, but you realised that you weren't actually feeling safe in yourself and you got your heart broken again,' Brutus says and his eyes insist that I look into them.

Safe. Whenever Brutus talks about sex, he mentions safety. Honestly, until I first talked to him, I had never made the connection. Of course you have to feel *safe* before you can enjoy sex. Before you can *want* sex.

Safety can mean a lot of things. When we think of sex and safety, the first thing that comes to mind is condoms and, especially if you're a woman having sex with a man, the risk of him being violent. Safe sex means: no diseases, no pregnancy. No consequences. Which I guess why 'safe sex' never seems to include 'no rape' because rape rarely ends up having real consequences for the guy.

But safe sex is so much more than that. It is about trusting that the person you are with will listen to you when you set your boundaries. That they will react to your body language; when you pull away, they will react accordingly. It is about trusting that they would not intentionally put you in a dangerous situation and that the aftermath will be respectful. That you won't suddenly get a text from the person's spouse or hear that they have told all of your mutual friends what you look like naked.

Sometimes, we need to feel safe in the knowledge that we won't fall in love. Or that if we do, the other person will treat you with kindness and not take advantage of the situation.

We need to trust that the person we are with will also communicate their boundaries and desires. That they are honest.

As I am putting this into words, I realise that maybe not everyone needs all of this. There are probably people who do not care if the person they are having sex with is lying or cheating, or whether they will treat them well afterwards. They feel safe enough in themselves, that however the other person acts, as long as it is not directly horrible, they trust they will be fine.

Maybe, at some point, you no longer fear that you will end up with someone who is going to be awful and toxic towards you because you just exude powerful boundaries and don't-fuck-with-me vibes, which mean toxic people just stay away from you. That is my dream. An inbuilt creep-shield.

Yet, Johnson was not a creep. Or toxic. He just fell in love with someone else. That happens. My first therapist once told me, 'It's not about finding someone who will never reject you – it's about finding someone who, if they do reject you, handles your heart with love and care,' and

I am still to completely learn that lesson. I gave too much of myself to Johnson, including the power to completely destroy me. That power should not belong to anyone other than me.

The person I was in 2015, in Johnson's bed, is a different person than the one I am today. So different.

3.

GENDER

P IS 36 YEARS old, a queer, trans nonbinary person who came out as trans in 2018. Before this, they were vocal about sex – both past and future prospects – and they were a lot more 'sexually open', despite not actually having a lot of sex.

'I met my current partner before coming out as trans, so she experienced the sexually "free" side of me at the beginning. We shared stories of past sexual encounters, partners and so on and I had this air of fluidity, confidence and experience in how I spoke and acted.'

P would boast and joke about their past sexual experiences, but once their new partner challenged them on this, they began unpacking it. 'I realised I had been wearing a big old mask my whole adult life. I explored my sexuality and gender, and it was clear: I had spent so long hiding behind a mask of toxic masculinity. I mean, I worked in kitchens at the time – need I say more?'

When P's partner got too close to their genitals, they would feel nervous. Sex always had an apprehension to it. 'There was a period of time where I had to become comfortable in my skin again.'

P never felt attached to any of the 'gendered parts' of their body: 'My body did not belong to me and so it was easier to put my tits on display, since they didn't feel like mine anyway. So since I came out as trans and began reclaiming my body, I have noticed that I am far less sexual and sexually driven. The mask is off. I no longer project desires or seek validation as I once was.'

The best sexual experience P ever had was the first time they had sex with their partner after coming out as trans. 'Before this, I had so much mental blockage, so much mind/body disconnect, that I just went through the motions. But suddenly, she knew and affirmed how I connected to myself and to her. I wanted to fuck like I have a dick, not a strap. A real fucking cock! So we did a little role play and she said she wanted to feel my dick inside her and we both came. It felt the way I always wanted it to feel. Phenomenal. Communication and honesty makes for excellent sexy times.'

P and their partner have been doing a lot of unpacking of their traumas, behaviours, desires and selves. And between a continuous existential crisis, a bad gag reflex and transitioning, they also found internalised fatphobia. P's partner is a fat woman and can become quite self-conscious of her body.

'In this unpacking process, my partner has developed "retroactive jealousy", where her intrusive thoughts would hyperfocus on my sexual past and she would compare herself to women in my past, to her own detriment. We have worked through some of those issues, but we both have shame and detachment issues in regards to our bodies. There is a disconnect between mind and body. Like, I want to get a boner but instead my clitoris gets engorged. And the process of stopping sex to put on a strap-on – and perhaps even having to clean it, if we were too lazy last time we used it... It just makes sex less appealing to me. Just being alive in this dumpster fire world is quite exhausting, so it would be nice to experience sex without the apprehension. Just loving blissfulness.'

P realises that sex used to be really important to them, before they started working on their issues. 'I think I was relying on sex to feel validated. It wasn't so much about the quality of the sex or the partner, but the fact that I felt wanted. I always felt like a novelty to people and I still wrestle with this insecurity. I was just thrilled if someone actually wanted to have sex with me, no matter who they were. I just needed to feel wanted.'

WILL I EVER HAVE SEX AGAIN?

The last time I had sex, I identified as a woman. Reluctantly, yes, but I assumed that was the correct label. As we were kissing and removing each other's clothes, it was a dress he pulled up over my head. My long hair was brushed away from my face and the next day, my mascara had left debris around my eyes. I wore a push-up bra and tights and dangly jewellery. If he had walked into the world and answered people honestly when they asked what he did last night, he would have said that he had slept with a woman, right after we had seen *Little Shop of Horrors*, shared a bottle of vodka and danced to the soundtrack. He would have believed he had just had heterosexual sex with a cis woman.

As I am writing this book, I have short hair. I no longer wear makeup or jewellery. I stopped wearing dresses a long time ago. I identify as nonbinary, which belongs under the trans umbrella. A lot has happened since November 2015. The next time I have sex, I will be a lot more myself than I ever was before. This is why gender is on the table, in this chapter. How can we ever talk about sex without talking about gender? How can we talk about anything, without talking about gender?

To fill you in on what happened, gender-wise, before and after November 2015...

Firstly, I have a chest tattoo, intimacy issues, I have mostly slept with men lacking emotional intelligence and my job is to stand on a raised platform in a spotlight and tell jokes to gain people's approval and applause, so I'm sure you're not surprised to hear that my dad left when I was a child. My mother was a single mother throughout my entire childhood.

My mother is an interesting person. She has hair that goes to her shoulders and she has breasts,[27] but that's as far as her appearance goes to let the world know she is a woman. If you stripped her down, you would see that she has a vagina, but please, I am begging you, don't do that to my mother. Just trust me on the vagina-thing. I've seen it up close,[28] I can vouch for it. Other than that, it is as if she deliberately rejects every notion of femininity. She wears exclusively men's clothing. Non-fitted jeans and shirts. Men's trainers. She has never worn makeup or touched her eyebrows. She escapes out of her bra every day when she comes home from work with a disgruntled moan, furious that society expects her to wear one. She uses a standard Nivea lotion on her face every night and a shampoo-and-conditioner for her hair (and body wash), and that's it in terms of products. She does not sway her hips when she walks; she mainly watches action films and reads Stephen King books. She never laughs at men's jokes and she is happy to be firm, ruthlessly honest and demanding.

One of the reasons my dad left was that she simply

---

27 It was never my dream, nor is it anyone's, to write 'my mother has breasts' in a book, I'll just say that much.

28 But enough about that time she got drunk at Christmas. I am kidding, calm down.

wouldn't take his bullshit. She demanded that he be as self-sufficient as she is and he was incapable of doing that. To be honest, most people – myself included – are incapable of being as self-sufficient as her. So he found himself a softer, gentler, more feminine and homely wife instead. A lovely red-headed woman who worked with children and liked candles and potpourri. My mother works in a factory, doing hard physical labour. She is in her sixties and I think her large, masculine coworkers are slightly afraid of her. My mother never asks for help. She will learn how to assemble furniture, she will find a way to carry a huge, heavy king-size mattress up four flights of stairs and god help the man who asks if she needs help. She will ask him why he considers her so weak that he has to berate her like that or why he is so insecure in his own masculinity that he needs to prove himself to her.

She is so comfortable with transness without having needed any education on it that I suspect that if she had been a teenager now and on TikTok, she would quickly have stumbled upon this new gender-inclusive world and probably come to the conclusion that she might not be a woman. She told me, matter-of-factly, about a time a friend of hers, whom she had believed to be a man, came over for dinner. This friend said to my mother, over a bolognese, 'I have never told anyone this before, but... I am a transgender. I am a woman.'

I held my breath as she said this, like a lot of us do when we fear our parents are about to be transphobic or otherwise problematic. But she calmly said, 'I was so relieved that I wasn't actually having dinner with a man, like I thought.' Her emphasis on the word 'man' was full of the tired contempt of a sixty-year-old person who has been around too many of them.

I was not raised as a girl. Not because my mother was intentionally raising me in a gender-neutral way; she simply refused to acknowledge gender as a thing. She was more practical. She would urge me to wear clothing from the boys' section because it was cheaper, had more pockets and seemed to last longer. She didn't introduce me to bras, even when I was thirteen and definitely had breasts, because she felt like it was madness that a child needed to wear a bra. She didn't teach me to shave my legs or to do makeup because it never even crossed her mind to do so. She would never make gendered statements about what girls should or shouldn't do. I don't ever recall her referring to me as a girl, only gender-neutral terms like child, kid, person or simply my name.

I remember being nine years old and asking my neighbour Martin at school if he wanted to play after school. He looked embarrassed and said 'No!' Later, he came to my house and asked if I wanted to hang out. He explained that he just didn't want the other boys to know that he was playing with a girl. I distinctly remember feeling confused. Like he was talking about someone else. I didn't understand why he couldn't play with a girl, but I also didn't understand why he thought of me as a girl. I didn't have the language or understanding of myself and gender to express or even consciously think this, so I just internalised it to mean that I am somehow wrong.

That followed me into my teens. I was bad at being a girl because I was the only one not wearing makeup, not shaving my legs, wearing my uncle's old clothes because it was more practical. I knew I was bad at being a girl and I externalised it by keeping to myself, showing great disdain for anything feminine. When I was 13, I won a competition to be interviewed in a teen girl magazine. When the journalist asked me about my makeup routine, I said, 'I don't wear makeup, I'm not like those whores in my class.' That was printed in the magazine. When it was published, I was called into a meeting with the girls from my class and accused of single-handedly bullying sixteen girls via the medium of mainstream press. And fair enough. I had reached Piers Morgan levels of nastiness, using the power of the press to oppress innocent people. Except I was 13, so it's a lot more excusable than Piers Morgan, who's technically an adult.

Every time I was referred to as a girl or a woman, I felt a knot in my stomach. Like I had been called by a different name. And when I referred to myself as a girl or a woman, I felt like I was lying. When I started doing comedy at the age of 21, suddenly my gender became seemingly The Most Interesting Thing About Me. Being called a woman was no longer just an occasional weirdness, it was daily. Please welcome the next comedian, she's a woman...

And you thought female comedians couldn't be funny! The female comedienne doing lady-jokes about woman things, probably. I didn't like it – but to be fair, neither did the actual female comedians. So I assumed that was the reason – that I was just being regularly annoyed at this weird focus on my genitals and what that is supposed to mean for my comedy.

I tried to distance myself from my own alleged womanhood by distancing myself from women in general. I would do incredibly sexist jokes, to impress the male comedians and show them that I was one of the guys, but also to create a thick boundary between me and the women. I was not aware of the actual reasons behind what I did, of course. If you had asked me back then, I would have just said the classic, I'm not a feminist because I don't hate men and I don't think I'm a victim and I've never experienced sexism. And blah blah blah.

I moved from Denmark to the UK and suddenly, a whole new focus on gender emerged. Cab drivers and shopkeepers would say 'love' and 'hon'; men would hold the door for me, walk me home, pull out chairs for me. On top of which, of course, my gender was still a Main Attraction when it came to comedy. First ever female comedian to win this competition. For a female comedian, that was very funny. Suddenly, I was 'Miss Hagen' or ma'am. Clothing was no longer just black and oversized, like I was used to in Denmark; now it had flowers and tight waistlines. At the exact same time,

I found feminist and queer theory.[29] I began to understand my internalised misogyny. I realised how ignorant my sexist jokes had been. I learned about the patriarchy and what it all actually means. I interpreted the way I cringed whenever I was called a woman as just internalised sexism and I fought it hard. I began to really claim my womanhood. As a woman... I would say that a lot. As a woman... It still felt wrong. I still felt like I was lying. I couldn't quite figure out why no one pointed out that I was clearly faking it.

When I published my first book, *Happy Fat*, in 2018, I was invited to a launch event at my publishers' office. I was to take the stage and read an excerpt from my book in front of an audience full of bookstagrammers[30] (that's people on Instagram who post about books and it's a subculture I love and appreciate). I was sitting in an office, waiting for the event to start, when Amrou Al-Kadhi walked in. I had been told that they were nonbinary and I felt nervous. I didn't want to say the wrong thing. Their book, *Unicorn: The Memoir of a Muslim Drag Queen*, lay on the table

---

29 I don't love revealing this but I didn't even consider looking into feminism before a man told me to. Pat Burtscher is now a successful comedian living in New York and each time his stand-up clips pop up on my social media accounts, I think, *goddamnit, that's the white, straight, cis man who turned me into a feminist.*

30 There are also booktokkers (people on TikTok loving books) and bookTubers (people on YouTube... you get the gist) and they are all really smart and cool. (Hi BookTokkers, my Instagram handle is @sofiehagendk and my TikTok handle is @sofie.hagen and remember how I love you so much? #WillIEverHaveSexAgain)

in front of me. Amrou walked in, dressed as Glamrou, their drag act. Wearing a beautiful, long Arabic dress with gold lace along the seams, a long, pink wig, a full face of silvery makeup and a unicorn horn right in the middle of their forehead, they moved with such grace and beauty. They said hello and sat down and I felt like I had to tread carefully. Somehow, we got to talking about Islam. I felt ridiculous for asking what was probably a question they were asked all the time: but what about Islam? Is Islam okay with you being nonbinary? I felt like such a regressive cliché that if Amrou had just taken the Quran and stuffed it down my throat, I would have fully accepted that as my punishment. But Amrou was patient and quoted a piece of the Quran that can easily be interpreted to say that Allah is actually nonbinary. And another bit that Amrou interpreted to mean that Allah was always accepting of queerness.[31] It made me incredibly emotional. I felt my eyes fill with tears. It was, of course, less about Islam and more about the sheer visibility of Amrou sitting in front of me, just being nonbinary, talking about queerness and transness in a way I had not experienced before. I just nodded and said, 'Wow,' and then I left my body in a desperate attempt to flee all the feelings I was suddenly feeling. It was too much truth.

Two years later, a couple of days before New Year's

31 'And the masculine people of faith and the feminine people of faith are spiritual protectors of one another: they encourage what is right and discourage what is wrong.' (Quran 9:71)

Eve, I had been ignoring the inevitable truth for so long. Whenever I was asked to give my pronouns, I found a way to avoid it. If I was asked to state my gender, I would mumble 'woman, I think, or...' and hope the other person left it alone. It felt like I was existing in some strange void where I was definitely probably potentially maybe certainly not a woman but also, surely, I wasn't trans. I was still under the belief that I had to be androgynous to be nonbinary. In November of that year, I had stopped wearing dresses. Before that, all I ever wore were dresses. I had gone to see a concert with some genderqueer friends and at the last minute I took off my dress and instead put on a grey top I bought in ASOS men's department and some burgundy trousers I had bought once but never worn. I felt incredible. I felt right. At the concert, a blogger wanted to take a photo of all of us but told me to step back because she'd get my photo later. She never did. And I didn't even care. I was almost proud. Better to be ignored as me than photographed as someone I'm not.

One of my best friends is a nonbinary performer called Jodie Mitchell who does a Drag King act named John Travulva. In December of this same year, I brought a friend to their drag show, Pecs, in Dalston, London. I saw people challenge and play with gender in ways I had not really seen before. Nonbinary and trans bodies that were used to being interpreted as 'female' wore masculine clothes, facial hair was painted on and their voices were made deeper. I had tingles down my spine. I turned to my friend and said, 'Isn't it funny how this kind of show just makes you wonder if you really are a woman or not?'

My friend shook her head. 'What? No, it doesn't?' and a tiny part of me thought, *Oh, but that is probably because you are a woman, then.*

A few weeks later, so close to the new year, I sat on my bed and listened to my new friend Travis Alabanza do an interview on the radio. They talked about how it felt to be nonbinary. I don't remember much because again I floated out of my body. But this time, instead of fleeing from reality and all the complex feelings that arose, I looked at myself from above and saw myself. My fingers were tingling as I unlocked my phone and opened WhatsApp, then pressed the little microphone icon and started my voice message to Travis. My voice was highly pitched and slightly shaky as I told them that I definitely probably potentially maybe certainly wasn't a woman. I took a deep breath and said, 'I don't know what I am, but I am not a woman. I am not a woman. I am not a woman. I am not a woman.'

I didn't expect it to feel liberating. It's not like anything had changed. The world was still the same. I was still the same. I just had a feeling of, *Oh. This is how the world is meant to look. This is how the world has always looked, now I'm just a part of it. Now I see.* Like the feeling of hearing your name said out loud by someone else in a loving tone. A feeling of being home, in yourself.

If this is all new to you, I do not blame you. Allow me

to briefly cover the basics of transness, so we can really get into it.

If you were born with a vagina and the doctors handed you to your mother and said, 'It's a girl!' and since then you've been absolutely fine with that, then you're a woman. If that just feels right, then you are a woman. You're a cis woman. Cis meaning, 'Yup, the doctors were right when they pointed at your baby genitals and decided your gender for you – lucky guess.' Similarly, if you were born with a penis and the doctors pointed at it and said, 'You shall forever be a man and, by the way, congrats, you are going to make so much more money' – and that still feels 100 per cent correct, then you are a man. A cis man.

But if you are like me, born with genitals and an adhering label that feels utterly wrong, you are probably genderqueer and/or trans. Trans is an umbrella term that covers anything that isn't cis. Anything, shall we say, out of the ordinary. And if you do not fit into one of the two simple categories 'woman born with vagina' or 'man born with penis', you may have to spend just a few pages in your book introducing this aspect of yourself. If I didn't, you would probably see my name, maybe my photo on the back of the book, and assume that I am a woman. That doesn't make you an evil transphobe, it just makes you a human who, just like me, was raised in a society where we were only taught about the binary genders: man and woman. Penis and vagina. To be honest, if I saw my name and my photo (and I wasn't me), I would probably assume 'woman', too. It takes a lot of time and effort to unlearn that automated response.

I hope you are reading this book in a future where it seems utterly pointless to be defending transness, but unfortunately, this is being written during a very dangerous time. Trans people are under constant and vicious attack from right-wing people, including women who claim to make these attacks in the name of feminism. When we start to challenge our ideas of gender, it is bound to stir up a lot of fear and anger, but there is a lot you can do with your frustration that does not mean bullying or threatening real people. These people could have sat down with their feelings and examined why this is so hard for them to accept. Sure, it will be harder, in the future, to know which colour to paint the nursery walls. It's easier when you just have to pick between blue or pink. The two genders, the two colours. If only someone would tell these distressed people that the fact that yellow, green, black, purple, red, orange, brown, grey and white also exist is a beautiful and exciting thing. The human eye is capable of seeing up to ten million different shades of colour, so why are we fighting it so hard?

According to Stonewall and YouGov's Trans Report: Facing Discrimination and Abuse, 41 per cent of trans people and 31 per cent of nonbinary people have experienced a hate crime because of their gender identity. A quarter of all trans people have experienced homelessness at some point in their lives. Twelve per cent have been physically attacked by coworkers or customers. Half of trans and nonbinary people have hidden or disguised the fact that they are trans at work because they were afraid of discrimination. A Trans Mental Health and Emotional Wellbeing Study in the UK and Ireland from 2012 found that 88 per cent of trans people were depressed or had experienced depression previously. This statistic lowered significantly for those who were undergoing or had undergone some kind of process of transition or gender-affirming surgery.

I am not a woman, a lady, a girl, a female. I am a person, a human, I am Sofie. I am me. My pronouns don't really matter to me. I am fine with she/her. They/them feels like a hug. He/him feels fun. Anything that is an acknowledgement that I am not a woman feels better than she/her. But then, you are catching me mid-gender journey. And honestly, you're probably always catching me mid-gender journey. I would hope that you catch most people mid-gender journey. I do not think we are ever done exploring and experimenting, as soon as we open our eyes to the multitude of things that gender can be – and doesn't have to be. Gender is ever-changing, fluid and such a ridiculous, fabricated thing that we get to decide whatever we do with it. There are few things we go through life without ever changing. We cut our hair, get a new sofa, paint our walls a different colour, move from the city to the countryside, we stop drinking, start baking, we change the way we dress, the way we speak, the people around us, and we evolve and readjust and grow into ourselves. It is the opposite of restrictive, if we let it be.

What is restrictive are the scripts we have learned to follow, based on our assigned genders. Like how the sexual scripts we have learned are restrictive too. Whereas broadening your mind and allowing more options to exist will allow you to take a more multifaceted approach to yourself, both in terms of gender and your sexual experiences.

Having to learn that gender can be more than just the classic man and woman is no more restrictive than learning that the guy from your work whose name you always thought was Steve Hansen is actually called John Hansen. You wouldn't say, 'But WHY are you named John Hansen? You look like a Steve Hansen!' or 'But it's so hard to change it, can I not just call you Steve Hansen?' because that would be weird now that you know that John Hansen has always been John Hansen. You and society just got it wrong. It's not your fault and you're not a bad person. There were times when even John Hansen referred to himself as Steve Hansen, so how could you have known? All you need to do is, you know, call John Hansen John Hansen. And if you later find out that John got married and has changed his name to John Williamson, you would just update your contact information. John Hansen is now John Williamson and that's just how it is.

I know I talk as if I have all the answers; I don't. There is a lot about my gender I cannot explain. What really makes a woman? I mention bras, beauty products, dresses, softness and the colour pink as somehow gender-defining things, but we know that womanhood is not defined by any specific object, characteristic or colour, so how do I know for certain that I am not a woman? I could be a woman raised in a gender neutral way and just not feel any attachment to what we consider typically woman-y. Is my discomfort with being called a woman just latent internalised misogyny? I get that one a lot, from transphobes. Unless you embrace the idea that there are just two genders, you simply *hate women*. I do not believe that I hate women. I feel in my heart a lot of love for women. Women are phenomenal. I would have had a slightly easier life if I was a woman instead of nonbinary. All I know and all I can tell you is that, right now, the label 'nonbinary' feels the least wrong of all the labels. 'Person' feels the most right. 'Man' feels funny, like I am wearing an interesting costume. 'Woman' makes my skin crawl, like I am being forced into a super-tight skinsuit full of itching weeds. 'Nonbinary' feels like you see that I am not a woman and I feel good about that. But did I grow up thinking I was 'nonbinary'? No. I just thought I was me. A person. I am still getting to know and appreciate 'nonbinary'. And who knows what will happen? Perhaps other labels will come along that will feel differently. Like I said, we are ever-changing.

The next time I have sex, I will not be cosplaying as a woman: I will be myself. But how do I have sex as myself?

How do trans people have sex? If you get rid of the labels, you get rid of the scripts you have been taught and then you are just two (or more, I don't judge) bodies... doing sex. I feel quite confused and lost, so I turned to an expert. Not someone who has read all the books and memorised the statistics, but someone who is an expert in being themself.

No one embodies this as well as Juno Roche. They are the author of four books: *Trans Power*, *Gender Explorers*, their memoir *A World-Class Family Ages Badly* and *Queer Sex: A Trans and Non-binary Guide to Intimacy*, which is the book I frantically picked up and swallowed in a day, as I tried to make sense of the world of sex from a trans perspective. As soon as I put down the book, having marked it to shreds with different coloured highlighters, I tracked down Juno Roche's email address and asked if I could speak to them for my book. On a Friday morning in October, we connected over Zoom. Me in my living room in London, them in their house in the Andalusian mountains in Spain, because, as they say, 'I find the mountains to be very trans.'

'The problem is gender. Once I freed myself from gender, I found my body incredibly sexy. I am nearly 60 years old and I find my body incredibly sexy and sexual, attractive and vibrant. I love to self-pleasure. I really love to feel my body and look at my body. And why shouldn't I? We were born into a world that wants us to hate our bodies because that's how they make money off our fucking asses. By us hating our bodies and then working harder to improve our bodies. I'm good, away from gender. I like being trans. Not transgender, not a trans woman or trans feminine or any of that shit. Just trans. Once I found that word I was like: oh god, finally, finally, finally, finally, finally. Even the way I wanked became specific to my trans body.'

Juno starts off incredibly strong.

'I feel like everyone would feel freer, if they freed themselves from gender, not just trans people,' I say, envying Juno's connection with their own sexuality, their own transness. The fact that they can just say 'wanking' to a stranger. I am not there yet.

'There was a time, believe it or not, when people would say: as long as trans people pass and look just like us, it's fine. As long as we don't notice them. And I thought, God, for me to do that, with my attitude and my politics... Because gender is not just a physical thing. It is the way you move, politically, in the world. The way you respond to people, the way you react to things. There is no way I am going to do that. It's just punishing.'

Juno had gender-affirming surgery back when they still embraced the label 'trans woman': 'When I first started this process, years and years ago, I had to start it privately because I was HIV positive and no one wanted to touch me. People were really mean – I mean, people are still really nasty, but back then, people were openly nasty. If you had the disease, you could fuck off. So I went to this posh place I couldn't really afford and they tried to send me away for wearing Converse. They said I was being difficult because I wasn't trying to be feminine enough. And I said, 'Well, what would have been feminine enough?' and they suggested that I could have worn pink Converse. Later on, I saw that in their notes about me, they referred to me as a 'butch lesbian'. Now, listen, I love butch lesbians, but there is no way under the sun I have ever identified as a butch lesbian.'

Towards the end of *Queer Sex: A Trans and Non-binary Guide to Intimacy*, Juno has interviewed trans and non-binary people in the search for answers to the question: how do you find intimacy, as a trans person in this world? They write:

I sometimes imagine that a kiss, a single kiss, would be so overwhelming that even thinking of its potential to link me to the world makes me tearful now. I miss being kissed. I miss feeling arms around me or a body pressed next to mine. I miss the warmth of another's breath on my neck. It's human contact I miss, desperately miss. I don't want to be overly dramatic, but it sometimes feels crushing – silent – and the noise from these interviews has ironically left me feeling that the silence of only being me is killing me slowly. We need contact, we need affection, closeness and I am writing it now, despite how painful it feels because I can't imagine that it's going to change whilst I pretend to be outside of this process.

Juno wrote this in 2015 and we are talking in 2023. I hope something has changed because I relate a terrifying amount to the pain in their words. I ask Juno what has changed since then.

'I have been looking through this litany of words that we have been given, like, vagina, woman, man, cock, submissive, penetration and all these words that just do not fit. But in the word 'trans', there was this expansive space that I felt like I could populate. And part of the way I did that was by only having relationships with people that are trans. And not because of any overriding dogma on my part but simply because I suddenly went: *God, we really are the attractive ones. We are the good looking ones. We are the ones who have bodies that are pulled and stitched and tightened and then loosened. We are the ones who have a wisdom about us, in the way we have tackled our bodies.* It is brave to tackle gender. It's so fucking brave. It is so brave to take your one way of being and then say: 'No, this is who I am.' It takes real courage to do that in a world that says that the closer you are to looking like Carrie Bradshaw and Mr Big, the better you're going to get on. And the further away you are from that, the tougher it is going to be. But what they don't tell you is that, actually, the joy is all over here.'

'I don't think I've ever heard anyone talk about trans bodies like this; I feel like we only hear about our bodies in relation to cis bodies, you know – how much or how little we look like either 'a real man' or 'a real woman,' I say, a bit out of breath with emotion. 'How do you get to the point where you feel so... at peace with your transness? So free from gender?'

'I was diagnosed with full-blown AIDS when I was first diagnosed, in the very early 1990s. I was told that I wouldn't live long. There were no drugs, so we all thought we were going to die. But how are you meant to receive that? I can't die, I've got stuff to do. I'm not saying I willed myself to live but I went to university and, in a way, I had a 'dry run' for people not wanting to touch my body. My body was seen as defective. I was untouchable. Back then, bodies with AIDS were terrifying to people. I had this notion that my body was a messy body that I'd have to take care of. I had a bad body. And luckily for me, I was also dealing with being trans at the same time, so I had other stuff going on too, but I did think: *My mind is beautiful. I am going to make my mind beautiful. I'm going to philosophically inhabit this world.* Even after I transitioned, there was this kind of internalised transphobia that made me feel like, in order for them to love me, I have to dismiss my body. I have always been bad at dismissing my body. I am a bit too punk to dismiss my body.'

'I feel like I am not looking for answers,' I say, 'as much as I am looking for scripts. It was such a simple rulebook I was given in my twenties. I must be a woman and I must be with a man and this is how I do that. Now, there are no more rulebooks.'

'The not knowing is a creative space. We are creative

beings. Artistic, creative beings. We go for walks in the countryside and pick up shells on the beach. We are eminently romantic, creative beings. And it is in the unknowing that we find the biggest kind of wins. That is not to say that all the sex I have had has been great. That's far from the truth. But what it has been is, it has had that element of the unknown. An element of "how will we do this?" and "how is this going to happen?" not in a spoken way. Because often what has happened is that my body has reacted and my body has been turned on. And I have just had to go with that feeling. Once I revelled in my transness, I had no desire to follow a script any longer. And there is something mildly terrifying about not following the script. You know, I'm getting older and I live in the mountains on my own with none of the traditional stuff around me. I don't have children, I don't have a partner, I don't really have much of a family. But what I do have is an intense joy that I know my cunt inside out. I know what turns me on. I can say to someone: "Please don't approach my cunt as if it was a biological cunt. It's a different kind. And you need to approach it on its own terms. Touch here, because I know that that piece of skin is from before. It has come across from before." I don't have a vagina, I have like an upcycled cock and balls that really looks like a vagina. Only with trans people can we have that kind of conversation. I have tried having these conversations on Tinder with cis men or cis women and they will act as if I am a freak, when really, I am just giving you pure, hard facts. I am telling you who I am and how I operate and how my body operates. That is because we are currently writing these scripts for the next generation. If we ask ourselves, where do these scripts come from – they come from somewhere. You know, I advocate for trans people taking over the world. I remember giving talks years ago and people would say, "Well, we're really worried that there are so many trans people now," and I'd say yeah, because we are going to take over the world. Of course we are. Being nonbinary is the only way to survive being in a body the world wants to gender. Because we have to survive gender.'

What Juno is saying feels radical and edgy. I have never heard anyone speak like this before, in this celebratory way, about transness. I realise that my go-to feeling is apologetic when I discuss my transness. Sorry, I know I look cis. Sorry, I know it's confusing. Sorry, I know I'm asking you to challenge a lot right now. Sorry if you forget that I am not a woman, don't worry about it, I totally understand. And I do totally understand, of course I do, but I can feel it tearing on my soul, having to constantly explain and minimise the importance of it, to coddle other people's feelings – presumed feelings they might not even have. Speaking to Juno, who is literally sitting in the mountains preaching love and celebration, makes me feel like Moses. I want to take my stone tablets up to Juno and have them write the new ten commandments. I like the idea of a deity who says the word 'cunt' a lot.

I am unable to shake what Juno said about only sleeping with trans people and only being attracted to trans people. I have no doubt that there will be people taking issue with this statement, claiming that it is discrimination against cis people or that it is counterproductive or hostile. But in a world where queer, trans, fat, Black, disabled and otherwise not-normative bodies are constantly dismissed to make space for classical and traditional Westernised beauty, it feels great to hear someone choose transness. It feels incredible to hear a trans person choose anything at all, instead of the internalised transphobia that tells us that we need to just wait and hope that someone wants us. There is an underlying nervousness as to whether the person I will have sex with will accept me and understand my gender, because I automatically assume that they will be cis and that they will take issue with it. I express this to Juno.

'I'll be completely honest, I had a weak moment in about year four of being here. I went to the market and I met this man at this knicker store and for some reason, I was looking at these knickers and I just felt really shit about myself. I don't know why but it all came flooding back. I ended up having sex with the man. It was the most awful experience of my life. My whole body, my cunt, my legs, just closed like that.' Juno claps their hands together hard. 'And you know when your body is closed and someone tries to fuck you, it's really painful. I just had that notion of like – I am never doing that to myself again. This was maybe six years ago. Since then, I have set my own criteria. And that tells me that I am only going to feel comfortable in bed with a trans person. I make no other assumptions as to whether they would be trans masculine, whether or not they have had surgery or they're nonbinary, none of that shit comes to mind. I have no right to create that kind of dynamic. I find transness to be a really attractive thing. I find the bravery of transness such a fucking turn on that I just want them to fuck me rotten.'

I wonder, out loud to Juno, if you can truly love transness, if you do not love your own transness. Or rather, if you can love your own transness and not automatically love other people's transness.

'I have a body that I know is sexual and I know it is desirable. It's taken years to get there. The other day, I said to someone, "I'm going to be 60 this year and I only just found all of this out." And they said, "Yeah, but you know now and isn't it always better to know?" And I agree. And the fear makes so much sense to me. Most of sex is all about am I going to be good enough? Is my body going to make a strange noise? Do I smell? And we need to be quite robust in terms of sorting out this stuff. When we hear ourselves think these things, we need to go: where is that coming from? Let's just pop that over there for a second. Let me park that there. And imagine, for a second, that I am perfect. What if this body is the perfect body? What if my body is a body that everyone would pay to have? What if my body was a body that everyone wanted to photograph? And touch? What if my body was the centre of the universe?'

'And do we need to love ourselves to be able to connect with our own sexuality?' I ask.

Juno smiles. 'I think it is really important to self-pleasure. Working out how to really self-please and enjoy it. I used to lie there in my courtyard with my legs out and just feel the sun on my cunt and it was just a feeling of: God, *how lucky we are, me and my trans cunt.* Just feeling that warmth. And that warmth flooding in, and, obviously, I then wanted to wank. Because it was just this moment of absolute oneness. The real pleasure happens when there is a oneness between you and your body. And if there is a oneness between you and your body, there can be a oneness between you and someone else. If that person has a oneness themselves. Which is why the man from the knicker store was the last time. I thought: *I closeth my legs to this world and I openeth my legs only to that which I know has considered its oneness.*'

That is one for the stone tablets, I think. Commandment number one: Thy shall only openeth thy legs to that which has considered its oneness. I am beginning to understand what Juno means when they talk about the beauty of transness and not taking the risk with cis people. It feels fairly certain that if someone is trans, they will have considered things that cis people can go through their entire lives without having to consider. Perhaps it doesn't have to be a trans thing. All genders could benefit from questioning the rules we have learned about bodies, genitals, gender roles, sexuality and, well, cunts. I am sure that the guy from the knicker store in the Spanish mountains could be a safe, exciting, beautiful fuck if he had spent some time contemplating that which Juno – and many of us trans folks – have been forced to contemplate for most of our lives. I am beginning to not just think – but feel – that my own transness is less of a burden and more of a gift to others. Which is a feeling that both terrifies and liberates at the same time.

'Trans people consider their oneness,' Juno says, 'much more than any other part of society. We work on becoming one with our bodies. When there is no oneness, you begin to externalise yourself and you go: look at me, I'm not good enough. I'm not slim enough. I'm too fat. I'm too this or that, you know. That affects everything. You are constantly trying to act a certain part – and that affects the wetness of a cunt or the stiffness of a cock. But if you occupy a trans body and you go: on every given day, this is as good as it gets. And it is better than I ever imagined. I'm not saying it's easy – I had to move to the mountains of Andalusia to be able to do this. I highly recommend it. They are beautiful mountains.'

Juno adds, with a grin, 'I hope that helps with your writing.'

We have spoken for an hour and I need to let Juno get back to the beautiful mountains that I can see through a window behind them. But there is just one more thing I have to say. I grab my Kindle and find the highlighted passage from towards the end of *Queer Sex*:

> At the very start of this book I owned up to being a 'virginal virgin', but now I feel that I need to own up to something that feels far more real and painful to say. 'I am an intimacy virgin.' I honestly don't know what real intimacy feels like, so I don't have a clue how to find it or even how to know that it's in front of me.

I tell Juno that reading this made me stop dead in my tracks. Despite having worked on this book for two years, by the time I read these words, the word 'intimacy' had never crossed my mind. Have I ever had sex with intimacy? Have I been too disconnected from it for it to be intimate?

What I had with The Comedian felt intimate, almost excruciatingly so. Not because of the secrecy of the affair but because I felt we were two people against the rest of the world. When we engaged in his fetish, despite never touching, it felt like the ultimate intimacy. He had shown me this deep, secret part of himself and I allowed myself to love him and trust him. And we shared moments I believed would keep my heart beating for the rest of my life. The relationship – and the intimacy – died retrospectively, when I realised that he shared this apparent intimacy with many people. That I was never shown any actual deep, secret part of himself – just whichever bits were enough to keep me close to him and to keep me obedient. When I realised how much had been a lie, the intimacy felt like a lie. True intimacy is surely only real if it is between two people showing up as themselves, in an honest and vulnerable way. We never did that. He pretended to be someone else and I repressed every boundary, every bit of personality that might scare him away, offend him or hurt him. He knew I was nonbinary but he never asked about it. It felt like he reluctantly accepted it, like you would accept a flaw in a partner. So I didn't bring it up much because I felt like it would ruin the fantasy for him. He liked strong, powerful women. Women. How can you be intimate with someone if they are not enthusiastically curious about who you are as a person? If they don't celebrate you in the way you are so rarely celebrated?

When I was pitching this book to publishers, and emails were flying back and forth between a bunch of people, I spotted that someone had written, 'It has been almost eight years since Sofie had intimacy.' It was very clearly just someone who felt awkward saying 'sex' and changed the word to something less crass-sounding. But it stung. It made me sad. I can talk about not having had sex in eight years without flinching. I feel no shame and, in some ways, I have not missed it that much. If you told me I would never have sex again, I would be sad but I would find a way to cope. But – intimacy. Saying, out loud, that I don't know if I have ever been intimate with someone, that is full of pain. If you told me I would never have intimacy with someone else for the rest of my life, all I would want to say is: then what is the point of living?

'I think we imagine intimacy to be between us and someone else but often, we can't be intimate with ourselves. Because we are so judgemental of ourselves. We are so tough and so hard on ourselves. We are brutal. We inhabit the language that others give us. We overlook the intimacy with ourselves all the time because we are chasing this intimacy between us and others. But what I really wanted was an intimacy with myself, between me and my cunt, between me and my body and myself and my sense of self. Between me and the spectre of self, between me and the projection of self. All of these things that are usually so fractured from us. How do people see me? How do they take me? Was I too loud when I walked into a room?'

Juno explains that when they had their gender-affirming surgery, the surgeon came into the room and did a 'depth test', where he shoved a dilator into the brand new vagina, only five days after the surgery.

'You've got stitches, you've just had packing taken out, you're not healed, you've never had anyone do that to you before. You have got this beautiful thing that has just been created and they come around and they push it in to test it. And the doctor said: "You've got enough depth for an average penis." And I remember thinking: *God, he thinks I'm only going to come alive when that happens.* I never imagined I would be lying underneath an old olive tree –

me! From south London! An olive tree that I own. Well, in truth, it owns me, it will outlive me by a thousand years as long as some fucker doesn't come and chop it down. But lying under that tree and saying out loud to my cunt: "I'm so joyful for you feeling the sun on you. It is helping you heal." I have got scars down the side, which I love. I experience bucketloads of intimacy now because I find it in myself and therefore I think I can be intimate with others. It is that sense of oneness.'

Commandment number two: Find oneness.

I thank Juno for their time and their beautiful words and I close down the Zoom conversation. I sit in silence for a bit, trying to process what I am feeling. I open my emails to find the break-up letter I sent to The Comedian. I find the specific paragraph I am looking for and read it again. But instead of reading it with him in mind, I try to read it to myself and it feels true.

You are the only person who is uncomfortable with your truth. Maybe that is why you lie so much, to everyone. You don't think you deserve to be loved, so you fuck it all up. You make sure we hate you, the way you think we should. I don't think you're a bad person, I think you're a deeply broken person. I think you're shitscared to look yourself in the mirror. You're not keeping the truth from us. You're keeping it from yourself.

Perhaps the reason I have not experienced intimacy during sex is not just that I am keeping the truth about myself from the person I am having sex with, but also that I am keeping it from myself. Perhaps I am so attached to these gendered scripts on 'how to have sex' because an actor without a script is what? Just a person? Or even worse, someone who does improv. Maybe this is why I dared to fall so deeply in love with The Comedian. He had no interest in the truth and, deep down inside, neither did I. I could cosplay as the person he needed me to be and he could do the same.

If I am going to follow commandment number two and find oneness, I need to be okay with who I am, on a fundamental level. I need to feel so at peace with myself that I can show up authentically with someone else. This slightly annoys me. I was half expecting my conversation with Juno and my exploration of gender to be more Here Is How You Use A Strap-On or How To Play With Your Boobs Without Feeling A Bit Gender Dysphoric About It All and less Dig Deep Into Your Soul And Heal Some Core Wounds So You Can Become One With Yourself. It would be easier to just buy a strap-on and find a new script to follow.

Juno's two commandments:

1. Thy shall only openeth thy legs to that which has considered its oneness, and
2. Find oneness are enough commandments for me, for now. It is enough to convert me into Junoism.

I Visited a Porn Shoot

June 2023

Six months ago, The Comedian with whom I had a five-year situationship slash groomership slash affair, slash whatever else you want to call it, turned up at my front door on a Sunday night. It had been a year since I ended it with him and I already felt like a new person. I had untangled myself from his toxicity and begun my Will I Ever Have Sex Again? journey. I was trying to find myself again – so to find him on my doorstep was not a welcomed surprise.

'You blocked me on all platforms, so I didn't know how else to contact you. Can I come in?' he asked, looking like a sad puppy out there in the rain.

I knew it wasn't a coincidence that he arrived today of

all days. A couple of days before, I had come clean to his now ex-girlfriend. I told her everything that had happened between us and when she asked for proof, I sent her one hundred screenshots. I had tried to do it in the best way possible, which I felt had to be upfront and apologetic but without asking for any kind of friendship or forgiveness. I owned up to my part of it, while trying to not make it all about me. It felt like the right thing to do.

He had broken up with her six months after I broke up with him and was now dating his other mistress. I had heard from someone that he was now trying to start an affair with his original girlfriend, while still being with his new girlfriend. I suddenly felt protective of her, which is admittedly approximately six years too late at this point. But it wasn't too late to warn her. She had finally got out of that relationship and if I could do anything to stop her from starting an affair with him, I would try. No, it's none of my business. Yes, I fucked up first. I wasn't sure if I had done the right thing by texting her. Nevertheless, I had. In the year I had spent recovering from his emotional manipulation, the only thing that had made me feel truly better was learning the facts. Every piece of evidence, any rumour that confirmed what I had already suspected, made me trust myself and my instincts again. I could give his ex-girlfriend some of the answers she probably needed. She told me that she had suspected us of having an affair but each time she asked him, he told her she was crazy.

For so many years, every time the doorbell rang, I had

hoped it was him. I kept my flat tidy, just in case. When it wasn't tidy, I felt anxious, because what if he showed up? I am not sure why I kept thinking he might do it; he never did apart from once during the first lockdown, when he brought me flowers, for no apparent reason. It had meant the world to me. He had no flowers this time, just a sad face and wet hair from the rain.

'Okay, come in,' I said. My flat was a mess and I was wearing an old, paint-stained oversized t-shirt and pyjama bottoms. I hadn't showered in a few days and I was living through what had been my worst nightmare for so many years but, surprisingly, I didn't feel the shame I would have felt back then. We sat down on my sofa.

'You really hurt her feelings by telling her that stuff,' he said in a serious tone.

I blinked a few times. 'Uh, by telling her what you did to her?' I asked.

He shook his head slowly and dramatically. 'She cried so much.' His tone was shaming, asking me to feel bad about myself. She hadn't seemed sad in her texts to me, but of course she was. Perhaps she wouldn't have felt that sadness if I hadn't messaged her, but she might have continued to feel crazy. And if I had to choose, I would rather feel sad than crazy.

'She deserved to know,' I shrugged, still in shock. He was sitting in front of me on my sofa. The first time we had been alone since before we ended it. The last time he sat on that sofa, I was crying my eyes out because I was struggling with his lack of affection and he was on the phone with BBC Leeds, while I tried to sob silently in the background. Now, it all felt so different. He looked pathetic to me. Less attractive.

'You could have just messaged me,' he said.

I frowned, 'What?'

'That's why you told her, right? To get to me?' he smirked.

I rubbed my eyes, trying to regain my senses. 'I'm sorry, what? What?'

'You even kept living in the same area as me. Why haven't you moved?'

Up until this point, I had seen the word 'guffawed' written down before but I had never truly understood what it meant, until it happened to me. I guffawed.

'Because I moved during the pandemic so the rent had been lowered by £200 and if I had to move now, when I have a dog, I'd have to pay £500 more and it would be impossible to stay in London, you absolute moron!'

His face revealed that this came as a shock to him. It filled me with anger that he had wandered around for a year thinking that it was just a matter of time before I let him back in and that I was just hanging around, waiting for him to come back.

'Oh,' he said. 'So when do you think you will unblock me?'

I started feeling my heart in my throat and my eyes stinging. The frustration went deep – six years deep.

I sighed, exasperated. 'You hurt me. I'm still recovering. You made me not trust myself, do you have any idea how bad that is? The cheating is… Whatever. But you made me lose trust in myself. I'm only just getting that back now. I'm only just beginning to feel like myself. You made me feel' – my voice broke – 'so unwanted and so… unloveable. I don't know how to… how to exist now. I don't know how to let anyone else in. I doubt every thought I have. You did that to me. And to her. And who knows how many others you've gaslit. I have no interest in ever speaking to you again.'

I wiped a tear away from my cheek and gathered myself. I hated that he was seeing me cry but at least he refrained from doing any press interviews while I was talking.

'Okay.' He seemed shocked. 'Well, I have to go now.'

I have a Ring doorbell and I saved the footage of him leaving. He took a few steps out the door and then looked back. 'If you did want to message me…' he trailed off.

'I have nothing more to say to you. Have a good night,' you hear me say in the grainy black and white video before the door closes. He stands there for a couple of seconds before wandering off.

I went to my bedroom and sat down on my bed. I started to cry. Only for a minute or two, then it was as if there was no more sadness in my body. I then got up and continued my life. Without him.

Six months later, I only think of him if his face is thrust upon me on social media or if someone mentions his name.

WILL I EVER HAVE SEX AGAIN?

His existence just annoys me a bit, but it doesn't even raise my blood pressure any more. Instead, my exploration of sex is in full swing.

It is June and I am in a Berlin hotel at the height of summer. After stepping out of the freezing hotel shower, despite the aircon being turned to ice cold, I instantly start sweating. I put my hair up in a knot and head downstairs. Cat, the porn producer of the radical, feminist porn production company Ersties, messages me the address with a 'see you soon!' I can't wait. I'm going to be witnessing a porn shoot. It is 2,769 days since I last had sex. There is something quite scary about going to watch people have sex. Why scary? It shouldn't be.

In the lobby of the hotel, I spot a man in a suit. He has a full beard and he is quite fat. He is incredibly attractive. I notice that my hips start... swaying. It occurs to me that this is something I do, when I see an attractive man. Almost as if I think, *Oh, better turn on the femininity because that is what they all want.* But – that is not me. I do not sway my hips when I walk. So why am I putting it on?

I look at the man's walk. He is sort of slumping along, seemingly a bit insecure and a bit geeky. I find it very hot. If I like this man, in all his fatty slumpyness, why do I put on a weird faux femininity to attract him? What if he just wanted me, for me? What if he also found my fatty slumpyness attractive? I make a note of these thoughts in my notebook and also add that these are not thoughts I would have had at the beginning of my journey. It is a positive step.

I get in a cab to go to the address in East Berlin, which turns out to be a block of grey cement flats. Cat comes to pick me up. She takes me upstairs to the flat in which they are getting ready for filming. It is not large and we can barely squeeze past each other in the hallways. There is a bedroom which has become the preparation area – this is where I will later help them by cleaning the toys they will be using. There is another bedroom which has a sofa up against the wall, covered with light pink fabric, and the rest of the furniture has been moved to the back of the room. They are using a flat that someone lives in, not a studio, like I had expected. Cat explains that not only is it cheaper – or well, free – to use someone's home, it is also a nicer place to have sex. Ersties' focus is on the models being comfortable and for them to have a genuinely nice time. You can tell, in their videos. You never doubt that they want to be there. It is what first made me say yes to doing their podcast a couple of years ago – I had just learned about ethical porn, porn you pay for because it's ethical and made by women and often for women. So when someone from Ersties popped up in my inbox, I was excited. Cut to a few years later and here I am – in Berlin, about to witness the production of one of their videos.

We are all boiling. The windows have to stay closed to keep the hot air out, that is how hot it is. I meet the models, Zina and July, two gorgeous and kind people. Today will consist of two shoots: 'How To Fist' and 'How To Use A Strap-On'. The films are going to be directed by Karyn Hunt, an American artist and director who sits confidently on the floor in leggings and a top that reveals her many tattoos. I am instantly amazed and a bit scared of her. She is clearly cool. I feel dumpy in the high heat in this sexy room next to these sexy people.

After explaining what I am doing here, I sit down on the sofa while the three of them sit on the floor in front of me.

'Have you always been just sort of a naturally sexually open or sexually self-aware person?' I ask July.

'Yes, I've always been super interested in sex and wanting to feel all the pleasure. It didn't make sense to me that people would ever see that as something negative. Like, why? It's the most pleasurable thing ever. How can you not want to do that every day and have that in your life all the time?' she replies with a huge grin on her face.

'How do you create a safe space?' I ask Karyn. I notice that her neck tattoo is a snake and that her shoulder tattoo is a rose.

'I'm just here to give the parameters of movement, you know, figure out what's good for the camera. Where can they move, what's the best direction for them to turn towards the camera? Other than that, I spend a lot of time just talking with them about their inherent actual desires, what makes them tick and what turns them off. When you begin with respecting the performer and their desire, the safe spaces basically create themselves.'

It feels like this is true for life too, and real-life, non-filmed sex. Safety keeps coming up in all conversations I have about healthy sex. Justin Hancock mentioned it, Chantal Gautier mentioned it. French Brutus. Now, Karyn, the porn director.

'The fact that so much of it is about talking ahead of time, it's just—' I pause, struggling to find the words. 'I guess, we grow up learning that if we talk during sex, you're a bit annoying. Like if you ask about condoms, you kill the vibe.'

'I talk a lot during sex, also when I do porn,' Zina says. 'You said earlier when we first met that you are like the opposite of a porn star because you are a comedian. But I disagree. Porn can be hilarious.'

I did say that earlier. I was feeling out of place.

'Please don't take my job,' I say. 'You can't be hilarious *and* look good naked.'

Zina smiles. 'When you have sex, you are playing with each other. It's fun. It's supposed to be fun. If it's not fun, it's time to say, "Hey, this is not working right now." Speaking can be sexy. Feedback can be incredibly sexy. What has really helped me is to have this mode of communication where when someone gives you feedback, you receive it by saying thank you, thank you for clarifying that. Thank you for being vulnerable so that I better know how to please you. And I have also noticed that when a partner does that with me, it becomes so much easier to speak because you know that whatever you are saying is really welcomed. And the other person is grateful – and they should be grateful because it is a gift that you are giving them. A gift of honesty. Not saying anything is the easier route to take. You don't have to be vulnerable when you are not putting up a boundary.'

I sit there for a moment, just taking that in. There is that vulnerability again.

'I was celibate for two years, from 2015 to 2017, and it was really, really powerful,' Karyn says. 'I fucked myself silly, though. People always said, "You were celibate but you still masturbated?" and I was like yeah, I didn't lose my sexuality. I just woke up one day and thought: *Oh my God, have I been performing for 35 years? And a role that isn't even inherently my own sexuality. Who am I? What do I actually like?*'

The shoot is about to start, so I go to stand in the doorway as Karyn begins the initial chat with the models.

'How is your body feeling?' she asks July. I watch July reply that her body feels comfortable and that she feels a little bit of nervousness, but she notices how the nervousness switches over to excitement. That she is feeling a bit shy but she is embracing it. A striking thought pops into my head: *I would not be able to say how my body is feeling because I don't know. I feel completely disconnected, almost paralysed with fear.*

'Today is all about communication and taking things

real slow before we escalate. If you need to take a break, just say, "stop"; don't worry about the camera rolling, okay?' Karyn says to the models. 'I have worked with you both before so I have a pretty good idea of what your boundaries and your desires are, but let's just go ahead and restate them so it's fresh in everybody's mind. What is on the menu today and what is not on the menu today?'

Zina says, 'Okay, so I like kisses on my neck. I like biting and if I am super aroused, I can actually take quite a lot of biting and it can be really nice, just don't go for it hard at first. I also like grabbing and pushing and feeling like my whole body is engaged. I also like some interchange between things because often when someone is just licking my pussy for 20 minutes straight, I would like for more interchanging stuff.'

July asks, 'Are there any body parts you don't like for me to touch?'

Zina says, 'Yes, I'm always paranoid because my hair is incredibly long, so I'd like it if you are a bit mindful of not being on top of my hair or not putting me in a position where I'm on top of my hair.'

'Are you okay with me moving your hair away from your face?' July asks, softly but curiously.

'Yes, but I'm not really into you doing too much with my hair. Some head scratches are nice though,' Zina replies.

I'm watching them in awe from the door. It occurs to me that when Karyn asked the models about their boundaries,

I felt scared for them. The first thought in my head was: *But what if my boundary offended the other person? What if they then pulled away or left?*

I make a note of this in my phone because it seems more than relevant: it feels *essential* to this entire journey. If I am afraid of stating my boundaries and desires in case they offend the person I am in bed with, then of course I panic when sex is on the table. If my entire body knows that we are unsafe, that we will not be able to say stop if we mean stop, of course it is not going to let me near another person in an intimate way.

Watching Zina, Karyn and July explain their desires and boundaries to each other is mindblowing. I feel like I am experiencing something incredibly healthy for the very first time.

'I can feel my outer energy body a lot, so if you hover around my body that can sometimes be even more intense than if you touch my body,' July is explaining to Zina, and all I can think is: *I want to know this about myself. How do you learn that you like someone hovering above your body and that it gives you pleasure?*

When the shoot starts, we close the door. The room is too small for all of us, so Karyn, July and Zina are left to start filming on their own while I go sit on the bed with Cat, the producer. We whisper about Edinburgh, where she is from, and Copenhagen, and about bodies and sex, while we hear moans and sweet laughter from the room next door.

Afterwards, Zina and July emerge, naked and sweaty, with smiles on their faces. A sweet, thick smell of sweat and sex fills the flat. Their cheeks are red, their hair slightly frazzled. They are giggling and seem a lot more relaxed than they were before the shoot.

I thank everyone for their time and for letting me chat to them. I get a cab back to my hotel, where I lie in my bed, thinking about what sex *should be* and what it, so far, *hasn't ever been*. I think about The Comedian and how, when I ever tried to state a boundary, he would get upset or he would disappear. For the first time in six and a half years, I am happy that I never actually slept with him. I am not sure I want to have sex with someone who not only can't handle boundaries, but who is not even curious about them. After today, I cannot imagine ever *not* being curious about someone's boundaries, especially if I am about to be intimate with them. How am I only learning this now?

4.

BODIES

A COUPLE OF MONTHS before I had My Last Sex in November of 2015, I travelled to New York for the first time in my life. I had just ended a very brief, three-week long relationship because it got too intense too quickly. Three days into deciding we were a couple, he had announced it on Facebook and he kept saying 'I lo— oops! Like you' and I panicked. I ended the relationship over text because my whole body was itching whenever I looked at him. There was nothing wrong with him – he was a lovely and quite handsome man. I was simply utterly incapable of being in a relationship with him.

It was with this new freedom that I went to New York. One morning, I sat down in my underwear in front of a full-length mirror, something I didn't have at home. My fat stomach rested on my upper thighs and, at first, its vastness filled me with shame. Then, instead of covering it, I kept staring at it. Until the shame disappeared and all I saw was . . . just a stomach. I had never really looked at it before. I had never seen it in a neutral light. It's *just a stomach*. I took a photo of it, which felt scary. Terrifying, even. I kept it in my phone for a week or so until, one day, I just decided to post it on Instagram. At this point, more people had seen my vagina than my stomach. I had sex in the dark. I got dressed quickly. I wore A-line dresses so my stomach was always covered by large amounts of flowing fabric. Very few men had been successful in convincing me that they found me attractive enough for me to actually stand in front of them naked. Posting my exposed stomach on Instagram felt like a massive step in the right direction. A direction away from shame and self-hatred. I thought, *Where will this take me?*

Four years later, I saw my first ever book in a bookstore. On the front cover, I sit on a chair with my fat stomach resting on my thighs, a smiley face drawn on it. People were walking past me, looking at the book too. A year later, I had a bit in a stand-up show where I took off my jumpsuit and danced a little in front of the audience, wearing nothing but a bra and pants. As I started to take off my clothes each night, I saw them staring in disbelief, many clearly thinking it was a joke, that I would not actually do it. But I did do it, and I felt free and joyful.

Cut to the year 2022. I am in New York again. I take off my bra and drape it over a chair. I then let my underpants drop to the floor and I step out of them. I exit the room through a big glass door that leads onto a Brooklyn rooftop. It is 35 degrees celsius and I feel the hot air on my entire body. I am surrounded by windows in skyscrapers but I notice no actual people, other than the photographer. I know her personally. It is Substantia Jones, a photographer and fat activist whose project Adipositivity has run for years. She has taken naked (and almost-naked) photos of fat people for the project, including many of my friends and people I look up to. It was a bucket list item for me to have Substantia take my naked photo. Behind her is a full camera crew, documenting the photoshoot for a documentary.

I realise that I miss having pockets more than I miss wearing a bra. I walk across the rooftop, not quite knowing how to pose for this naked photo. I try lifting my hands above my head, so I can feel the air underneath my arms. I suggest to Substantia that it might look cool if I go to the end of the rooftop, by the railing, so she can shoot me from behind, with the Manhattan skyline in front of me. When I grab the railing, it is hot and I have to wait for my hands to adjust to the heat. I then raise my arms out from my body, to the side, and close my eyes. *I'm the king of the world.*

I hear the clicking of Substantia's camera and I think back to the full-length mirror in 2015, when revealing *just my stomach* to *just myself* felt groundbreaking and wild.

WILL I EVER HAVE SEX AGAIN?

I open my eyes again and see the Manhattan skyline and the sun setting behind it. I lower my gaze and see... Oh. I see around 50 cars all lined up to watch the outdoor cinema that starts soon, projected onto the wall right below where I am standing. Inside the cars, on top of cars, on benches and chairs below me people are sitting, staring up at me, like a very fat miniature Statue of Fat Liberty. I am not sure which movie they were about to watch but I hope I provided decent pre-movie entertainment. I have never been more naked in my life.

I am a fat person who has spent more than a decade learning about fat positivity, fat liberation and body politics. I wrote an entire book, *Happy Fat*, solely about this topic. And, as described, I confidently flashed what felt like half of Brooklyn just a year ago. This is why it makes no sense to me that I still, despite all of this, have a little voice in my head that narrates my life and which still holds quite fatphobic thoughts at times. Not all the time. Not like when I was a teenager, when the voice had a megaphone and would shout toxic statements as if they were truths, and it would make me self-harm while taking turns binge-eating and starving myself. I believed what the voice told me: that my worth was related to how thin I was, that I was inherently unlovable, that I was lazy and gross. I trusted that the voice was just telling me the truth and the solution would be to lose weight.

Whatever the situation, I would always blame myself. In my early twenties, I wanted so desperately to hook up with people and find a partner, but I was just not receiving the same level of attention as my (thin and conventionally attractive) friends. I remember complaining to a friend, who always seemed to become the centre of the universe whenever she stepped into a room. Her response was, 'It is all about energy. Confidence is sexy, happiness is sexy.' I believed – and still, to some extent, believe – her. Only, this meant that I would focus super hard on having the right energy when entering rooms. I would hype myself up, incessantly repeat positive affirmations, try to contort my face into the biggest smile I could muster. I would pull my shoulders back, swing my hips and confidently sway into a room – and still, no one would even look at me. Meanwhile, my friend would walk in behind me and even if she was in a bad mood and had her arms crossed all night, she would not be able to move for men wanting to flirt with her. My energy is so wrong, I would think. I learned that blaming the size of my body was just an excuse.

I spent years unlearning that my mood and my confidence was the problem and learning all about the fatphobia in our society instead. The voice is now quieter. But smarter. Sneakier. It will take all the knowledge I have accumulated and turn it around on me. 'This world is so fatphobic. Fatphobia is ingrained in every single person, so why would anyone be attracted to you? Not that they *shouldn't* be, of course, we think you're brilliantly beautiful, but *they* probably don't because, you know, systemic fatphobia. It's not that you are worthless per se because you are fat, but we also know that fat people are paid less and hired less than thin people, so in a *way* you are at least *worth less* because you are fat, so maybe you should really think about that. Yes, you were very hot when you wrote that book but you have gained even more weight since, so maybe there is a limit, just for you, of how fat you could get before no longer being hot. Just saying.'

It is hard to describe the frustration you feel when you google 'how to love your fat body', because you are suddenly feeling bad about yourself, and all the articles that pop up on Google are written by you. I have literally become the old joke about the man who goes to the doctor and says he is depressed. The doctor replies, 'Treatment is simple. The great clown Pagliacci is in town tonight. Go and see him. That should pick you up.' And the clown says, 'But Doctor, I am Pagliacci.'

Sad fat activist goes to Google and says, 'I have negative feelings towards my body,' and Google replies, 'You should read something by Sofie Hagen.' And the sad fat activist says, 'But Google...'

In reality, I generally feel good about my body. When I look in the mirror, I very rarely feel hate towards it. I like it, even. Other times, I just feel neutral. The negative thoughts only appear when I am in relation to others. I can love my body – but *can anyone else*? I can look myself in the mirror and feel positively, but once I am standing next to someone else, I am *fatter* than them, *bigger* than them. *Too much, too big.* And when it comes to sex that is not just solo sex, that bit – the *relation to others* – is fairly important. How are we meant to have sex with someone, be present and mindful, if we are scared that they have negative thoughts about us?

I recall what I have learned about the nervous system. When we detect danger, we tend to go into fight/ flight mode and when we do that, we cannot be present. Being vulnerable with a person who you suspect might criticise you or reject you can feel very dangerous. And for a lot of fat people, vulnerability is often punished by the outside world.

I was once sitting in a nightclub waiting for a friend to finish dancing so we could go home. A man sat down next to me and talked at me for a while, until I indulged him. He seemed lonely or socially awkward and I was already quite bored. We talked for around five minutes and it was dreadful. The music was so loud, I could barely hear a word he said. But I remember his face changing as he burst into laughter and said, 'I can't believe you thought I was interested!' before he rushed over to a table of guys, all laughing too. I am quite lucky that I had not actually thought he *was* interested, nor was I interested in him. It had all happened very quickly, but he also had not seemed that flirty. Like he was too chickenshit to commit to the prank fully, so as to not be teased by his friends about it later. But I understood what had happened – I had played the role of the fat person who is just so desperate to be loved, to get attention, who is so low in the pecking order, that a conventionally attractive man talking to her would make her day. Apart from reeking of desperation, she is, of course, also unintelligent, so she does not pick up on the subtle cues that this man is actually playing a prank on her. I am not saying I am above being pranked – but it would definitely take more effort than this particular guy was willing to put into it. Nevertheless, the lesson was clear: trust no one. People will quite literally fake intimacy in order to mock you. Because you are fat. Because they see you as less than.

In an experiment popularly referred to as 'Cyberball', psychologist Naomi Eisenberger and colleagues placed virtual reality headsets on their test subjects. In the headset, the participants would see their own hand and a ball, plus two characters, who, they were told, were two fellow participants playing from another room. With the press of a button, each participant could toss the ball to another player. Meanwhile, the scientists were measuring their brain activity. In the first game of Cyberball, the ball flew back and forth between the players normally, but soon, the two other players started passing just to each other, ignoring the first player. Of course, these two players were fake – the experiment was about the feelings and brain activity of the person being ignored. The participant was experiencing being rejected by computer-generated characters so that Eisenberger and colleagues could figure out if there is a deeper connection between physical and emotional pain.

The brain scans showed that when participants were excluded from the game, several brain regions lit up, including the anterior insula (AI) and the dorsal anterior cingulate cortex (dACC). These are both regions that we know light up when a person experiences physical pain. Basically, being socially rejected triggers the same neural circuits that process physical injury. Rejection truly, physically hurts. Like with many neurological studies, I am sure we are all tempted to say: well, of course. Did we really need science to back us up on this? We have all experienced rejection and we can surely all attest that it hurts. Yet, I know for a fact that I have said the sentence, 'It feels like my heart has literally broken' to describe the pain I felt post-break-up. It is comforting to know that my brain agrees.

I wonder if being continuously exposed to social rejection throughout your life has the same effect on you as if you had been exposed to physical violence. Someone raises their hand and you flinch because your body expects the hit. Someone flirts with you – do you emotionally flinch? Shut down to protect yourself? Dissociate and disconnect because the rejection and social exclusion is most likely imminent?

Learning to love my body is a tricky journey but it is easy, compared to learning to trust that other people can love it. In a vacuum, where it is just my mirror and myself, I can look at my fat stomach, fat thighs and my double chin and I can love, love, love it with all my heart. Which is why I enjoy my vaccum. I enjoy being alone. Trusting that there is someone out there who would *also* love my fat stomach, fat thighs and double chin is a whole different battle.

I decide to speak to my friend Miranda Kane. Miranda is a former BBW[32] sex worker, a comedian, a host of the *Metro* sex podcast *Smut Drop* and she runs events called Club Indulge. Club Indulge is a nightclub for fat people and the people who love fat people. Miranda is a delightfully loud, confident powerhouse of a woman. She once taught me a very valuable lesson, almost ten years ago.

I was seeing a guy, let us call him Xavier. The first words I ever said to Xavier were, 'I want to have your babies.' He smiled and said something like, 'I love you too.'

We went on a date. He took me to Chiswick where we got drunk in all the bars along the Thames. I knew that he was really into horror films, so every time I went to the bathroom I googled information about specific films so I could go out and say things like, 'What I find fascinating about Rodrigues' movies is his use of shadows and how it takes after early Hitchcock.'

He would say, 'Did you just google that?' and I would say, 'No, of course not.'

---

32 Within sex work and adult sites, BBW was typically used to describe either Big Beautiful Women or Big Black Women. Miranda, who is white, used it to mean Big Beautiful Woman.

He would smile and I would blush into my beer. It was, quite frankly, class A flirting from my side. I was adorable. So was he. We took the night bus back into central London, where we would eventually part. He lived in north London, at the edge of zone 8, and I lived in south London, at the edge of zone 3. I didn't know at the time that relationships between north and south Londoners rarely work out. It takes pretty much as long to get from Streatham Common to Enfield as it does to go from one end of Denmark to the other.

We lingered around Trafalgar Square. Walked to Leicester Square. I let several 159 buses to Streatham pass us by. Eventually, he kissed me and I flew home on a pink, optimistic cloud.

Before our third date, which was to take place at his flat, I was waiting for him to pick me up at Euston Station. I was crouching under a staircase, gasping for air, in a full panic attack, hoping he wouldn't spot me. I felt like throwing up. I took some paper out of my bag and started writing the words, 'IT IS OKAY. IT IS OKAY. IT IS OKAY' over and over again, until the pen poked through the paper and onto my thigh, in a desperate attempt to calm myself down. I had no idea why I was reacting this way and, eventually, I managed to crawl out from underneath the stairs, brush Tube station dirt (primarily rat faeces, I assume) off my leggings and stand up straight, feigning self-esteem. I saw him, we hugged and got on the train together. He placed a lump of cheese in my hand and

I looked at him, puzzled. 'Red Leicester cheese,' he said in a matter-of-fact way.

'Oh! Oh yes!' I said, remembering our conversation from a few days ago. I had been in Leicester and he had made a joke about cheese. I, being a new arrivee in the UK, had no idea about this type of cheese, so he explained it to me. And now, on this train, he had given me some. It was a cute and nice gesture, a little reminder of an inside joke. I was, however, still breathing quite frantically and trying to compose myself, so my brain had no access to any knowledge about how to behave like a normal human being. So I quickly unwrapped the block of cheese and took a big bite of it. 'Mmmmm,' I said, nodding, as his face fell into a confused state.

'You don't... have to eat it,' he said, puzzled, as I gnawed down on it again. Still chewing but now so embarrassed that my cheeks were bright red and my eyes were slightly wet with shame, I said, 'No, no, it's good!' I noticed people on the train staring at me, wondering if he had just picked me up from under the stairs at the Tube station where I had grown up raised by rats. I finished the entire block in silence, just the sound of me chewing wildly mixed with British people tutting and the occasional posh voice saying, 'Mind the gap.'

Xavier (un)fortunately turned out to be as bad at intimacy as me. When I arrived at his place, I saw he only had two armchairs. No couch and no dinner table. He cooked delicious food but served it on a tray, from which

I ate, sitting in an armchair, looking at the TV, like we had both aged fifty years overnight. He fell asleep during a Wimbledon match and I saw myself out.

Over the following three years, we would play the frustrating game of 'will they/won't they', taking turns being the person who's suddenly open to a relationship and being the person shutting the other one out completely. It worked for us, in a strange way. We would be at the same party, each flirting with other people. As soon as we saw the other person flirting, we would manage to sabotage it, ending up two single people standing outside the pub calling each other 'impossible' and 'annoying', after which we would either go to his and have sex or go home, furious and alone. We let each other in exactly as much as we both could handle. Which was not that much.

He could only really be turned on when I wasn't showing interest. And I could only really be turned on when it felt like a challenge. I remember enjoying sex in silence, trying to keep it from him so that he wouldn't stop. At first, I was confused, but once he said, 'Stop pretending you like it,' I realised that this was very much his issue. He thought I was lying to him if I made any sound at all. When he would show initiative, I suddenly felt strangled and like I wanted to push him away. I would tease him a bit, making jokes about pregnancy and marriage because I knew that would scare him.

His penis was the first circumcised penis I ever met. I quite liked lying between the legs of someone and just getting to play and examine their penis and balls. It's just not something I had general access to and it's usually so soft and squishy. I loved that the penis head is shiny and the foreskin is almost silky smooth. I liked feeling the veins inside of the penis and I felt giddy when the blood makes it harder. It's fun. Exciting. A new experience. The balls remind me of those plastic toys you could buy in petrol stations when I was a child, with a little ball bouncing around inside of a bigger ball.

Despite having played for quite some time with Xavier's balls, I was still surprised when he brought up having only one testicle, because he had had testicular cancer years prior. I just hadn't noticed. I also didn't immediately notice that he was circumcised. I didn't know what to look for. I remember saying, 'Oh, is that it?', which is not what anyone wants to hear when you look at their genitals.[33] I was nervous about giving him a handjob, since usually I would use all the lovely excess skin as a 'sleeve' I could move up and down (or from side to side, depending on position). I was afraid that if I just moved it up and down without the 'sleeve', I would just be causing friction. I didn't want to start a small bonfire or give him first-degree burns. At one point, I just held it in my hand and squeezed it. Like it was a clown's nose.

---

33 I never know what to say when you see genitals for the first time. I feel the need to express something. But I don't want to sound crass and overly horny, so I am not going to throw 'Oh yeah, that dick is so hard and big' in their faces. I'm also not going to say 'Aw, cute'. So I usually end up putting on an odd Six O'clock News reader's voice and announcing, 'That is a very nice penis and I am very satisfied with it.'

'Yeah, you like that?'

'Not really.'

A few years after we stopped attempting to make a relationship or even a sexbuddyship work, a mutual (married) friend of ours tried to kiss me at a party. Drunkenly, he said, 'Sofie, I just want to save you. I know that deep down inside, you're just really insecure and I want to be the person to comfort you when you're scared.'

I have been told many unflattering things by drunk men but that one remains the worst. I was so offended that I just said, 'The only thing I need saving from is you,' and then I left.

On the night bus to Streatham, I texted Xavier. 'Do you think I need to be saved?' and he instantly replied, 'You? Fuck, you're Rambo.'

So while Xavier and I had officially stopped trying to make it work between us, I was devastated when he told me he had kissed our friend Miranda. I was completely wrapped up in dramatic feelings of jealousy and anger, and I took it out on both of them, angrily severing all ties to them. Miranda asked me to meet up with her.

We met in a Wetherspoons and got drunk on their cheapest bottle of wine. I remember her saying, 'No man is worth a female friendship,' and it struck me because I had never considered choosing a friendship over a man. I saw male attention as this incredibly small pitcher of water in a world of people dying of thirst. Not only that, but one of the things I had really liked about Xavier was that he liked me… despite me being fat. It made me feel safe, knowing that he would not reject me because of my fat. And then Miranda waltzes in, also fat but more confident, more fun, more sexy. And it made me want to eliminate her. Until she got me drunk and made me laugh and apologised for kissing the man I had already decided I didn't want to be with. The feeling of connecting with a friend on that level felt better than any attention I had ever gotten from Xavier. We took a selfie and sent it to him and he texted back, 'I'm moving to Yemen.'

Neither of us kissed him ever again and we are still friends.

'Are you going to write explain our friendship in the book?' Miranda asks, at the beginning of our conversation in November of 2023.

'Something like that,' I say and lunge into my thoughts and all of the embarrassing questions I haven't ever dared to ask her. 'I think because I haven't had sex for so long my brain has gone back into the same old track, where, on some level, I don't believe anyone wants me because I am fat. And yet, even as I am saying that, I am thinking that's ridiculous. And you have the evidence. Not only have you been a fat person who people have paid money to have sex with, but with Club Indulge, you see it happening all the time: fat people showing up and dating and being wanted.'

'Oh yeah,' Miranda laughs loudly, 'We have had marriages, kids, engagements. We see people hooking up all the time. And these are not guys that fetishise fat women; I vet them really carefully. I personally hoist them out of there if they behave disrespectfully. The whole reason I started Club Indulge was because through sex work, I saw that there were plenty of good guys who just preferred bigger women or bigger people. They wanted to meet them but they didn't know how. They wanted a safe space to do it in. I obviously didn't start it just for them but I knew that those people existed and I thought fat people deserved to meet those people in a safe space, in an environment that said: 'You must behave and you must be respectful.' Often, fat women can be super self-conscious, but at the last speed-dating event we had, there were more men signing up than women. The thing is, the men are a bit older – by that, I mean, they're in their late twenties, early thirties. They have moved to London, they are no longer surrounded by their fucking "banter" schoolmates. They are a bit more mature and they just want to meet someone they actually want to meet.'

It reminds me of a podcast episode I listened to the day before this chat. Aubrey Gordon, a queer, fat lady known around the internet as @YrFatFriend and author of *What We Don't Talk about When We Talk about Fat* and *You Just Need to Lose Weight and 19 Other Myths about Fat People,* and Michael Hobbes, a gay journalist and podcaster, are behind the wildly popular podcast *Maintenance Phase*, which debunks myths and 'junk science' behind health, nutrition and wellness. In an episode called 'November Bonus: Big Victories!' a woman emails in with a story in which her boyfriend initially acted in a fairly fatphobic fashion towards her, but after listening to the podcast and educating himself, he changed and became an ally. The following conversation ensued between Aubrey and Michael.

'There does seem to be this thing among straight dudes where a huge number of straight dudes seem to be into larger ladies and are attracted to thick or fat women,' Michael says.

Aubrey states firmly, 'Yes, this is true.'

Michael continues, 'And their bros give them shit about it. There is this weird thing where it's like, "I'm attracted to you, but also for your health or for my boys, I need you to look different," which is super fucked up. So I'm assuming from this that (HE) is fucking into her, HE thinks she's hot as shit, but he has this kind of ingrained thing of like: oh yeah, I just really need you to lose weight. But, no. Your girlfriend's hot, you're having a nice time, you're attracted to each other. This is just the way it's going to be. And if your fellas give you shit about it, like, fuck your fellas, find new fellas.'

'I am completely in that camp with you,' Aubrey replies enthusiastically. 'I will say, there are dudes that think they're doing that, and that are actually being utter total creeps.'

'Oh yeah, you've gotta draw the line between that weird fetishisation and being fucking weird about it,' Michael agrees.

Aubrey adds, 'Yeah, totally. Consent is really important. But yeah, man, if you are in a loving relationship with someone and you think they're fucking hot, even if other people around them fucking don't, and maybe especially if people around them don't, be fucking loud about it.'

Your teen years and early twenties is when you will usually begin dating or taking an interest in people romantically and sexually. It is incredibly unfair that this is also the time people are the most insecure. And insecure people tend to lash out. I remember receiving an email in my early twenties from a guy who used to bully me in school. He politely apologised for having been an asshole. At this point, I chose to thank him for the apology but not offer forgiveness. His second email was flirty. I was not in any way interested in him – he had been really cruel – so I again thanked him but rejected his advances. The third email was abusive: he called me fat and disgusting. If you were to look at this guy through an empathetic lens, which I honestly still struggle to do, you would probably see someone who feels incredibly insecure and who is most likely into fat people. But the idea of actually going for it – and risking rejection – is so terrifying that instead, he bullies. His insecurity makes him assume that rejection is impending, so he rejects the fat person before they can reject him. Or whatever. It is pocket psychology, but it makes sense, in an incredibly sad way. And now, we are all adults. Perhaps he has changed. Perhaps he is confident and happy. Perhaps he respectfully flirts with a fat woman at the grocery store. But her formative years were spent being bullied by people just like him, so she rejects him, because anything else feels too risky. As with everything else to do with toxic masculinity, insecure male behaviour is not just harming women and the wider world, but it harms men themselves too. No one wins.

'We did a speed dating event in Birmingham,' Miranda says. 'There were 15 blokes and three women, so they were exhausted. I think it helps that we are seeing bigger people on television, we're seeing bigger people have a voice, we're seeing bigger people feeling themselves and being unashamed and unabashed being who they are. And I think guys really— Sorry! I realise I am being very heterosexual, it's just my nature,' she laughs.

'I think a lot of fat people just stay the fuck at home,' I say. 'I'm not going out there where people are annoying and uncomfortable to be around. I think a lot of women wouldn't even know where to find these men you talk about. Just like the men need the safe space you talked about to meet fat women, fat women need the safe space, too, to meet non-fatphobic guys.'

'When I say men needing a safe space, I mean that men need a safe way to approach women because they don't know how to do it. They do it in the most disgusting ways, and you're just like, oh fuck off. The first thing they say on dating apps is, "I love a woman with curves." And you immediately go, "oh no no no no". They think the best way to flatter you is by saying how much they love your body. It's like, 'Mate, I know I'm fat, you don't have to tell me I'm gorgeous. I just want to talk about me, rather than about how hot you think I am,' Miranda says.

'Yeah, but,' I interject, 'at the same time, if someone just said, "Hi, how are you?", I'd immediately be like, "I am fat! Do you know I'm fat? Have you seen my photos on my profile? Are you aware?!" I think what I want is impossible. I want you to treat me as if my size isn't a thing, but it will always be a thing because of society's perception of fat people. Mention it and I feel weird. Don't mention it and I also feel weird.'

'But they know how you look, Sofie!' Miranda takes a firm tone with me. 'They obviously do. Where does this stuff come from?'

There is the obvious answer: fatphobia. Society. TV. Growing up watching shows like *Friends*, where Fat Monica is the butt of the joke. *Desperate Housewives*, where Gabby tricks her chubby daughter into running next to her car because she wants her to lose weight. Shows like *The Biggest Loser*, where thin people get to shout abuse at fat people just because they are fat. The same message has been drilled into me from the moment I could understand words. And even in the past ten years, when I have been actively working on unlearning it, it still appears in the comments under any post I do on the internet or whenever

I look at the news. Who can really, realistically, resist all of this messaging?

There is also the fact that my relationship history has been with inherently avoidant men. Men who have not necessarily kept me a secret because I am fat, but because they had wives or girlfriends. Or, because I am fat. Their girlfriends were always thin. I was once waiting at a bus stop late at night and a guy stopped his bicycle to talk to me. He looked excited to see me, like a little boy at the zoo seeing a real-life giraffe for the first time. He asked for my number so enthusiastically that I gave it to him. As he called the number to check I had given him the correct one, he said, 'This is great. I got just engaged but I've never tried sleeping with one of your kind before, so I want to try that before I get married.'

I never did sleep with him but I wonder if the difference between him and many of the people I did sleep with was that he was upfront and honest about it. The others – those who claimed they were just stuck in loveless relationships and that, in time, we would be together – probably knew that it was never going to happen. Or perhaps they believed the lie themselves, too.

The truth is, the underlying insecurity that comes from an entire lifetime of fatphobia is a huge part of the reason I have behaved in ways I do not like. I have never wanted to be the person someone cheats with. I have never wanted to sleep with people I do not fully respect. But the voice in my head – the one that refuses to let go of the fatphobic statements – will whisper things like, 'But what if this is your last chance to ever have sex? What if he is the only one who wants you?' and then it blurs my ability to make the right decision. This is not to excuse that I have been the person that another person has used to cheat on their partner with. I was never completely and utterly helpless. I definitely made bad decisions, out of desperation. Desperation to be loved and wanted. And yes, I would justify it because I knew that if it wasn't me, they would find someone else to cheat with. Their partners would be cheated on regardless. So why not me, who felt so desperate for the attention?

When I was in my early twenties and just starting out in comedy in Denmark, I received a booty call from a comedian I had slept with a couple of months prior. We had been incredibly drunk and the sex had been bad, but I was so in awe of him as an artist that I had somehow still enjoyed it. After the sex, he had been so excited that he rushed to his laptop to start writing new material. I, a true fan of comedy, just watched him naked, crouched in front of his laptop. In the blue light from the screen – the only light source in the room – I could see that his face was still sweaty, and my heart skipped several beats. *Wow*, I thought, *what an artist*.

But when he called me a few months later, I immediately said no. I was sober. I was scared. The voice in my head offered helpful explanations for his phone call: *he is just desperate, it is a prank, he is waiting in his flat with a camera crew to humiliate you.* All the things alcohol would usually drown out. I had never had sober one-night-stand-type sex before. But I was also flattered. And I worried that if I kept saying no, he wouldn't ask me again. I ended up saying yes, reluctantly, and going to his place. On the way, I stopped at a petrol station and bought a bottle of some kind of booze. I swallowed as much of it as I could but I was too nervous to feel any of the effects. The sex was bad again. We never spoke outside of his bedroom. I watched him on stage be absolutely brilliant and I felt incredibly lucky to have shared a bed with him. He would call me after that, occasionally, asking me to come over, but it had been so bad the last time that I said no.

A year or so later, the Danish comedy club had a comedians' Christmas party. By this point, he had gotten famous and rich. I had seen him in the magazines dating models. His fanbase had grown. He had a newfound confidence – I wonder if the fame, money or models were mostly to thank for this. That night, someone had brought in a karaoke system and comedians took turns singing on the stage where we would usually be doing jokes. Most comedians sang in pairs and even those who could actually sing did it deliberately badly in order to make the rest of the room laugh. Then he went up. He chose an old, slow Danish song. He couldn't sing, but he did. He stood there, in his own world, simply not giving a fuck about how he sounded or what the other comedians thought of him. He oozed confidence and, I thought, sex. I suddenly felt warm all over. It was the most attractive thing I had ever seen. Even when – or, rather, especially when – the other comedians rolled their eyes at him.

For the first time, I spoke to him outside of a bedroom. I told him he looked good and he asked me to leave with him. I nodded. We ended up going to a hotel because, as he said, he was rich and didn't know what to do with all the money. At this point, I had £4 in my bank account that had to last till January, so I found it hard to relate to this particular problem of his. When we got to the hotel room, he was different to the first two times we had been together. This time he was confident. Commanding and firm. This time, it was good.

In thinking back at all the sex I have had in my life, this is placed in the top three. In reality, it was probably because of the lack of insecurity. His confidence removed my need to be insecure. I had no doubt that he wanted to have sex with me. I knew it was only sex. Regardless of how much I looked – and still look – up to him as a comedian, we never had an emotional bond. Another aspect that probably added to the greatness of the sex: I wasn't being emotionally manipulated. In a way, it felt respectful. Equal. He left straight after we had had sex, but he urged me to stay, since he had already paid for the hotel room. I knew I should probably feel taken advantage of – that is what TV shows told me – but I was too excited to be staying in an actual hotel suite all by myself.

Before he left, he said something along the lines of, 'You only wanted to sleep with me because I am famous now,' and I realised his confidence probably was only skin deep. I reminded him that we had sex twice when he was unknown and, besides, I wanted to have sex with him because he serenaded himself completely out of tune on stage, in front of our judgemental colleagues, which signalled to me that he had very big balls that I would like to see and play with.

The next morning, when I checked out, the woman at reception said, 'That will be £45.'

I confidently said, 'Yes, can you just take that from the card that paid for the room?'

'I'm sorry,' she said, 'we are not allowed to do that.'

When I had emptied the minibar, I really thought it would be automatically charged to his card. I had no way of paying.

'I was told that it would be possible,' I lied to her face.

She looked at her computer for a while and then back up at me. 'I would need permission from the gentleman whose card it is. Do you know him?'

I conjured all the acting abilities I could, for the sake of £45, and gasped, 'That is my husband! What are you implying?'

The thing about posh hotels and rich people is that if

you just pretend to be confident and difficult at the same time, you are quite likely to get your way.

'I'm terribly sorry. I have used the card now. Have a nice day,' she said and I rushed out. He didn't mind; he didn't know how to spend all his money anyway.

I tell Miranda this story and say, 'I can't figure out if it's a great story about some great sex I had or if it's a sad story about a one-night stand with someone who just left me behind afterwards. If he was super hot and confident or if he was just faking it, like I faked it with the receptionist.'

'What if both things are true at the same time?' Miranda says and I am forced to reframe a lot of stories in my head. What if sexual experiences can be both good and bad? What if I am allowed to enjoy them in some ways and dislike other aspects of them?

'I think it's about knowing what you want because otherwise, you can't ask for it. I have a friend who gets really turned on by being called a fat slag by this guy she is sleeping with. She told me that he is this incredibly lovely bloke but she loves it when he is dirty. So she was confused as to why she was so upset when he left, after sex. Then she realised that what she needed was aftercare. So she asked him: "Hey, would you like to stay for breakfast?" And he said, "Sure! I love breakfast." And it can be so simple as soon as you know what you want. Do you know? Do you, Sofie Hagen, know who you want to have sex with? Or what sex you would like to have?'

I stare at Miranda's face for a long time.

'I don't think so.'

'Well, we have to figure that out before we can make any decisions. You can't just not have sex because you don't know who you are. We need to talk about affirmations – and I know it sounds really, really airy fairy and like "put it into the universe".'

If you read the book *Happy Fat: Taking Up Space in a World That Wants to Shrink You*, written by Sofie Hagen – you know, the book in which she confidently tells you how to love your body – you will read something similar. That affirmations work, even though it seems like a 'wishy washy' thing. So, that being the case, maybe we should actually be doing them, rather than just telling people to do them?[34]

According to leading psychologists on the subject, there are specific ways of doing it. David Creswell, a psychology professor, said in an interview with the *Washington Post* in 2022 that making broad statements like 'I really like myself' most likely will not cut it: 'It's more about really identifying, in really concrete ways, the kinds of things about you that you really value.'

Creswell and his research team at Carnegie Mellon University wanted to find out how affirmations affected

---

[34] The book also has other excellent tips on how to learn to love your body, such as: Unfollow all social media accounts that make you feel bad about yourself, consume media that features fat people in a positive way, leave and unlearn diet culture, let go of the idea that you will ever be thin and seek out communities full of fellow fatties. Don't tell my former publishers that the whole book could be summarised in a footnote, please.

students' ability to solve problems. He asked the participants to rank a list of their values (art, business, family and friends, and so on). They were asked to write a couple of sentences about why the value they chose as number one was the most important to them. Then were then asked to complete a challenging problem-solving task under time pressure, one that required creative thinking.

The results were clear. Students who said that they were chronically stressed but who had done the self-affirmation exercises performed at the same level as participants with low stress levels. This means that people who are highly stressed can reduce their stress by taking a moment to think about what really matters to them.

Natalie Dattilo, a clinical psychologist with Brigham and Women's Hospital in Boston, similarly points out that the words of encouragement you use in an affirmation have to align with your inner truth. So you have to first identify things about yourself that you like and then you have to remind yourself of them. This should then increase how much you like yourself. And in a research article by Janine M. Dutcher, other benefits of self-affirmation are listed. Self-affirmation has shown to improve self-control post rejection, promote a general increase in well-being and enhance feelings of relational security. So this stuff works. Miranda has her own version of self-affirmations:

'If you keep saying to yourself, "I want to have sex with Ryan Reynolds" then you are making that a goal for yourself. Then, in your mind, you start thinking about, well, how am I going to have sex with Ryan Reynolds? Let's see, I'm an award-winning comedian, maybe I can ask my agent if he can connect me to Ryan Reynolds. Maybe I write a really amazing script and get Ryan Reynolds on board. You know what I mean?'

'And then I cast myself in the role of his sex partner in the movie, so he has to fuck me? Isn't that... coercion or entrapment or something?'

Miranda rolls her eyes at me. 'You know what I mean. You're on apps or you go to a nightclub, you have to think to yourself: *Who do I want to have sex with?* You have to know these things and then go for it. It's like, you go to a restaurant and then you order. You don't just sit there and wait for them to bring you food.'

I sigh. 'If sex was a restaurant, I would go there and then think, *Oh no, what if someone spat in the food? I should just go home and eat my own cooking.* And then I'd go home.'

'You're just afraid,' Miranda states and she has never been more right. Much more right than when she laid out my plan to sleep with Ryan Reynolds.

'Oh, definitely,' I agree.

'That sounds like trauma stuff. That's above my paygrade,' she says, with a compassionate smile. 'But I also think one of the things that I think is really handy is to masturbate more.'

Miranda mentions the orgasm gap, where studies have shown that in a sample of more than 50,000 people,

95 per cent of heterosexual men said they usually or always orgasm when sexually intimate, while only 65 per cent of women say the same. Though 92 per cent of women orgasm when they masturbate. In Laurie Mintz's book *Becoming Cliterate: Why Orgasm Equality Matters – and How to Get It*, she asks thousands of women what their most reliable route to orgasms is. Four per cent say penetration; 96 per cent say clitoral stimulation, either alone or paired with penetration.

When you look at queer relations, the statistics are not incredibly different. Gay men orgasm 89 per cent of the time, while for bisexual men it is 88 per cent, lesbian women 86 per cent and bisexual women 66 per cent. Laurie Mintz explains that part of the reason is that women need to feel entitled to pleasure and they need to know what turns them on, so they can ask for it.

'This means heterosexual couples must rid themselves of the old script that calls for foreplay followed by intercourse after which sex is over. Instead, they can take turns having orgasms using oral sex or manual stimulation where she orgasms followed by intercourse. Alternatively, women can touch themselves with hands or a vibrator during intercourse,' writes Laurie Mintz, in an article on The Conversation website from 2023.

She goes on to cite studies that show that feeling entitled to pleasure increases a woman's agency in telling partners what they want sexually – and their agency in protecting themselves sexually. When you feel more entitled to sexual pleasure, it increases your confidence in refusing to engage in sexual activity that you are not comfortable with. Not only can masturbation lead to more orgasms during sex, regardless of who you are having sex with, but it can seemingly help protect you from harmful sex as well.

'It is so easy to get into a state where you think you are not worthy of pleasure and the easiest way out of that is to have a wank,' Miranda says. 'A lot of people who feel ashamed of their bodies or who are worried about how they look forget that they can give themselves pleasure and that they deserve that. It helps you feel sexy, it helps clear your head. And it's free serotonin, for God's sake. It's important to know when you feel sexy, too.'

I wonder when I feel sexy. The first thing that comes to mind is, weirdly, oversized clothing. When my sleeves hang below my hands and the shirt is baggy. I wonder how much of that is to do with internalised fatphobia – perhaps I need to feel smaller to feel sexy. I go to the folder on my phone that I have named 'oh dear', which is photos of all the people I have had sex with (minus the ones I don't want to remember and the ones I never saw again or whose names I didn't know). The ones that aren't tall are broad – either because they are fat, muscly or just built bigger. The shorter they are, the broader they are. The thinner they are, the taller they are.

You often hear men complaining that women refuse to date them if they are short. And without a doubt, short men have it harder than tall men. But I remember seeing an analysis of this issue as being related to fatphobia, which theorised that women are not necessarily looking for a man who isn't short but just for someone taller than them, because it is less about finding him attractive and more about being smaller than him. Because we have learned and internalised that being big, as a woman, is bad. Similarly, while it is always difficult existing in a fat body, it is slightly easier when you are a man. Or rather, as a fat man, you can weigh a lot more before you are discriminated against than a woman can.

So do I feel sexy when I wear oversized clothes because it makes me feel like I am a thin(ner) person? Or do I just like oversized clothes? I have a very distinct memory of watching the American TV show *The Fresh Prince of Bel Air* when I was a child and teenager, and there is an episode where Hilary – who is usually dressed up often in designer clothing, always wearing perfect makeup and heels – has a night in on the sofa. She wears grey sweatpants and a faded blue baggy hoodie and her face is less made up than usual. It is so out of character that the butler, Geoffrey, comments, 'You know, Miss Hilary, I have never seen this side of you before. Baggy clothes, no makeup, tousled hair,' he says.

'I feel really comfortable like this too, Geoffrey. I mean, I don't need to hide behind cosmetics, I'm beautiful just the way I am.' The punchline arrives when her new boyfriend, who is as superficial as she is, turns up and she shouts, 'Oh my God, it's Trevor, quick, get my hot comb!'

But Geoffrey says no. When Trevor sees her, he looks at her and says, 'Oh my, you look beautiful.' And she truly, fucking does.

I had never seen Hilary as attractive before this – of course, I can see that Karyn Parsons, who plays Hilary Banks, is stunning, but I had never been attracted to her before she showed up in sweatpants. In fact, whenever a woman on TV wears her boyfriend's shirt after sex or staying over, I do a double-take. Perhaps it is just that I like big clothes on people, including myself. Or, again, is it a fatphobia-thing? It could also be a queer thing? A woman wearing a large sweatshirt is culturally a bit queer-coded? Or is it all of the above? It can be all of the above. I note down 'oversized clothing' in my notebook under the headline 'things that make me feel sexy'.

'Are you having sex?' I ask Miranda. She starts chuckling endearingly, a bit taken aback.

'No, I'm not, but it's more of a choice. I know I can have sex, if I wanted to. I am really lucky that I run a club night for fat girls, where the men who fancy them pop along. It's so important to be able to go to events where people are. I don't recommend the apps – they do not work in your favour. Get into the real world. I joined an am-dram group recent—'

'A what-now?'

Miranda cackles. 'An amateur dramatics group! Because it's so much fun doing something creative that I am not depending on to pay my rent, you know? I just get to play. And because I'm playing, I feel so much more confident. And I am meeting guys through that. I'm making friends and making friends with their friends. It's wild – I have found a whole new section of people who aren't the people that come to Club Indulge, who are not necessarily wrapped up in the fat activism bubble. They do not dismiss me in this group. I get offered the sexy roles. It is such positive affirmation to learn that I can go out in real life and mix with just "normal" people and they will still find me attractive. So, I say, sign up to a class. I know it sounds boring and I know that there are socioeconomic reasons why some people can't, but sometimes you will be able to find something that is free to join and only takes a few hours a week. It is so nourishing for the soul and the mind and for your libido. You feel like you're out and doing something rather than sitting at home on the apps. When was the last time you flirted with someone in real life?'

'I think I flirted with someone over Zoom, in a meeting recently,' I say.

It had felt really great to flirt with this person. Afterwards, I had called my friend Jodie, explained the interaction and asked if I had misinterpreted it, if that was indeed flirting. Jodie said, 'Yes, that is very obviously flirting,' and I felt warm and fuzzy inside. 'I think I flirt by teasing then,' I told Jodie. I was really just kindly and gently mocking them, and they were laughing and blushing. I make a note that you can flirt 'in real life' over Zoom too. Which is probably good to know, if you, for

WILL I EVER HAVE SEX AGAIN?

whatever reason, cannot leave your house to go into the world and face-to-face flirt.

'There is an excellent flirting coach named Jean Smith. She does flirt classes,' Miranda offers. 'She talks about noticing body language and stuff. Like, sometimes you just touch the other person's elbow to see how they react. If they pull away, that's fine, but they never do. People like flirting.'

'I feel like the biggest, most general difference between you and me, Miranda, is that my mindset is very much: what is the worst that could happen? Meanwhile, your mindset is: but what if everything was just amazing? Because if I imagine touching someone's elbow, I'm imagining them flinging me across the road in disgust. Whereas I think you're just like: oh, this is probably a positive moment. I think I live my life believing that if I asked 100 people to sleep with me, one, maybe two, would say yes. And I think, if I just chose to believe that 100 of them would say yes, then I would live a much happier life.'

Miranda laughs. 'Fifty of them could say yes and that would still be great. And don't get me wrong, I'm not one of those "everything's awesome all the time" people. I do feel like shit a lot and I absolutely believe the worst is going to happen. But I also know that every time I have taken a chance, good things have happened. And I truly believe that you always regret the things you didn't do. I don't want to say that you have to be positive about everything because, obviously, not everything is positive.

I think it's just that I know what I'm looking for. And I keep my mind open as to how I can get that. I've spent so much time – fuck it, all women are brought up to believe that one day our white knight will show up and rescue us, and then we get married, we get the kids, we get the house and then that's all fine. It wasn't till I was 30 that I finally sat down and thought, *Fuck, what if this guy isn't going to show up? Who the fuck is going to look after me?* And I realised: I have to do it. From that moment on, that was the biggest shift in my life. I realised that I was going to have to start doing things by myself and for myself, rather than doing things to try to attract someone so they could help me and save me. From that moment, I thought, *Let's just give it a go. Let's just try.*'

I have one last question for Miranda. One I hate asking – or rather, one I hate wanting to ask her. But I need to shut up the voice inside of my body that keeps whispering negativity. I have to ask her because I need to hear her answer, even though I know the answer. I know the answer with my brain, not with my body. My body needs to hear this.

'So, you claim that there are people out there who are normal, kind, maybe even interesting, maybe even smart, maybe even hot, maybe even hygienic, who actually want to have sex with fat people?'

'Yes,' Miranda says, looking a bit like the straight-mouthed emoji. 'Yes, Sofie, there are hygienic, nice, kind, normal people who fancy fat people, who want to have relationships with fat people. But what you tend to find is that those fat people know what they want and they have said what they want. They probably know what makes them happy.'

'Do you have any of their phone numbers?' I ask.

Miranda smiles. 'Come to Club Indulge.'

'You know what? Maybe I will,' I say and grab my calendar. 'When is the next one?'

Miranda tells me and I promise to consider it, which I do. But while I am not sure what makes me feel sexy, I do know what makes me feel anxious – nightclubs. That is Miranda's scene. She can shout over loud music, she loves to dance and have fun. I feel quite confident that I will not meet my future partner in a nightclub. We will meet wherever Ryan Reynolds usually hangs out, I guess.

It feels important to acknowledge that my body is inherently treated as undesirable by society, which means that it is harder for me to find and date that other person who is willing to get intimate with me. There is a definite value and importance in paying attention to the big picture and in not gaslighting myself. I need to be allowed to be realistic about my prospects or I will begin to doubt my own instincts and experiences. But there is a difference between acknowledging society's inherent fatphobia and assuming that everyone hates you. Staying inside, because what if everyone hates me. Not dating, not flirting, not being open to sexual experiences, because what if everyone hates me. Yes, it is hard to date in a world where fatphobia is so rife because it will have shaped a lot of people's attraction and preferences. But at the moment, I do not challenge this idea at all, so instead it becomes a self-fulfilling prophecy, where I can say, 'See? No one is having sex with me!' while my front door is bolted shut and I snarl defensively at anyone who looks at me in the supermarket.

Miranda inspires me to live a little bit more like her. Sure, there are people who won't find me attractive but what if *this* person did? Someone will. Might as well be him or her or them. Miranda has such a tight grasp on her own agency and that is inspiring. That is what I want.

E is a 33-year-old cis woman who describes herself as white, British, non-disabled, straight-sized to small fat and queer/sapphic/bisexual. E did not have sex until she was 31. She grew up in the church, as her mother was a Christian, and she would, as a teenager, attend evangelical church camps, where she was taught that sex outside of heterosexual marriage was a sin that would send you to hell.[35]

'I was never fully committed but I was terrified in case it was true. A bigger impact was that I never wanted to

---

35 I need to acknowledge here that a lot of the stories that were submitted to me come from people who were somehow affected by religion, especially different branches of Christianity. I am not sure if this is just coincidence – because we are all affected by religion to some extent – or because my form asked about what shaped people's understanding of sex and included 'religion' as an example, and thus pushed it to the forefront of people's minds, or if it just shows how our society is less secular than we think it is.

do anything that would disappoint my family, such as go to parties or drink, which meant I was almost never physically in places where hooking up happened. I didn't believe that sex before marriage was wrong, but I did believe that sexual experiences should be 'special' and with people I was attracted to. I avoided things like spin the bottle because I wanted to seem 'proper' and, honestly... I was scared Jesus might be watching.'

E was also chronically shy and found it challenging to make and keep friends. E only had female friends in her life and while she eventually, in her late twenties, realised she was queer, she attributed her feelings of queerness to a sense of being 'deviant' and 'gross'.

'I discovered masturbation pretty young,' E explains, 'just by accident. I remember being about 12 and reading about it in a sex education book at my friend's house and realising that that was what I did. I was horrified. And ashamed. I mean, I would still masturbate, but just with huge feelings of guilt and shame. It was never talked about among my friends until much later. In my twenties, as personal essays became more popular, hearing from other women who started young – and could even laugh about it – radically changed my self-perception as some gross monster.'

E is tall, almost six feet, and that happened at a very young age. E was taller than her male teacher at the age of 11 and it would take most boys in her class several years to 'catch up' with her in height.

'It's okay to be tall and willowy, like a model, but I'm tall and... not willowy. I always felt like I was taking up too much space and wasn't attractive to men. I always felt that there was no reason anyone would choose me over all the other girls, who were so hot and funny and petite – I mean, hello undiscovered queerness. When I did find out that tall women were actually a good thing in the queer community, that also had a huge impact on my perception of myself as someone who could be fancied by anyone. Like that bit in *Wicked*, the musical, where Elphaba's all 'this weird quirk I have tried to suppress – or hide – is a talent that could help me meet the wizard!' That. It was that. Because I felt like nobody could find me attractive, I felt very detached from my own sexuality. It felt grubby and gross to be a sexual person when I was totally single. Almost like it was embarrassing to want something I wasn't allowed to have. I wanted to be having sex, in an abstract way, but there were literally no opportunities presented to do so, and I had no idea how to seek it out.'

E tried dating apps with not much success. She met up with a handful of men with whom she had zero chemistry. She kissed one of the men and he wanted to go further, but she was not into it at all: 'I found the kissing to be weird and emotionless. I once got drunk and tried to kiss a man in a club; about five seconds in, he put his hands on my shoulders and walked away, looking embarrassed.'

E started taking SSRIs, which initially completely removed her sex drive and she was relieved – 'It was inconvenient to get turned on with no outlet for it, that felt good.'

Today, E is in a happy relationship with her girlfriend, but it has been a long process of unlearning and learning things about herself. 'It has taken the whole two years to go on a journey together to where I am today, which is I'm much more in touch with my sexuality than I was at the beginning. Well, even where I was months ago. If you watch TV, movies and read books, you'd think literally everyone is having sex all the time and it's just not true. I had never really seen anything about not having sex for most of my life and it's incredibly isolating.'

Rejection hurts. Around 2011, after I slept with a guy, I ran into him at a bar. We ended up dancing and having fun. I bravely assumed that he wanted to sleep with me again, since we had already done it and we were dancing. So when he moved his face closer, I went in for the kiss. I remember what happened next in slow motion. My lips touched his but continued to travel across his face, like a dehydrated slug, as he turned his face away from me. By the time I was almost kissing his ear, I was so embarrassed, I wanted to die, so I created a new dance move which consisted of squatting on the floor while covering my face with both hands until he left, because he realised I would not be getting up until he did. The memory still turns my entire face red with embarrassment and makes my body itch from the inside.

In 2014, I appeared in a show at the Edinburgh Fringe

Festival, where I was paired up with a fellow comedian as a 'couple'. We would jokingly pretend to kiss and be in love, all for the sake of the magic of the show. Later on that night, in one of the artist bars, he – a chubby, bordering on fat guy himself – kissed me. I remember being very aware that we were at risk of being discovered by other comedians, which I wasn't too excited about. At one point, my agent walked past us and gave me a look that said, 'Really? Him?' And I tried to communicate with my eyes that 'Yes, I know he is a bit of a dick, the kind that interrupts people and objectifies women, but he does it in a really cute way and he is quite handsome so can you just let me make out with him, please?' but I am not sure it translated. I wasn't embarrassed to be kissing him but I was aware that a lot of other people would be. I enjoyed it, the kiss itself. It was hot and he was hot.

Around 4am, I informed him that I had to go because I had to go to Denmark for twenty-four hours to shoot a TV thing. In between kisses, he said, 'Okay, fine, but when you are back, I want to take you on a date. No, wait. Two dates.' He continued to lay out, in great detail, the plans for these two dates. I laughed a bit and assured him that I wouldn't be needing these dates. I was fine with us just having kissed a bit. He insisted, 'We will go on two dates, Sofie Hagen.' And I said, 'Okay, sure, I will message you when I am back.'

Two days later, I was back in Edinburgh and I texted him. No reply. I was profusely annoyed that he had lied, when the lie had not even been necessary. I felt like he could now walk away thinking that he had somehow rejected me, when I had not even wanted what he offered in the first place.

The next time I worked with him, a year or so later, he saw me from across the room and walked over to me. He put his hand on my arm and tilted his head to the side and said, 'Hi. How are you?' as if the devastation of his rejection still had not left my heart. As if seeing him for the first time since the kiss would bring me to my knees in sorrow. It has been almost ten years since the kiss now and he still talks to me in this tone. It still fills me with a cold, white rage, but even more so, it makes me full of doubt.

He made me think, *hang on, am I actually desperate?* He treated me so much like I was in love with him that I started thinking, *am I?* Because surely, this doesn't come from nowhere. And then I think that it has to be a fat thing. He must see me and think that I get so few offers that of course I fall in love with any D-list comedian I kiss.

Extensive research has been done into biases within dating, with most of it surrounding race. OkCupid co-founder and data scientist Christian Rudder even said, 'When you are looking at how two American strangers behave in a romantic context, race is the ultimate confounding factor.' Studies show that white users of OkCupid are more likely to receive messages or replies to their messages than people of colour. Asian men and black women are, overall, least likely to receive messages and responses. White people of all ages are least likely to date outside their racial group. The fact that racism is rife in the dating world should not be a surprise to anyone – and since it has been so well-documented, it is impossible to dismiss. While research into ableism, fatphobia and ageism in dating is less extensive, the existence of these societal biases cannot be denied either. Yet, I sometimes feel like I am losing my mind.

Australian actress Rebel Wilson is undoubtedly one of the more charismatic people you will see and when she, in 2020, lost a lot of weight, she noticed a big difference in how she is now treated. 'Sometimes being bigger, people didn't necessarily look twice at you. Now [...] people offer to carry my groceries to the car and hold doors open for me,' she told Australian radio show *The Morning Crew*.

Shonda Rhimes, producer of *Grey's Anatomy* and *Scandal*, reflected on her weight loss in one of her Shondaland newsletters:

Women I barely knew GUSHED. Like I was holding-a-new-baby-gushed. Only there was no new baby. It was just me. In a dress. With makeup on and my hair all *did*, yes. But...still the same me [...] And men? They spoke to me. THEY SPOKE TO ME. Like stood still and had long conversations with me about things. It was disconcerting. But even more disconcerting was that all these people suddenly felt completely comfortable talking to me about my body. Telling me I looked 'pretty' or that they were 'proud of me' or that 'wow, you are so hot now' or 'you look amazing!' After I lost weight, I discovered that people found me valuable. Worthy of conversation. A person one could look at. A person one could compliment. A person one could admire. You heard me. I discovered that NOW people saw me as a PERSON. What the hell did they see me as before? How invisible was I to them then? How hard did they work to avoid me? What words did they use to describe me? What value did they put on my presence at a party, a lunch, a discussion? When I was fat, I wasn't a PERSON to these people. Like I had been an Invisible Woman who suddenly materialized in front of them. Poof! There I am. Thin and ready for a chat.

On Lisa Lampanelli's podcast *Let Lisa Help*, actor Josh Peck talked about the reactions to his weight loss and he said, 'This is my favourite comment that people would say to me after I lost the weight, they'd go, "You have blue eyes!"'

Lisa Lampanelli jokes, 'Oh because they were wrapped in the rolls of fat?' before saying, 'No, because they weren't looking you in the eyes.'

I reach for these stories because they are told by Hollywood people whose entire jobs require them to have great energy and to be charming, and yet, being fat did not keep people from treating them worse. It is oddly validating to hear that you are not making this up, that you are not just making excuses.

It just is harder to date, to flirt, to engage with other people, when you do not fit into the Westernised beauty standards, be it because of your race, looks, body size, disability or age. When talking about sex, or, not having sex, we have to discuss how these inherent biases affect us. How am I meant to feel safe if I am terrified that the person I am having sex with does not actually find me attractive?

A couple of days after I announced this book on my TikTok account, a comment appeared that said, 'If you ever have had sex, he was just doing it as a joke! But I bet you're lying, no one would ever touch you!'

What if they are having sex with me, as a joke? It may sound unreal, if you have not lived as a fat person, but when you have experienced people kissing you as a joke, flirting with you to make their friends laugh or dancing with you to win a bet, it is something you have to consider as an actual, genuine risk. How are we meant to feel safe, when a simple internet troll's voice can appear from anywhere at any time, to say, 'But what if you are actually not safe right now?'

While we can do our very best to do the work – work on our traumas, unlearn the damaging messages about sex we received, seek out flirting courses and self-affirm ourselves silly – we will still be trying to find love in a world that is constantly trying to make us feel unloveable.

In this book, I am trying to look inwards; I am trying to do anything in my power to live a better life that involves a lot of hot, healthy sex. And I believe it is valuable for everyone to look into what they can control and do for themselves. But this should never detract from the bigger picture: that fatphobia, racism, ableism, homophobia, transphobia and sexism are all fuelled by capitalism and fascism. There is a direct connection between social politics and our sex lives. The same fatphobia that causes me, and so, so many people, to hate how they look naked, also leads to fat people being paid less and hired less. It leads to medical neglect, which can – and has – lead to deaths that could have been prevented.

There is probably a whole book in the topic of how the sociopolitical climate affects the sex lives of individuals – you only have to skim the 1,800 responses to my questionnaire to see people mentioning the cost of living crisis as the reason they do not have the sex life they want. Either due to needing to work longer hours, feeling stressed about money or because people have had to move back in with their parents or children in thin-walled flats. If you are wondering how you're going to be able to pay for your electricity bill, how are you going to get the juices flowing?

Another trend in the submissions I received was the effect of the overturning of Roe v. Wade in the US. Several people with vaginas stated that the fear of getting pregnant while living in a state that had banned abortion was enough to keep them from having sex with people with penises – no condoms or birth control pills could make them feel comfortable enough to go through with it. A 26-year-old from Texas said, 'It is no longer a case of "worst case scenario, I get an abortion", it is now "worst case scenario, I am either a parent to a child I can't take care of or I end up being sentenced to death." How am I meant to have a fulfilling sex life when I feel like my government has waged a war against my body?'

Our individual sex lives are not confined to our individual bedrooms.

I cannot ignore the fact that while it is definitely harder for me to meet someone who will make me feel desired, it is not impossible. I just like to treat it as impossible. Staying home because I will probably not meet that person. Because the odds are slim and I am not. But then I scroll on social media and I see fat people in happy relationships and I think, *Fuck, this invalidates my entire theory: that I am unloveable because I am fat.* I speak to friends like Miranda, who is fat and has sex and who is surrounded by fat people who have sex. I found a really inspirational quote on this topic: 'Fat people are not desexual. Fat people fuck. I am walking, living proof that fat people have sex.' – Sofie Hagen, *Happy Fat: Taking Up Space in a World That Wants To Shrink You.*

If comedian Sofie Hagen says it, it must be true. If only I knew her in person.

Two things can be true at the same time: it is hard for me to find people who will find me wildly attractive AND I am hiding behind that to avoid going out there and attempting to create a meaningful connection with another human. The fact is, I am not trying to sleep with every person on earth. I would be absolutely happy with just one or maybe two, down the line. Also, I am not attracted to bigots. I find their lack of intelligence to be inherently unsexy. Empathy is sexy. Kindness is sexy. Not needing society's approval to sleep with someone is sexy.

Even if the majority of all people do not find me attractive, I do not want to let that keep me from meeting the ones who do. The ridiculousness of this trend in behaviour becomes only more obvious when I scroll through the many submissions I received – hundreds of people who are kind and loveable being too scared and nervous to go out there, because what if they get rejected. Meanwhile, there are probably enough of us that we could all gather in a massive hall and just meet each other. Like at Club Indulge, thanks to Miranda Kane, for example. Because I refuse to believe that the right people don't exist. It might just be a matter of finding each other.

The Sexy Workshop

Spring 2023

A month before I go to Berlin for the Ersties porn shoot, I find myself attending a workshop put on by a woman I follow on social media.

No one turns off the loud music when the workshop begins. The facilitator, a sexy woman dressed in sexy clothing, just starts talking and me and the rest of the participants, who all paid £30 to be there, have to lean forward and narrow our eyes, as if that helps you listen better. We are all there to learn how to get over our sexual problems and to be sexually liberated, but we cannot hear anything other than some sultry Drake.

Eventually, the music stops and we can hear her. She asks us to take turns and share with the group why we are having issues with our sex lives. But not before we tell everyone our porn name. I panic and write down 'Banglord' on a piece of paper.

'Orgasm Fairy?' a woman shrugs when it's her turn, 'And I guess I'm here because it's really hard to date when you're a plus-size woman.'

There are murmurs and nods from the whole room. I catch myself nodding, too.

It's my turn.

'Banglord,' I say and people chuckle (I would have preferred a laugh). 'And I don't know – I just haven't had sex in almost eight years and I feel like there is a blockage between me and sex.'

There is one man in the room. He is sitting by himself. When it is his turn, he clears his throat nervously and says in a quiet tone, 'I was married for 14 years and in the last couple of years, I just... I just didn't want to have sex with my wife. We weren't in love anymore and I felt bad about myself. But I forced myself to have it anyway, because I didn't want to let her down. We got divorced. And now I struggle to have sex at all. I think because I forced myself to do it so many times when I didn't want to.'

A beat of silence. Then, a voice from the back, 'Sorry, I didn't hear a word he said.'

This workshop really could do with a microphone.

'Right, would you please share that again and louder this time?' the facilitator asks the man, whose face has now turned red. Please repeat your sexual trauma for the entire class, sir. There is nothing this man wants to do less than this.

He tells his story once more, this time louder.

'Okay,' the facilitator says. 'Now – we're going to be playing games!'

We are asked to go get drinks from the bar. It is a Tuesday early evening and we are in a brightly lit basement with a bunch of strangers whose sexual traumas have very much been left to hang in the air, like a thick fog. Most people get a glass of water.

We are then divided into groups. The facilitator makes sure to separate people from the people they came here with, to ensure we are all strangers and no one has any friends (read: safe people) around them. I am placed in a group with a young-looking trans person who looks at me with terrified eyes and says, 'I think I am having a panic attack. This is like school.' I nod. I can already feel myself building up mental walls around myself.

We are asked to pick a leader and the choice naturally falls on a woman who works for a sex toy brand. She is asked to go up to a large table full of sex toys and choose a bunch for our group. She comes back with whips, handcuffs, dog leashes, feathers and stuff that vibrates.

'Right – now you have to go together two and two. Take turns being the dom and the sub. Go,' the facilitator says and claps her hands excitedly.

This feels awful. I fundamentally, on a very real level, do not want to do this. The trans person next to me also does not want to do this. But I see them being handcuffed by the person next to them. I lock eyes with the leader of our group who raises her eyebrows, 'Shall we?'

I guess. I take the dog leash and say, 'Okay, how about, uh... What if I... like... Walk you? Like a dog? I mean, only if you feel comfortable?'

She smiles. 'Yeah, let's do it!'

She lets me know that her sex toy brand sponsors the event and that is why she is there – that she is not there to fix a sexual issue. She is kinky already, so she doesn't mind being walked by a stranger in a basement, like a dog.

I attach the leash to her jeans and start walking her around the room.

'Do you want to call me a whore?' she asks, kindly.

I smile. I do not particularly want to call her a whore. I want a professional sex therapist – or even just any adult with a basic knowledge of kink and consent – to attend this workshop and stop people from being traumatised. I want the word 'consent' to have been mentioned at least once. I want people to be able to do this exercise with their safe friends. I want people to have the option to say no. I notice that the man who had to shout out his trauma has left. I am happy for him.

'You are... such... a whore?' I say, weirdly, my face scrunched up.

We are asked to switch. I am now the sub. We stay seated this time and my partner grabs a leather whip. She takes my arm and starts stroking it gently with the leather strands. It tickles and it is nice. I get goosebumps.

'Are you okay if I use it?' she asks. I nod, 'Yeah, go for it.'

'Okay. One. Two. Three.' She lets the whip snap over my wrist. I feel like my body jumps but I know I do not move from my seat. It feels like my entire body was infused with a burst of heat and adrenaline.

'Oh,' I say, 'That's... That was nice.'

'Yeah?' she says and starts stroking me again. I become very aware of how lucky I am. I have coincidentally been partnered with the only person in the room with experience of kink and consent. I feel safe with her.

She cracks the whip again, and this time, a bit harder. Again, my body twitches as I feel the pain quickly become excitement.

'I get it now,' I say, mostly to myself, but she smiles. The contrast between the gentleness of the stroking and the biting and surprising pain when she uses the whip is incredible. It makes my body extra aware of all sensations, probably because it is now in a state of anticipation.

'You are doing very well,' she says and I feel my cheeks burn. My brain stops producing words in English and I struggle to reply. I just smile and keep my eyes on the leather stroking my arm before it, again, slaps down over it, sending electricity into every nerve.

The last game we have to play is one where the facilitator starts singing a 'sexy song' and the group that can finish the song gets to go up and pick a free sex toy. One group gets no toys because they are seated so far away from her that they cannot hear what she is singing. Another wins all the toys and then we are done with the workshop.

I thank the woman I was partnered with and she gives me some free lube from her sex toy brand. We politely exchange social media information. I am desperate to talk to someone about what we all just went through together, but people quickly scatter and disappear.

I understand the need for aftercare now. And microphones.

In the Uber, on my way home, I wonder what constitutes sex. I was undoubtedly turned on when the stranger whipped my arm. If we had met on a dating app and had arranged to meet up and I had walked her like a dog and she had whipped me, I would have left that interaction thinking, *that was sex. I just had sex.* So what is the difference?

We know that sex is not just penis-in-vagina or penetration of any kind. That would invalidate a bunch of queer sex. You can have sex whilst fully dressed, so nudity is not a descriptor either. If an orgasm meant that you had had sex, a lot of hetero women would technically be virgins. Just being turned on by a person will not make something sex either – if it did, I would have had sex with the lead singer from Imagine Dragons several times.

When I met up with Justin Hancock, sex educator, I asked him to define sex. 'I don't define sex,' he said. 'You define sex.'

But do both people need to agree that they had sex, for it to have been sex?

When Bill Clinton had an affair with White House intern Monica Lewinsky, he would push her away from him when he was about to cum. In his mind, it was not cheating if he did not ejaculate. She would be absolutely right to call that sex and, in theory, based on the 'you define sex' definition, he would also be right when he said he'd had no sexual relations with that woman. We define what is sex, right?

I do not think I have had sex with the Sex Toy Brand Woman at the workshop. I am just not quite sure why.

Then it strikes me. *Oh no.*

I have been on this journey with a very clear mission statement: I have not had sex since 19 November 2015, where I left the bed of Johnson, the love of my life, six months after he ended it with me.

But that is a lie.

In January 2016, I attended a friend's leaving party in Brixton. I remember snippets. I remember that I knew that he was in a relationship. I also remember seeing him flirting with a woman who was not his girlfriend – in fact, his girlfriend was not even at the party. I felt jealous. When the party ended, I spoke to him outside of the venue. He told me that he was in love with this other woman and had been for his entire life, but she had just rejected his advances again. I decided, firmly, in my head, that I would not ever touch this man sexually.

He then suggested that we should go get a hotel and something happened in my brain. A little voice appeared and said, *Do it! He chose you over her and, well, the other her. You don't know when you will get this opportunity again!*

We walked till we found a hotel. At the reception, we were told that one night would be £450. 'I'll go to an ATM,' he said. I thought nothing of it – in retrospect I can see that, yeah, a hotel charge on a potentially shared credit card would not look good.

As soon as he was out of eyesight, I realised how much I wanted to go home. I wanted to sleep in my own bed, alone. I had no desire to check into this hotel. I had no toothbrush. I had an early morning the next day. I just – I wanted to go home.

He came back and told me in a hushed voice that the machine took his card because he had insufficient funds. As if I was seeing myself from the outside, as if I was controlled by something else, I witnessed myself paying the full £450 for a hotel room I did not want in order to share a bed with a man I did not want.

I have snippets of memories from the next couple of hours. There was no penetration. He tried to insert a flaccid penis into my vagina at one point, but it was not happening. I think he went down on me. I know he wanted to spank me; he is into kinky stuff. I tried so hard to want it. If I'd had to admit to myself that I did not want to be there, it would have devastated me. Instead, I told myself that I loved this. I had to love this or I was an idiot.

He changed his voice. It was now deep and pretend-sultry as he tried to be domineering. I do not remember what he said, but I remember being actively turned off by it. He was insecure – of course he was, who isn't? His credit card had just been declined, he had been rejected by a woman who he was trying to cheat on his girlfriend with and he felt like he had to change his voice to be sexy. I felt like he was pretending – and I ignored the fact that I was also pretending. I wonder if he wanted to be there as little as I did. Were we just playing the parts of two people having hot hotel sex, when, actually, neither of us was happy?

The next morning, I began to reframe the evening in my head. First of all, I decided that we did not have sex because his penis did not enter me. I also decided that it was a wild, crazy night of hot passion. I laughed – no, I gloated – when I told friends, 'Oh my GOD, I just spent £450 because I was so horny, lol.'

A year or so later, we repeated the same mistake. We got a hotel, he couldn't insert his flaccid penis, he spanked me. I tried to ignore that I did not want this to happen. He gave me a sentimental present. The kind of present that says, 'I know you, deep down inside, and I have put a lot of thought into this', and it would have meant a lot, had it not come from him. It was not reflective of me and who I am, but of who he would like for me to be.

After we had Sex That I Decide Is Not Sex, I left. I said I had an early-morning start. He was disappointed and asked if I would at least come back for the hotel breakfast. I lied and said yes.

A year later, he asked to meet up. We went out for pizza. He dramatically sighed, took my hand and said, 'Sofie, I did not want you to find out from the internet – I am proposing to my girlfriend in the spring.'

Mouth full of pizza, I said, 'Oh congratulations, that's great!'

He pursed his lips, 'I want to be a good husband. So, we can't see each other again.'

I blinked a few times and nodded. 'Okay. That's... I guess I will have to just... learn how to live with that.' Though I couldn't help but laugh a bit. He looked at me with the kind of disappointment you have in a child that is being naughty. 'I mean, now that you have so viciously broken my heart, I assume you will pay for the pizza.'

'Fine, of course I will,' he said. 'I'm glad you are taking it so well.'

We finished eating while he described how he was planning to propose. If anyone proposed that way to me, I would take out a hit on them for being so annoying. But fine – I guessed she would like it because she actually liked him.

We left the restaurant and he announced that he 'should really get home'.

'Cool, it was good to see you,' I said, and gave him a

hug. He lingered, his arms around me. He then sighed and dramatically took out his phone. He looked at it and then closed his eyes as he put it back in his pocket.

'Okay. One more drink,' he said. Half an hour later, he suggested a hotel.

'I thought you were going to be a good husband,' I reminded him. He made a face that suggested that he thought I was just teasing him and that it was the sort of sexual teasing that he simply could not resist, despite how much he loves his girlfriend.

I said no. We left the bar and hugged goodbye. As I walked away, I grabbed my phone and pretended to make a call. 'Mother,' I pretend-cried into the phone, 'he is getting married! I lost him forever! What shall I ever do with myself?'

'Fuck you!' he shouted after me, defeated. I felt elated and grateful that I could say no, finally.

So it now occurs to me, as I am on the way home from the workshop, that the last time I had sex was in 2017. However, weirdly, having a woman platonically whip my wrist for two minutes felt a lot more intimate, a lot sexier.

I think there are several reasons why I do not want to claim what Hotel Spanking Guy and I did was sex. I did not want to have sex with him – I knew that, even in the moment, despite trying to repress those feelings. So by claiming that we did not have sex, I have a faint illusion of control, still. There is also some deeply internalised bad sex education still lurking – the kind where you do think of sex as a penis entering a vagina, and everything else is just foreplay. Under all those layers, there is another truth that I am very slowly acknowledging. There is a part of me that likes that Johnson was the last person I had sex with, because it meant something. He meant something. And I meant something to him.

Justin's definition of sex being 'whatever you decide it is' frustrated me because the lack of a clear definition meant that I had to think about these experiences. If sex is what we say it is, were the fetish experiences with The Comedian not also sex? We never touched, we never kissed, we were never naked. But we were both turned on. We engaged in an activity for sexual pleasure together. If we define that as sex, I have had sex several times in the last eight years. The entire premise for this book crumbles before me, if that is the case.

At one point, I thought it would be funny to have a 'Days Since Sex' counter made, so I could flip a number each day and see it get bigger and bigger. You know, as a funny, funny joke. But sex is proving to be a tricky one to nail down. Instead, I should get several of them made. Days Since Touched Sexually. Days Since Kissing. Days Since Enthusiastically and Willingly Participating in a Sexual Experience with Someone. Days Since Penis in Vagina. Days Since Flaccid Penis in Vagina Attempt. Days Since Sex with Someone Who Wasn't Cheating on Their

Partner With Me. Days Since Intimacy. Days Since Sex I Didn't Regret. Days Since Being Reluctantly Spanked at a Workshop Which Ended Up Actually Being Quite Hot and Exciting.

5.
SEXUALITY

i will allow myself to overreact this time. i don't want to deny this for what it can be. friday night I went to the movies with this girl from my class <3 <3 <3 The Girl is somewhat like me, and i've always liked her more than all the other girls. anyways, while we were watching this film i felt like kissing her. it grew stronger on the way home. i saw her saturday night as well, and it's getting stuck on me. i still love my boyfriend... but I'm really crazy about this girl. i have never felt this way before. is this like falling for a boy? cuz that would be wrong. i don't know. i'm actually scared by this emotion. i hope it will pass, i really hope so. i haven't told my boyf. i don't know how to. or if i should. this may be a phase only. it may pass.

– My diary, November 2005

i just focused on her lips on mine. ladies and gentlemen, she is a wonderful kisser. i love the drinking game 'pandora's box'. everyone at the party put three notes each into the box and they either ask a question or give a dare. i put in three notes that all said 'kiss lisa'. i was lucky enough to draw the last one left. the kiss lasted about four seconds. she is so beautiful<3<3<3

– My diary, January 2006[36]

I'm doing research for my book, I tell myself, as I find Lisa's Facebook profile and look through her photos. A couple of months after our intense kiss, at the house party in 2006, I told her that I thought I maybe liked her. She thanked me for letting her know and told me that she was straight. I was confused. I had not told her I was *gay*, just that I had a crush on her. *Why is she even bringing sexuality into this? I am straight too, of course. I would just like to marry her, in an incredibly heterosexual relationship. Just two straight people with vaginas, making love.*

The following year in school, she told everyone that I was in love with her. When people asked me, I made a

---

36 Yes, I wrote my diary in English and often in all lowercase. I thought it was dramatic and exciting.

face like I was confused. I told them that she probably just wanted the attention and, for some reason, they believed me over her. It probably helped that I had a boyfriend at the time. My boyfriend, by the way, did not at all factor into my crush on Lisa. I even told him about being in love with her, a testament to how I viewed queer relationships and feelings as 'not real'. My boyfriend was completely wrapped up in the men's magazine idea that 'girls only kiss other girls to please the men' and that if his *kæreste*,[37] who he considered to be a woman, wanted to kiss or have sex with another woman, he had to act like a horny caveman and cheer it on. In this particular case, the patriarchy worked out pretty well for me. I got to kiss girls at parties and my boyfriend never considered it cheating, even when he knew I fancied them. Likewise, I thought of myself as *as straight as they come*, even as I wrote declarations of love to them in my diary.

Lisa is still unbelievably beautiful, in her profile photo, next to her two children and husband. The business she works at just won a big award and she is very proud. I am 17 again.

After Lisa, there was Sally. I was 19 and had just

---

37 In Danish, we do not have two separate gendered words for 'boyfriend' and 'girlfriend'. We just have kæreste, which covers both and all genders. Kæreste stems from kære, which means 'dear'. Kæreste is, directly translated, 'dearest'. Except, 'dearest' sounds very 1920s and kæreste just sounds like 'boyfriend/girlfriend' but without the gender aspect. Since I very much took the role of 'girlfriend' at the time (going along with being a 'girl'), but we now know I am nonbinary, I would like to just refer to myself as kæreste. I hope we can contain all of this, in reading this part of the book.

moved to Copenhagen, where I got a part-time job in a kindergarten alongside my studies. One night, my housemate had a friend over. Sally. We started talking and we did not stop for two months. We slept in the same bed, held hands when we walked down the street and when I ran into her ex-best friend, I felt the jealousy bubble up. We would kiss whenever a man was nearby, telling ourselves that it was for him. We joked about threesomes with men but the focus was always *us*. The man was just an excuse. Some old classmates of mine lived with three other men and we ravaged their little commune. She slept with one guy while I slept with another guy, in the room right next to them. We would then go home together, discussing the sex we had had, close to but not with each other.

Within a month of knowing her, I was fired from my job. I had fallen asleep while playing with the children because I had been up all night with her. She told me I would look good with a labret, so I immediately let someone in a dodgy basement pierce the space underneath my bottom lip. It got infected and I still have a scar. Every time my tongue touches the back of my bottom lip, I feel a little bump and I remember Sally and how it ended. After a whirlwind two months of being completely enthralled with her, I found out that she was having a manic episode. I had been swept away by her spontaneity, her fast-paced, confident ideas and, let us be honest, her very beautiful, green eyes.

One day, I told my therapist at the time that Sally and

I had been out drinking, and, when the pub closed, Sally suggested that we break into the flat of an acquaintance, because they would *just love* to wake up and see two women lying on their kitchen floor. *What a wild, exciting and sexy idea.* We walked three miles, found the key under the mat and unlocked the door. We woke up on the kitchen floor, when a 20-year-old man in a bathrobe turned on the lights. He was not at all impressed. When I told my therapist, she calmly asked me if Sally had ever mentioned having borderline personality disorder. I said yes, because she had. She had told me it was just this condition that sometimes made her sad. My therapist told me to be aware that this might just be a manic episode.

A bit spooked, I reached out to the friends I had been ignoring for two months and began seeing them more. Sally became controlling. She started 'punishing' the men we had slept with by faking pregnancy tests and demanding money from them. I felt uneasy – these were men I had introduced her to. They were my friends. On New Year's Eve of 2008, my best friend got hit in the eye by a piece of firework and had to urgently go to A&E. Sally screamed at me that I was abandoning her and that I was being selfish. I went with my friend to the hospital and stopped speaking to Sally. I moved out of the flat I shared with our mutual friend because Sally kept showing up and walking into my room.

It felt like a break-up. A complicated, messy break-up that left both emotional and physical scars. The only way

I knew how to explain the intensity of it to people was to refer to her as my ex-girlfriend. It had felt that way. We had kissed and held hands and I was utterly and absolutely obsessed with her. Until I was no longer obsessed.

The fact that she had borderline personality disorder worked as an excuse for me to not question the sexuality aspect of it all. *Oh, I wasn't gay in a gay relationship, I was just caught up in someone else's manic episode.* In the same way as I denied being queer as I was declaring my very queer love to Lisa. I even introduced Sally to my mother as my *kæreste*, and it felt normal and natural, because it felt *heterosexual*.

When I was 14 years old, a friend came out to me. It was the first time I ever heard the word 'bisexual'. We sat on a bench in the small Danish village where she lived and she seemed so scared to be telling me this. 'Sofie, I'm bisexual,' she said.

'What's that?' I asked.

'It means I'm attracted to both boys and girls... You know? Sexually and... romantically,' she said, her face red and her eyes wet.

I laughed. The whole thing seemed ridiculous to me. 'Okay? That's so dumb,' I said. 'That's how everyone feels. I'm straight and that's how I feel. Of course I want to kiss both boys and girls, but I'm straight so I just choose the boys.'

I have no memory of the rest of the conversation; I doubt my friend felt particularly supported. I wish someone had sat me down and said, 'Hey, you're quite possibly queer and you need to deal with that because you're confusing a lot of people here – including yourself,' because I needed to hear that.

(Again, for research's sake, I just looked her up on Facebook. She just had a baby with her Norwegian husband.)

(And I looked up Sally. She is now working at an LGBT+ organisation, as a mental health counsellor.)

I kept postponing writing this chapter because, honestly, I feel a bit like a fraud. While I have proudly embraced the label 'queer', it comes with feelings of complicated guilt and confusion. I do not feel like I am 'queer enough' to claim it. Drunken kisses with women at parties, ostensibly for the sake of boys watching, is the only thing I have to show for my queerness. I am a queer virgin. And now, I look back at everything I have written about the men I have had sex with and it feels different. I wonder why I ever cared about them. I wonder if I am even actually attracted to men. And how can I possibly know, when I have not tried sex with anyone other than them? I am in a no-man's land between the only thing I have ever tried, which no longer feels right, and that big scary thing I really want to try, but I have no idea how to go about it. I left the Straight Woman club ages ago and now I am standing outside the Queer Trans club trying to find my membership card, and I don't know if I left it at home or if I haven't earned it yet.

I know, logically, that no one can gatekeep sexuality. I know I have been in love with and attracted to women, trans people and nonbinary people. I know that that is technically 'enough' to be queer. But somewhere deep inside, I feel like the next sexual experience I will have will not be with a cis man. So I need to figure out where I exist within queerness. I call my good friend, Jodie Mitchell.

I met Jodie Mitchell in 2017 at a show in Edinburgh, where they lived at the time. After the show, we had fish and chips on the Royal Mile and we have been friends ever since. In 2018, we launched a podcast together called *Secret Dinosaur Cult*, an obscure, cult podcast about daddy issues[38] and dinosaurs. It was on this podcast I first came out as nonbinary. Jodie had already come out at this point and was performing as their Drag King alter ego, John Travulva, with their drag group Pecs. They were a huge part of my gender journey, as they helped me to realise that something gender-y in my body was vibrating. In 2023, I directed Jodie's first stand-up show, *Becoming John Travulva*, a show about *their* gender journey. As I am nearing the end of the book, I want to speak to Jodie about queerness.

'I think it started exceptionally early. I had several close friends when I was very young and we would be –

---

38 My dad left when I was a baby and came back when I was around five years old. And then he left again. Jodie's dad left and their step-dad appeared. Then the step-dad left. So my dad left twice, while Jodie's two dads both left. Perhaps not the funniest base for a comedy podcast, but we somehow made it work.

I guess at the time we used the word "tomboys". We were tomboys together. And we would explore each other's bodies, but not in a sexual way, if that makes sense. We would be playing Husband and Wife, which, looking back now... That's gay as fuck. We were dressing up as little boys, playing Husband and Wife. But during the process, we were actively discussing the fact that there would be no wife,' Jodie explains one night over Zoom.

'So, you were playing Husband and Husband?' I ask.

Jodie laughs. 'Yeah, basically.'

'When we played House, I was always the dog,' I say, with a very clear memory of being on all fours in the kindergarten, next to the miniature play-pretend kitchen.

'So even then you just wanted to be told you were a good boy?' Jodie teases and continues, 'I had a best friend at the time who was a cis guy but he saw me as another boy, so I felt safe with him. I was always comfortable when I was seen as a queer person. Of course, I wasn't conscious of this at the time. Because I always – I don't like the word, but for simplicity's sake, let's use it in this context – 'passed' as a boy. The first time I actually thought of myself as queer was when I was 13. I had developed a huge crush on a girl in my year. I really wanted to be bisexual. I remember thinking, *hopefully I'm bisexual. Because then I don't have to put myself in a box*. And that was the message I got from people around me whenever I told them. They'd say, "Are you sure? You can't go back, once you come out." I know now, as an adult, how ridiculous that is.

Then when I was 16, I had my first kiss with a girl, who I fell head over heels in love with, and who was also my best friend. It was like being hit by lightning. I remember feeling it all over my body. I'd never experienced anything like it; it was like synesthesia. I could almost picture the lightning running over my body. And I thought, *fuck. I can't argue with that*. I had been so slutty with boys and it was never like that. I mean, I really hadn't ever hopped off a finger for long enough to even think about it, but I knew it was shit, in comparison.'

I chew a bit on the sentence 'hopped off a finger' and try to put that aside in my mind, where it will fester and become an uncomfortable nightmare. 'When you kissed your best friend, was it a real kiss? Or one of those teenage kisses, where you do it to impress boys?'

'Oh, it was a kiss-kiss. I told two people about it and one of them then came out to me as bisexual. Her response was to make out with me, because there was no one else to make out with, right? She took the opportunity. We had this terrible makeout session that we were both disgusted by. And then at parties, it happened again but always in front of people. Using your sexuality to impress men was so grim. But it also meant I got to make out with women, so I indulged in the silver lining of it.'

'I don't think I would have kissed a girl yet if I couldn't have excused it as a drinking game or because I was trying to impress whatever guy was nearby,' I admit, feeling a teensy bit of shame. 'I would start kissing them under the guise of impressing the boys but then get completely wrapped up in the kiss and forget that the rest of the world existed. You say you slept with boys too?'

'Yes, I thought I had to check,' Jodie says with a sly smile. 'I slept with a guy when I was 17 and it wasn't very good, even though he brought whisky-flavoured condoms because I am Scottish. So I thought I'd better check again. I bootycalled a guy who was a close friend. I was still like, right, that was bad. I then tried again with the original person. Then I finally had sex with a woman. And to be fair, it wasn't very good. But I think that's what cinched it for me. The fact that it was still not good but it was still infinitely better. Even though she went out in the garden afterwards and cried because she was incredibly religious. She believed it was okay to be bisexual because Jesus says to love everyone, but once she had sex with me, she thought she was fully gay. And she couldn't be fully gay because Jesus would not be okay with that. She ended up telling everyone she'd had sex with a woman – I called myself a woman at the time – and everyone knew it was me. She never said it was but they knew. I had a red mullet; I mean, it was fairly obvious. This happened right before I went to university, so I skipped the whole coming out process. When I arrived at uni, I was wearing leather, had a back-combed red mullet and I was covered in piercings. I looked queer as fuck, so it wasn't hard to convince people that I'd always been out.'

'Compulsive heterosexuality', often shortened to

comphet, is the idea that society has pre-decided for us that we are all probably heterosexual. We see it so often. A little girl plays with a little boy and the comments begin: look at those two, they are going to get married one day. What a charmer, what a flirt. Meanwhile, in the 1800s, two women would live in the same house and sleep in the same bed their entire lives and they will still be described in the history books as 'two single spinster friends, hanging out in their singledom, longing for husbands'. Heterosexuality is the norm, the expected and the assumed. If we then turn out to be queer, we almost need to make a ceremonial announcement that we are *not* this thing that was foisted upon us by society. Compulsive heterosexuality is 13-year-old me telling my friend that she is silly for saying she is bisexual – because why would she not be straight? Why would we *both* not be straight, even though we desperately want to kiss girls?

The Lesbian Masterdoc, a 30-page document that has circled the internet since 2018, was originally created by a Tumblr user with the handle @cyberlesbian who in real life is named Angeli Luz. Luz was just 18 years old when she created the Googledoc. The Lesbian Masterdoc explores the difference between genuine heterosexuality and compulsive heterosexuality, posing questions like: 'Do you like the idea of being with a man, but every time a man makes a move on you, you get incredibly uncomfortable?' and 'Do you think all straight girls feel at least some attraction to women?' The document does not pretend to have all the answers – it is really just a list of questions that can help you reflect on your sexuality. And while it began as something for and about lesbians, it has since then embraced the existence of bi- and pansexuality too.

The reason the document is worth mentioning is that its existence went viral during the first pandemic lockdown in 2020 and it seemed like hundreds, if not thousands, of women realised that they were some kind of queer just based on what they read in it. What it goes to show is that compulsive heterosexuality goes deep – and we could all benefit from actively challenging what we think about ourselves. You may learn that yes, you are definitely straight, but what if you learned something exciting? That perhaps there is an entire world, an entire community you have not yet explored? And potentially a whole new sex life you have so far missed out on?

I say this as if I am not, myself, in the middle of this untangling.

'Okay, I'm going to be embarrassingly honest, Jodie,' I say. I hate that I am about to ask this question. 'When you say you "had sex with a woman"... there is a missing piece of the puzzle in my head. I know it is ridiculous, but when you said you had sex with a man, I could conjure a visual in my head: the porn script. Blowjob, missionary, orgasm. Penis in vagina. He comes, you don't. Classic penis-in-vagina-sex. But as soon as it is two vaginas... I'm like, how? I do know, logically, that there are a million different ways that it can happen, just as the penis-vagina sex, but in my head, I just don't have the script. Did you? Did you have the script? Are you just meant to be able to know how to do it?'

'Honestly,' Jodie says and matches my embarrassment, 'I think it helped that I had watched a lot of *The L Word*.'

'Wait, do you see them have sex on *The L Word*?'

'Not explicitly, but there is a season where – God, I can't believe I'm talking about *The L Word* – where Jenny and Shane get a housemate who is a cis man and he wants to make a documentary about lesbians. And he asks them what the primary lesbian sex act is. He says, 'When it's a man and a woman, it's fucking. So what do you do?' And Shane goes, 'What the fuck is wrong with you? It's completely possible for us to fuck.' It blew my mind completely. And it really stayed with me. It helped a lot because I don't think that *is* the primary queer sex act. But from an early age, so much of what we learn about sex is so penis-centric. We didn't learn about lube, which is also great for a penis, by the way. The phallic-centrism of sex is really damaging for everyone. Straight people, queer people. Because sex is so much more than that. So once I was in the moment, I wasn't too worried about it because I was like, *oh, it's about enjoying bodies*. I hadn't gotten that before because I had only slept with people whose bodies I wasn't interested in. This is just my own experience, of course. I used to think going down on each other would be *the big thing*, because it felt so intimate. I really sucked at it.' I note down 'it's about enjoying bodies' on a Post-it note because it feels incredibly relevant. I can just stop writing this book now – it's done, we solved it. *It's about enjoying bodies.*

I say, 'It feels like what we learn from normative, toxic, PornHub-style porn is that sex is a performance. You're *performing* a blowjob and there *is* a wrong way of doing it. I am afraid that I will take that mindset into queer sex, where, if I am bad at it, it will be embarrassing.'

'Well, porn is a performance. And that is not what sex is.[39] And at least with queer sex you can't hide in the script. You have to think creatively and you realise that *oh, it is a lot more than that.* There just isn't a one-size-fits-all, especially with trans sex. It is about finding what you are comfortable with. It's scary for everyone, I think, before they do it. You're not alone in that, whatsoever.'

I better not be alone with it, I think, *because then this entire book is incredibly embarrassing.* But I am in my mid-thirties and I am asking my friend how to have sex. I have a career, I own a slow cooker and a dog. I pay taxes and have an ISA and I am essentially a *queer virgin.*

'The people I am going to have sex with are going to be around my age. How do you say to someone that you haven't done it before? I don't want to be fumbling around being like *oh what does this thing do?* when I'm in my thirties.'

'I get what you are saying and I truly empathise,' Jodie

---

39 Not the first time in my life I have been told that the porn I watch isn't real sex. Flashback to the day after my 11th birthday.

says. 'But at the same time, you are a body that has had sex with other bodies. And you are nonbinary, so, in a way, you have never had non-queer sex, between a man and a woman. So what you are really just nervous about is potential new genitalia with a lack of examples to follow. But you do know what it is like to have sex with someone and it shouldn't be *that* different.'

'God, I hope it's different though,' I sigh, remembering all the ceilings I have stared at, impatiently waiting for the sex to end.

A few years back, I had a big crush on a woman and there was a brief window in which I thought she might like me back. I panicked. I thought, *I can't do this because if we get together, I would have to be present in my body. She would be able to tell if I'm not. I would have to be gentle and careful and curious.* And then it hit me. *I should be all of these things when I have sex with anyone, though.* Is it that I am scared of having sex with people who are not cis men, or is it that I am scared of having sex when I am not dissociated and disconnected from the act? And do I just tend to see men as people who will not notice if I am not truly into it or not? If this is the case, I would need to have sex with different men, because that should be the very bare minimum. Or, do I tend to see women as particularly caring, aware, soft and gentle? Because that also feels like a very single-faceted view of quite a lot of diverse people.

I recently drove to a gig with a lesbian comedian and

she told me about a one-night stand she had had. She said, 'I fucked this girl and it was so great playing with her boobs.' And I realised that this was the first time I had heard a woman talk in an objectifying, horny way about another woman. I tell this to Jodie. 'It was so great. It took off like, 20 per cent of my nervousness around queer sex because I thought, *oh yeah, sometimes it's just – hey, I love tits and I want to play with them*, rather than this idea that you have to gently and carefully caress a nipple while jazz is playing.'

Jodie is smiling. 'I feel like porn presents us with this idea that lesbian culture is *for* the male gaze. So often you watch lesbian porn and they are fucking each other with stilettos. I'm yet to meet a woman who wants to fuck someone using a stiletto. It's either that or this super sensual version, which is *also* for the male gaze, because it is so purist. Like, you don't want to fuck, you want to look pretty. So much of this porn just really sucks. When you pay for porn, though, where it's actual queer people enjoying each other, it's great. Or, well, sometimes it's not, but you still never see the stiletto.'

There was a 'fun fact' that went viral earlier this year which said, 'You know what it feels like to lick any object you can see' and it really freaked people out, including me. I now wonder if everyone with a vagina instinctively knows what it would feel like to be fucked by a stiletto, even though you have never been fucked by a stiletto. I feel like I know how it would feel. I am not a fan of the sensation.

'How do you go from A to B, then,' I ask Jodie, wanting to get some practical answers. 'Where do you find people to, you know, date and... fuck?'

'I think it's about finding your community,' Jodie says. 'For me, it was about finding performance communities because that's where my interest is. Through *The LOL Word*, our queer comedy night, I met a bunch of new queer people. And through PECS, I met Drag Kings. Through community, and all the confidence it gave me, I did end up finding people to fall in love with. Oh, look at this.'

Jodie picks up a card from the shelf in front of them and shows it to me. It is a beautiful card with the words 'Thank you from your local lesbian' written across it. 'This is from my friend, because she just came out and I helped her. Speaking of community, right? Existing in these communities enabled me to explore gender in a way that I think would have taken me so much longer if I didn't have supportive people around me. At the same time I also grew in confidence because I had previously received so much messaging around being butch and how that was a bad thing. Being both fat, masculine and queer is quite different to being femme presenting and you're so often seen as a predator.'

(Community, *again*. Miranda Kane mentioned finding a community too. Juno Roche talked about the trans community. It can't be a coincidence. I write down 'community' in my notebook.)

'Yeah, I feel like Shane from *The L Word* is portrayed as this *ideal* type of masculine lesbian. Whereas we see Boo from *Orange Is the New Black* as this predatory, gay, butch lesbian.'

'And I was so afraid to be Boo!' Jodie exclaims with a laugh. 'I was terrified of being Boo. I needed these spaces. I needed spaces that celebrated someone like me and where I could watch other people be platformed and celebrated and feel safe. Celebration gets rid of shame. Tolerance and acceptance are not negative things, but they are not positive things, and it's not enough to heal all the harm caused by shame, homophobia and transphobia. We need celebration. I am not saying that everyone needs to become a Drag King and comedian to find a community, but that is what worked for me.'

'I was just about to say,' I add, 'we're quite lucky to be living in a big city where this is all a possibility. If I had stayed in the small town I grew up in, I can't imagine what I'd do. But there are queer and trans people everywhere, so it *shouldn't* be impossible, right?'

'Oh yeah, we're super privileged to be able to find these communities because if you live in smaller places, there will be fewer queer people. I was actually just speaking to a friend of mine about this because she used to be really upset that she couldn't find any queer spaces where she lived, in Edinburgh. There were nights but they were primarily for gay men, and she wanted a space dedicated to radical intersectional queerness, especially ones that

WILL I EVER HAVE SEX AGAIN?

prioritised AFAB[40] people. So she set up a reading group called Get Lit With a Lesbian and it exploded because there was such a need for it. It's so cool. They get together and they read books and they do cute outings together,' Jodie says. 'How do you feel when you're in queer spaces, Sofie?'

'I still feel I haven't earned my badge. Like I need to prove myself. I just have so many questions. . Queer spaces feel *more right* than other spaces and I love being in them, but I don't know if I'm allowed to be there.'

Jodie nods. 'The community is not welcoming enough to people who are questioning. And I understand why – a lot of us carry around a bunch of trauma and straight cis people flooding queer events is a very real thing. And people should be aware of that. But that shouldn't divert away from queer spaces welcoming bisexual people and people who are questioning, or other members of the community who are less visible. I think that's counterproductive and not in the ethos of the space. If you don't welcome people who are exploring, you won't have people who realise that this *is* who they are. And there will be far fewer of us being visible in the world. It's such a necessary part of the journey. Those spaces are specifically meant for people who don't feel safe and who don't feel celebrated. And quite often, the people who feel like that are in the beginning of that journey. So I understand where you're

---

40 Those who are Assigned Female At Birth. AMABs are people who have been Assigned Male At Birth.

coming from and I just want to say that you so deserve to be in those spaces. Those spaces are for you.'

It's just about enjoying bodies. I thank Jodie for their input. And friendship. I am convinced this will help more people than just me. As I am about to shut down the Zoom window, I stop.

'Wait, one more thing! Are you meant to carry dental dams with you wherever you go?' I ask.

'Listen, I've never used a dental dam. But I also have contracted chlamydia of the throat once, so maybe I should,' Jodie laughs. Jodie has a history of weird illnesses, like the time a budgie spat in their eye so it was red and swollen for weeks. I was incredibly confused when they told me about this because I thought a budgie was a type of dog and I have never seen a dog aim a spit before.

'I would suggest regular STI testing and checking in with your sexual partners that they are engaging with the same health practice,' Jodie clarifies.

'It would just feel like such a typical "queer virgin" thing for me to do, to show up to My First Sex with a box of dental dams and a strap-on. Like, *let's get ready to rumble!*'

Jodie laughs. 'Listen, There is a great company called RodeoH. They sell pants that already have the O-ring, where you can just put a dick through. So you don't have to have a strap, you can just keep your dick in your bag. You can get like a dog-tag that says 'RodeoH' – that way people know that you have a dick in your bag.'

'In case they need to borrow one?' I ask, confused.

'No!' Jodie laughs. 'So people know you have a dick. And you're, you know, ready to go. Listen, there is nothing wrong with prepping. I think it's super hot when people do that. But it's also very valid to show up with nothing and just have a chat about what you like. My favourite discovery recently are these little lube sachets that you can take with you. Because so many people don't have their own lube, so it's very convenient.'

'I love practical advice,' I state and remember, 'Six years ago I bought 100 condoms, *just in case*. I got an email a year later that said: "It's time to order more condoms!" I didn't. So I don't think I want to buy lube sachets just yet, I think I would be jinxing it.'

'Do you still have those 100 condoms?' Jodie asks.

'No, no, they expired.'

'Good, because I was going to offer to come round and ritualistically burn them with you.'

I laugh. 'I doubt that's great for the environment.'

'We could bury them?' Jodie suggests.

'Imagine the next person living here digging them back up. Finding 100 condoms. They'd be able to conclude, *look, someone sad lived here.*'

Jodie smiles. 'They died a spinster.'

After speaking to Jodie, I go to Google Images. I look up a variety of people. Cis men, cis women, trans women, trans men, nonbinary people, people with different gender expressions, femmes, butches, mascs, gay men, gay women, androgynous people – and I notice that my attraction to people isn't based on their gender or gender expression. I think Chris Pratt playing Andy in *Parks and Recreation* is hot. I think Lea DeLaria as Boo in *Orange Is the New Black* is hot. Kerry Washington in *Scandal* is hot. Sara Ramírez playing Che Diaz in *And Just Like That* and Sara Ramírez playing Callie in *Grey's Anatomy* is hot. The singer Meat Loaf was hot. Steven Tyler from Aerosmith. Yoga teacher and fat liberation activist Jessamyn Stanley might be the hottest. Jason Momoa, Jesse Williams, Angelina Jolie, Kevin Bacon (when dancing in particular), Gillian Anderson, Aubrey Gordon, Tim Curry in *The Rocky Horror Picture Show*... Just, hot. I find so many people hot. There are people who I have seen on TV and never noticed, but when I met them in real life, they became the hottest person in the world. Because of a look, an energy, a vibe. I have known people for ages and not seen them as hot until I saw them on stage. I have found people unbearably hot until they opened their mouth and started talking, and it went away immediately.

'Queer' seems to cover this experience perfectly and I will always be queer, even if I end up dating Kevin Bacon (when dancing in particular). And yes, in theory, labels should matter a lot less than they do. But they provide a comfort. A community. A sense of belonging, which is essential to feeling safe.

When I first announced this book on my social media, a lot of people asked me if I was asexual and if that was the reason I hadn't had sex in a long time. I would say 'No, I'm ...' and then realise I had no idea what the word is for 'not asexual'. I looked it up. Allosexual. Allosexual being when you have sexual attraction towards others and asexual being when you do not feel sexual attraction to others. I am allosexual. But a lot of people feel like they fit into neither and they have claimed the label 'greysexuals'. One of these people popped up in my survey.

G is a 44-year-old man who has been disabled for 20 years. His spine is bent and fused. He cannot move his neck and he has had both hips and his right shoulder replaced and all of his larger organs removed. It has been 20 years since he last had sex.

'I was taught that men had the right to sex with women, that women could have anyone they wanted, and that all other men were child predators. I told my parents I was gay at the age of 12, and they told me that I shouldn't worry as they would always love me, and that I couldn't be sure I was gay. These things change, they're just phases. From this, I thought my parents were telling me that I would eventually be interested in children. When my friends send me photos of their family, their kids doing goofy things, I always think, *No! You shouldn't be sending that to strangers*. I think I might always think of myself as a stranger.'

Before G became disabled, at the age of 24, he was a very thin young man who was mainly attracted to 'heavyset bear types'. He felt like he should look like that himself and the self-hatred caused him to self-harm. He attempted to be sexually active, 'But somehow it just didn't work. I struggled to maintain an erection, would lose interest halfway through. Then I changed my body to become larger. It's fascinating that the fact that my disability changed my body in quite extreme ways, never impacted the body issues I had.'

G saw penetrative or masturbatory porn of all kinds before he saw just two men holding hands. When he finally saw that, it was like something unlocked in him. 'Just seeing this piece of extremely boring, barely intimate comfort. I know a lot of men now who would only half-jokingly describe themselves as cuddle-sexual – the strange grey area of greysexual where gay domesticity, or dressing a certain way and contacting in a certain way, is gratification enough. I know men who pay to watch videos of other men walking their dogs in the park.'

Some people describe themselves as greysexual if they are completely asexual but still have sex. Others describe being able to go months or years without feeling sexual attraction or having any desire to have sex, only to wake up one morning feeling turned on.

'I think one of the largest problems was the understanding that sex means penis-in-vagina and that gay sex means penis-in-anus,' G explains. 'I had nobody to explain to me that this doesn't matter, that virginity doesn't matter. I felt like you had to want to do these things and I did not want to do them. As soon as I saw those two men holding hands, my sexuality widened again and I became more interested in "traditional sex". It's almost like I craved an adolescence, the fumbling normalcy of spending a few years dating boys with no expectations and without knowing what either of us wanted, that I could never have at the age of 14.'

One of the most confusing things to G was the fact that while he knew that he was definitely gay, he had no interest in penises or genitals of any kind. 'That was quite hard to bring up in casual conversation, so I simply acted as if it wasn't the case. I would now – finally! – describe myself as gay and pansexual, because I very much prefer a masc-presenting person, but I am quite superficial about it.'

The internet really transformed G's ideas around his sexuality. 'Most of my realisations needed the space of not having sex. Of reading and watching and understanding. If I wasn't disabled, I think I'd have a sex life that I was perfectly happy with. But I do think I can say: I'm pretty happy with myself now. Discovering other people who have spoken about their indifference to the received wisdom about what is the correct way to feel about sex and bodies and body parts, trans people's lived experiences...The idea that as a cis person, I could experience gender dysmorphia because I was not presenting the type of masculinity I wanted to be or that gender performance, gender euphoria and gender affirmation were universal. As for why I don't have sex now and haven't done for years – it is just because it's really uncomfortable and tiring.'

The topic of asexuality came up regularly among the many responses to the questionnaire. Some said they have had periods of wondering if they were asexual, since sex was utterly unappealing to them, while others found great comfort in realising that they were. For years, they had felt like there was something wrong with them. While compulsory heterosexuality refers to society's assumption that we are all probably heterosexual, compulsory sexuality, or allonormativity, means that we are all assumed to feel sexual attraction towards others and if you stray from this, you are somehow abnormal.

Amatonormativity is how we are all expected to seek out heteronormative, monogamous romantic relationships. Even though, just like some people feel no sexual attraction towards others, other people (or sometimes the same people) are aromantic and typically experience no romantic attraction. Some people are polyamorous and find that a monogamous lifestyle doesn't suit them. This is fine too. It is important to note that not all asexual people are aromantic and vice versa.

Also, both aromantic and asexual people can and often do have relationships. The term aceflux, for example, means that while you remain on the asexual spectrum, your sexual orientation fluctuates. Similarly with aroflux. You can even be aroaceflux, which means that both your romantic and sexual orientation can fluctuate, although you remain on the aromantic and asexual spectrum. Now, chances are, if you are a boring allosexual or alloromantic person like me, this might feel confusing. Which is why the asexual (and aromantic) community is fighting so hard to be understood by the rest of the world, so we should perhaps think twice before we try to impose our ideas of 'normality' on the next generation. I hope someone picks up this book in a vintage book shop in many years to come and, reading this, they are amazed to learn that there once was a time when we needed to have explained to us that not all people experience interpersonal relationships in exactly the same way.

B is a 31-year-old woman who describes herself as 'gay and maybe demisexual', mixed race and fat. She realised she was gay when she was 24 and until then, she'd had a low sex drive. 'I didn't realise it until my friends got older and hornier, then I just felt like the odd one out. But I figured stuff would happen when it would happen.'

B enjoyed sex with her girlfriend. 'Even if it was a bit of working everything out because I hadn't had sex before then. I don't buy into the whole idea of virginity, so I won't be using that language.'

Since then, B has only had one one-night stand with a woman: 'Which was nice, but I didn't really feel that sexy or turned on during it.'

For the longest time, B was convinced that a magical switch would just flick on and she would be as sexual as her friends. She found herself still thinking about sex, relationships and being in love a lot, so it was confusing to her that this did not translate to her body and desires.

'Sex with women also feels a lot less scary than sex does for my straight friends, who have to negotiate masculinity and the constant threat of male sexual violence. A lot of women close to me have been sexually assaulted or raped and that really coloured sex for a while. I feel much safer with women, so I kind of thought that maybe it is just about moving past that leftover fear – and perhaps with therapy and positive male friends, some of this fear would pass and sex would be on the table again. I also think the queer community is often hyper sexualised, or that in order to be accepted in the community, you have to want the same things as the heteronormative people – marriage, babies, being a couple, being in love and so on. It is all bollocks stereotypes, but it is so hard when your own community is based on a lot of sex-based stuff and you don't fit into that idea yourself.'

B found a therapist and brought all of her angst around sex to the sessions, with thoughts like: I should be having sex, I should be dating and why don't I feel sexy?

'We talked a lot about it and figured that I may be demisexual.'

Demisexuality is a term used to describe those who typically do not feel attraction to others unless they form a strong emotional bond with them first. They may still feel a romantic attraction but not usually a sexual attraction until the deep connection is formed. Some demisexual people define their demisexuality as them not being attracted to anything that is to do with sight, smell or other instantly available aspects of another person. They will only feel sexual attraction once they know more about the person. Simply put, it is the inside that counts. The word 'demi' means 'half' or 'partially', which is why it is often described as something between allosexual and asexual. Because we love a black and white world. We prefer a straight line from A to B. And we still refuse to see sexuality and gender as an ocean full of possibilities.

'Realising the nuances of asexuality has been really helpful for me,' explains B. 'It's like throwing the shackles off myself and realising that my brand of sexuality is different and valid. I guess my initial idea was that asexuality was: you're not into sex and that's that. But having had a partner and enjoyed sex with her, and thinking about sex too, made me assume asexuality wasn't right for me. However, demisexuality describes something much closer to my experience – having a strong romantic attachment that may lead to sexual feelings. It means I have accepted that I don't need to have sex to be an erotic being – it's just different. I realised that I'm not particularly interested in sex. I say I think about sex and relationships a lot, but if I really interrogated that, what I was thinking was, *this is something I should be doing*. If I actually concentrated on me, I was like, *oh, I'm not horny and I'm not actually desiring to be with another person.* Actually, shagging a person feels gross a lot of the time. I love the idea of love and romance, but I'm not that concerned if sex is or is not involved. I enjoy consuming media about sexual and romantic relationships – not porn, just books and films – but they don't reflect my feelings or my experiences. I am still disentangling where my feelings start and end and where the bullshit expectations from everyone else comes in.'

When B tries to tell people about this, she feels weird. A lot of people just assume she hasn't met the right person yet or they will compare it to their own experience of 'not really wanting casual sex either'. 'That's not how demisexuality works! This is why I feel weird when I tell people that I don't date and I don't want sex, particularly, but that I'd be open to a relationship if it happened. It's a work in progress. I do feel freer, though. I know myself better and I know my body better. I am cultivating the kind of life I want to lead outside of heteronormativity and the assumed sexuality of queer – and well, all – people.'

In my conversation with Miranda Kane, she asked me, 'Do you know what kind of sex you want?' and I hesitated for ages. The potency of this question shows up now, again, as I am curiously googling the vast list of sexualities. Knowing what kind of sex you want is hard, if you don't know who you want it with or what it takes for you to want it. Knowing that you are asexual or demisexual or greysexual – or queer or aromantic or even allosexual – can shift something inside of you.

I was so confused as a teenager, falling in love with my female classmates and friends without understanding what was happening or why. I wonder how many experiences I have missed out on because I wasn't open to all of the possibilities.

Labels are often criticised as being 'too restrictive' and perhaps they are. But they are also options. And explanations. Having a word that describes what you feel on the inside, in a world that expects you to feel differently, is liberating.

Finding a label, a word that fits, also helps find community. I cannot imagine anything more helpful to someone on a sexual journey to not only know what you want sexually (or don't want) and then find a room full of people who fit into that same category. What is community if not the antithesis of being and feeling alone?

6.

NEURODIVERSITY

I AM, TO SAY the least, reluctant to even look up the flirt-ologist who Miranda Kane recommended I speak to. The word 'flirtologist' reminds me of the word 'mixologist', which essentially just means 'fancy bartender'. I wonder what a flirtologist is a fancy version of. A Pick-Up Artist? A Love Coach? There is something about it I don't trust. Did you get your Flirtology Degree, studying Flirtology at the University of Finding Love? Stop making 'wink at someone from across the room' sound like a science.

However, this entire journey has been about learning, so I stop being stubborn and judgemental and instead buy her book. And while it is immediately clear that *Flirtology* is not directed at me – a nonbinary, fat, socially awkward, introverted, anxious, neurodiverse comedian – I decide that it is foolish of me to cross my arms and refuse to take *anything* on board. And as soon as I speak to Jean Smith, over Zoom, I understand why she is successful. She is good.

'I wrote a book called *The Flirt Interpreter,* where I used anthropological research,' Jean tells me. 'And I interviewed people in New York, London, Paris and Stockholm. And it's about the unwritten rules of English culture, about not being too familiar, about giving people space. And it's hard getting to know strangers if you're worried about being too familiar. It's a reserved culture. But on the other hand, it is a very polite and considerate culture, especially compared to the US, where I'm from, where it's very much every man for himself.'

I had not considered that my whole 'not being British' could be part of the reason I am in this sexless situation, but it makes sense. I come across *differently*, maybe more brass, too *familiar* because I still struggle to understand the British unwritten rules.

For example, one of the first things you are meant to learn when you arrive in the UK is that there is a pre-written script, a ritual if you will, that you have to follow every time you meet a person. They will say, 'Hi, how are you?' and you will say, 'I'm good, how are you?' to which they will say, 'Good.' If you stray from this script, you are booted straight out of the country and you will never see a Yorkshire pudding again in your life. It took me six months to learn this. In Denmark, if someone asks you how you are, it is because they want to hear how you are. When I first moved to the UK, I would answer honestly. *I am actually quite hungover today and I am feeling a bit homesick.* And then, quite crucially, I would not ask them how they were. To me, *that* would be the rude thing to do. They would know that I only asked because *they* had asked me. Instead, I logged it in my brain: *Bobby asked how I was, remember that.* Then, later that night, I would find the person and say a heartfelt, 'How are you?', hoping they had forgotten that they asked me earlier. If they just said, 'Good, how are you?', I'd probe. No, really, *how are you?*

I found it very hard to make British friends for the first six months I lived here, before I learned. It took me longer than normal to learn all of this because I am just not good with subtext.

You don't have to be Danish to be oblivious to British subtext. If you are neurodiverse, the social codes that underpin interactions like flirting may feel like a complete mystery. I am often (potentially mis-)diagnosed by strangers on the internet as autistic because I share many of the same difficulties and traits. There are several Venn diagrams online that show the vast overlap between PTSD and autism. Both autistic people and people with PTSD can experience dissociation, impulse control difficulties, difficulty managing intense emotions, sensory overload, intimacy difficulty and stimming. According to Dr Megan Anna Neff, an autistic psychologist, researcher and writer, the traits that are exclusive to PTSD sufferers include hypervigilance, nightmares, intrusive memories and flash-backs, and avoidance behaviours. Whereas autism includes repetitive behaviours and self-soothing through routine difficulty reading social cues and special interests.

According to PTSD UK's article, 'Can Childhood PTSD be Mistaken for Autism?', this overlap makes it easy to misdiagnose folks. For example, their Venn diagram shows that both autistic children and children with PTSD can experience outbursts, but for autistic children this could be due to their inflexible adherence to routines and insistence on sameness, whereas for sufferers of PTSD, it could be because of high irritability and hypervigilance.

It is of course possible to be *both* autistic and have PTSD or C-PTSD. Not to mention that autism, PTSD and C-PTSD all share symptom overlaps with other disorders like ADHD and BPD (bipolar disorder). I find it important to state that there is of course nothing *wrong* with having either of these conditions. When I say that I am not sure that I am autistic but that I think I just have C-PTSD, it is not because I look down on autistic people or because I *prefer* to have C-PTSD. It just feels like an internal knowledge that while I have a lot in common with autistic folks, I do not think I have it. That being said, give me another couple of years in trauma therapy and who knows what I will learn.

I know I have social anxiety which also, surprise surprise, has a big overlap on the Venn diagram with autism. According to Dr Neff, both autistic people and people with social anxiety share a discomfort of starting conversations, discomfort with parties, and social withdrawal and avoidance. Social anxiety, C-PTSD or autism – I cannot say.

'You say you can learn to flirt? That it's a skill? Is it something that always came naturally to you or did you have to learn it, too?' I ask Jean Smith.

'What I have discovered,' she replies, 'is that everyone has some things that just come really easily to them. But they come so easily that they don't actually realise it's a skill, or that it's anything special. I travelled the world when I was younger, backpacking, and I quickly learned that it was all about human connection. You know, I'm backpacking all by myself, so I can either sit in my room alone or actually meet people. So I forced myself to go out and speak to people and that required me to get through my 'mental models', which are these thoughts you tell yourself all the time – like, *if I go up to them they will think I am weird*. Basically, we do everything to not be rejected. And what I learned is that generally, for the most part, people don't reject each other, because as humans, we are born to connect. So yes, it has always come easily to me, but it was definitely made stronger because of my experiences. So what I have been trying to do is distil what exactly the steps are so that I can teach other people to do this, in a practical way. I cannot stress how powerful it is to work with these mental models, rather than just accepting them as they are. Like, this is just the way it is and there is no other way.'

I keep switching between two main thoughts: *Oh yeah, you're a beautiful, extroverted person, this is all easy for you to say* and *oh no, she might be right.* Since Covid in March 2020, I have spent the majority of my time indoors, whenever I can. I like my alone time, I like hanging out with my dog. And when I go out, I love headphones and looking at my phone. And one of the things I love doing when I am at home all alone, is telling myself that the outside world is full of people who are not interested in me. Yet, the day before my conversation with Jean, I filmed something for TV. After the shoot, a handsome man from the production team struck up a conversation. I was giving myself a headache trying to decipher if it was flirting or just kindness. There was definitely *interest.* And human connection. I realised that if I had been at home and seen a photo of him, I would have had an internal voice telling me that he would not look in my direction, even if it was just to be polite. As I have been writing this book, the presence of this voice in my head has become increasingly obvious and I am getting quite sick of it now. I wonder if it is boring to read an entire book that consists of one comedian asking hundreds of people if the voice in her head is right when it says she is unworthy of love and sex.

Jean Smith knows what she is talking about. She is an American who has managed to teach British people how to flirt. My curiosity gets the better of me and I ask, 'How on earth did you teach British people to flirt?'

'Actually,' Jean replies with a smile, 'I've taught Danish people to flirt and that was even harder.'

Oh. Oh, my smugness backfired.

'I do these Fearless Flirting Tours and I took them to Copenhagen. I have done them in so many different countries but I have never experienced anything like it. Before the tour, I was standing with two women in front of a supermarket during rush hour. We were just trying to stop people to ask them normal questions, like, 'Can you recommend a restaurant to go to?' just to get it started. And I could not stop anyone. People were in their bubbles. I couldn't even – I mean, I *created* this tour and *I* couldn't get anyone's attention. And what I realised about Danish people is that everyone has these big protective bubbles. Once you poke the bubble, people are so happy, they want to connect. But you have to persevere to get to that point.'

When I was in my early twenties, I worked in street fundraising. For several months, it was my job to stop Danish people in the street – and not just engage them in conversation but get them to donate money to charity. I feel oddly proud of my stubborn, socially hostile home country. And grateful that I was fired from that job because it *was* incredibly difficult getting people to stop.

'I find that it's so much easier to flirt in Denmark,' I say. 'I don't know how to explain this. Sexism is rife in Denmark, it's quite a backwards country in many ways, but gender roles are not as obvious as in the United Kingdom. Here, you are always referred to as "miss" and "ma'am" and "luv" and whatever; men hold the door for you and it's kind of 1950s in many ways. In Denmark, I am treated more… like a man? So I find it easier to flirt in Denmark because I can just be myself and flirt like myself and it isn't seen as a weirdly masculine thing. In Denmark, I can just say, "Oh hi, you're hot and I want to make out with you," and the other person will either laugh or say, "nah" and it will still be fine. If I did that here, I fear that the British people would just freak out because someone actually said something *real* to them.'

Jean laughs. 'The thing is, everyone wants someone to talk to them, they just don't want to be the ones to do it.'

Jean's Fearless Flirting Tours would not be fun for me. They would be Fearful Flirting Tours and would consist of me walking around sweating on strangers, avoiding their gazes and running away, faking a phonecall to get out of it.

I decide to be honest with Jean. 'When I first saw your book, I thought, *this isn't for me. I don't belong to the group of people that this is written for*. I don't think it's for the socially awkward, the neurodiverse, you know… Those of us who don't read social cues. Or even just for those of us who don't fit into the, sort of, heteronormative beauty standards.'

'Of course, you are right, Sofie,' Jean says, smiling. 'I am a heterosexual, 49-year-old, white woman. And I am not a millennial, so I look at the internet and think, *no. Let's all just go outside.* Because I am a social person. So you are right, it is written by me. When I was recording the audiobook, I asked the sound guy, "Do you think this book is for both men and women? Is it biased? Or is it just more of a female perspective?" I realised that most flirting experts are men. So there I was, one of the only women in the field, not even knowing if I was talking to *just* women, because we think women only talk to women, right? So I totally understand what you are asking.'

Internally, I am arguing with myself again. Yes, Jean is right, we're all treated differently based on whatever biases are associated with our gender or class or whatever, but there must be *some things* that surpass society's normativity. On a very basic level, human connection *must* be utterly universal. And while there are elements of Jean Smith's experiences and advice that will not make sense to me, some will.

'You've travelled the world doing this work,' I say to Jean. 'By now, you must have an answer to the question: what *is* flirting?'

'Other than my work in Europe, I have also lived in Japan for a year, I lived on the west coast of Ireland, I have lived in Istanbul. I spent almost a year in Australia. Six months in Singapore. And basically, flirting is about two people making each other feel good. Flirting is not a construction worker yelling, "Hey sexy" at a woman – that is harassment. Flirting is always *between* two people.

It doesn't have to have intent but it will have a bit of...
Oh, hang on,' Jean laughs. 'Look, even after all this time,
I'm still not 100 per cent sure!'

'Well, what's the difference between just being friendly
and then being flirty?' I ask.

'When you flirt you put a bit of sexuality into it. Now,
I know sexuality is a *big* word and people immediately
think of sex, but no; it's just that I am being a bit extra – I
don't even want to say "extra girly" because I am not being
girlish. I'm just being extra *me*. I put something extra into
the conversation that isn't necessarily nice or friendly.'

'I'm trying to figure out what the difference is between
saying to someone, "Hey, you look good, and then" –
I lower my tone, squint a bit and say – "Hey. You look
good." I think what scares me is that I can't always see
if someone is flirting or not. I hear it often from fellow
neurodiverse people – this fear that we will misunderstand
someone's intentions.'

Jean smiles excitedly – it is clear that this is her favourite
topic. 'Here's the thing, we will need to flip this around.
Instead of thinking, *how do I know if someone likes me?*,
we need to think, *how can you show someone that you
like them?* That is what we need to focus on. Now, when
I was writing *Flirtology*, years ago, my beautiful editor – I
love her so much – said to me, "Jean, we need to talk about
what happens when flirting goes wrong. For you it's easy,
you know your boundaries and you will just say 'fuck off'
if you need to; you can do that. The average person can't."

This is how I came up with the "test and assess" method and I think every person, every human should do this. Okay, so, let's say you're in a supermarket. The "test" is to say to someone, "Oh, have you tried this?" about a product. The "assess" is to give them space and see how they are responding to you. What's their body language? Have they moved towards you? Are they smiling? Are they asking you a question back? Or do they back away from you?'

It slowly occurs to me that I tend to make flirting about me. Understandably so, as I am terrified of the rejection, so I go into self-protection mode, which means that I only notice what affects me. Am *I* reacting perfectly? Am *I* showing them that I like them in a good enough way? It becomes a one-way performance rather than a two-way *connection*. I say to Jean, 'I like the idea of flirting being like a gift. You know, when you give a gift, you don't necessarily expect to get anything back. You are just giving someone something because you like them. If flirting is just telling someone they look good because you want them to feel good, then that's quite nice. If I knew that this person did not like me back in a romantic or sexual way, would I still want to tell them that they are pretty? And if you really like them, you would, wouldn't you? You'd want to give them that.'

'And then they can't reject you because you are not asking for anything,' Jean says.

'Right, but,' I offer, 'let's talk about rejection, though.

It feels incredibly crucial to my entire journey here: this incessant fear of rejection.'

'One of my friends recently divorced,' Jean begins. 'Her confidence was very low so she thought, *I need a confidence boost*. She signed up for a dating app, bought a new dress and spent a lot of money to travel into London and spend an evening with some random dude she met on this app. He wasn't a jerk, he was fine, but there was no connection and they were never going to see each other again. She knew this, he knew this. She went back home and was completely depressed because he never contacted her again. What this story tells me is that the problem with rejection is that we are giving other people the power to judge our self-worth. Another way she could have gone would have been to go to a yoga class at the gym, cook her favourite meal, take a bubble bath, drink some wine and go to bed early. Which of those two scenarios would have made her wake up feeling great about herself?

'So in a way, it's very simple, but what we end up doing is giving other people the power to judge if we are worthy, attractive, nice... So one of the things I do with my clients is we make a list of how we can nourish ourselves. On my own self-nourishment list are things like taking an epsom salt bath with lavender oil. Watching some of my favourite shows. Cooking my favourite food. Yoga. Rejection is a complex issue but I believe it starts with us taking care of ourselves. We tend to walk around with holes in ourselves and we go up to other people and say

"Can you fill this?" But if you are nourished, if you have done your self-care, we can fill it ourselves. And if we are not dependent on others to do it, then when we *do* go out and join the dating and flirting game, we can accept it a lot easier when someone is not interested. It's just like, okay, no problem, good luck, man.'

I used to do that a lot, which is probably a big part of the reason why I ended up letting so many toxic people and bad sex into my life. At times, I have to admit, I felt like I would die if I did not get that external validation. After a number of serious heartbreaks, it was as if I built a wall around my heart. I tell this to Jean. 'I feel like I am finally completely independent and I enjoy being alone and on my own. I have almost put it on a pedestal, that I can be alone and not rely on anyone else. And I am struggling to admit that human connection with other people really matters. And it is so difficult to separate needing external validation from still needing people. And I want these little connections, not to boost my self-worth, but to boost my mood. It's all about being seen, isn't it?'

'It gives me a spark,' says Jean. 'It makes me happy. And I like making people feel good.'

'Me too, actually. And if that is what flirting is all about, maybe it's not that scary.'

Before we end our call, Jean challenges me to stop wearing headphones in public and to try starting conversations with strangers. I tell her I will definitely consider it, even though the idea of standing in a supermarket saying 'DO YOU LIKE THIS ONION' sends my anxiety levels through the roof. I still cannot imagine doing that without coming across as a serial killer. And I am not sure I *want* to attract people who like being quizzed in the produce section on a Tuesday afternoon. Yet, in the following months, I keep thinking of it. I find myself *noticing* more people. Flirting is a *gift*. Rejection does not matter. Self-worth is not dictated by other people. And not even a leading flirting expert can get Danish people to stop in the street to have a chat, which makes me think that maybe my heart isn't cold and dead – maybe it is just Danish.

Jean's advice sounds eerily similar to Justin Hancock's comments about micro-moments of positive resonance. Noticing the little things, appreciating human connection. That sentiment has echoed throughout the book. Sex is about being in the moment, existing fully with another person. Yes, there is misogyny, trauma, horrible sex education, cowardly Comedians, societal biases, voices in our heads, gender and body dysmorphia, and it all takes us away from 'living in the moment'. It makes us believe we are unwanted and undesirable. And it takes up space, in the bedroom, with us. In our minds and bodies and relationships. The road to a (better) sex life was never about ignoring these very real issues. It was about circumventing them, fighting or dealing with them, facing them head on, coming to terms with them.

And then, when the dust has settled, all that is left

is the simple fact that underneath it all, we are all just humans wanting to connect with each other. It is about the moment. Sitting underneath olive trees wanking in your oneness. Reclaiming your sexuality and agency. It's about finding community. It's about *enjoying bodies*.

AFTERWORD

I AM PUTTING THE final touches to the book. Checking again and again that all names have been changed. Two months ago, I cut off my hair. When the barber shows me the new, short haircut from a mirror behind me, I cannot stop smiling. I run my fingers through my hair and make it sit in different ways and say, 'I can make myself look like each member of Westlife.'

I make spikes. 'Look, Nicky, *ano* 2001.'

I ask, 'Do you think, if people walked behind me, they'd sometimes accidentally say, "Sorry, sir"?'

'...Would you like them to?' my barber carefully asks.

I smile and say, 'Yeah, that might be nice.'

The next couple of days are confusing. Almost instantly,

I do not feel like wearing makeup. My long, dangly earrings that I loved only a few days ago suddenly seem old. Like artefacts I have recovered from a buried treasure from another life. Perhaps another universe, one in which I would put on makeup, have long hair and wear earrings. I put most of my makeup, all of my hair clips and hair bands, and all of my long, dangly jewellery in a box and put it away. It takes an afternoon.

Three days ago, I would have felt unattractive if I left the house without makeup on. Now, I can only feel attractive if I leave without it.

For a week, I am in bed crying. I cry to my therapist that I am *not* sad, so I don't understand this. She suggests I could be grieving the loss of something. I add that I am also scared. There is something vulnerable about my new look. I am *more me*.

I am editing the book and it feels strange that I used to care about these people, these men. I want to delete any mention of them. I try to embrace the person I used to be while coming to terms with feeling so different now.

I have not yet had sex. It has been 3,000 days today. When I originally pitched the book for the first time, three years ago, I wanted the book to end with me going to an orgy. It would be fun, I thought. I would gradually, over a year or so, work towards being confident enough to go to an orgy, where I would probably engage in some kind of hot, sexy gangbang.

I am sitting in my living room, listening to music,

finishing the book while drinking hot chocolate, and feeling my dog napping by my feet, and I am thrilled that I am not at an orgy. I thought the goal was to have sex, when really, it is to become emotionally ready to have sex in a safe way with a safe person. I believe I am there now. I am not at an orgy, I am just in a place where I can say 'no' (or 'maybe') to sex if it doesn't feel right. It is not as exciting an ending as 'and then I was railed by ten people in a basement', sure, but for me, it is a much bigger deal.

There is a person I am flirting with. It is no more than flirting and it will probably not become more than flirting. They are nonbinary, like me, and it feels effortless and safe. I am not anxiously pining for them and we are aware of each other's boundaries and we respect them. It doesn't scare me. It makes me confident that if not them, then someone will come along, and I can flirt with them and maybe we will kiss and maybe we will do more. Small, exciting steps, of which some will be sexy steps and others will be comforting or safe steps. Maybe some of the steps will be a bit scary. I am sure, when the sex does happen, it will feel like the very first time.

THANK YOU

MOST IMPORTANTLY, I NEED to thank my dog, **Hank Hagen**, for pissing on the floor to warn me about shitty men, even when I wouldn't listen. For patiently sleeping by my feet when I was up past our bedtime finishing this book. For listening to *The Little Shop of Horror* soundtrack on repeat because my brain decided that's the only music I can write to, when he really prefers Chopin. For being a better man than most human men I have met.

I owe my editors **Susannah Otter** and **Lucy Tirahan** a huge thank you, both for their help with writing this book, but also for their patience and kindness. You received a broken writer who flat out refused to actually send you the book for ages, out of fear that you would hate it and somehow you never shouted at me to calm the fuck down. You made me feel confident enough to write again, which is really nice, when I would like to be a writer some day. People can say what they want about this book, but no one can say I didn't finish it.

Everyone else at **Blink Publishing** has been equally great and deserves my gratitude and love.

Thank you to **Liz Marvin** for copy-editing this book with a lot of patience and thoroughness. Sorry That I Like Writing Sentences Like This So You Had To Change All Of It Only To Have Me Change It Back Because I Think It Looks Funny. I'm Sure This Sentence Annoys You, Especially Because It Suddenly Changed Tense As Well. Wasn't That Annoying? Also, I'm Writing This After You've Finished The Job, So You Won't Even Get A Chance To Edit This.

Carly Cook, my super cool literary agent, I can't figure out if I admire you more than I fear you, but it is all surmounted by love and appreciation.

A huge thank you to **Justin Hancock, Chantal Gautier, Miranda Kane** and **Jean Smith** for taking time out of your schedules to let me ask you a bunch of questions, some of which I am sure made you want to roll your eyes. Your contribution to this book and thus my (sex) life means the world to me. Thank you for wanting to guide me and others. A big thank you to **Ersties** too, and particularly **Cat,** for letting me into your little porn world, where sex is beautiful and fun. Thank you for trusting me.

Thank you, **Juno Roche,** not just for letting me chat to you for the book, but for existing in this world, just like you are. And for *seeing me* in a way I have not often been seen. I cannot thank you enough for your words.

Jodie Mitchell, I am singling you out, too, because not only did you let me chat to you for this book *and* do the sensitivity reading, you are also one of my best friends and I love you so much. I consider it a privilege to exist in your orbit, daddy.

My manager **Chris Quaile,** my comedy agency **IAM** and my content creation agent **Charlotte Euzenat** – a big thank you for letting me say, 'Sorry, I can't do that, I'm writing a book' for almost two years, when you then clearly saw me posting about watching *Desperate Housewives* on Instagram Stories. Um, excuse me, but a lot of writing is actually *thinking about writing* and I consider *Desperate Housewives* to be *research, actually.* Thank you for being so supportive and cool.

Quentin Le Fevre (French Brutus) – fuck me, these past two years did not turn out the way we thought or hoped they would, but I am endlessly proud of you for being a person who grows so consistently and gracefully. Thank you for awakening my ovaries enough that after we met for the first time, I went home and wrote 10,000 words then and there. While I am thankful for your general friendship and all of that, blah blah blah, I am slightly disappointed that this book didn't have a romcom ending where we ended up making love and getting married. It would have been *SO GOOD* for the narrative, but probably *SO BAD* for our friendship.

My therapist, **S.**, who is so good, I am not going to put their name here, in case you all swoop in and offer them more money so they leave me for you (yeah, yeah, we will need to work on those abandonment issues, S.). Or kidnap them and force them to tell you how my face looks when I cry. But S., I can confidently say that this book would not exist if it wasn't for you. That's a risky remark because what if it utterly stinks and gets awful reviews? Then this feels like I'm blaming it all on you? Yeah, yeah, we will work on those catastrophising thoughts (but what if I'm right? Some books DO FLOP!). I can't wait to spend the next (probably) decades solving everything in this brain of mine with you. Also thank you so much for checking the whole trauma-chapter to make sure I wasn't spreading misinformation. One day I will win therapy and never cry again, I promise.

Thank you to my good friend **Daniel Foxx**, who just so happens to be texting me nice things while I am writing these acknowledgements, so I feel like, fuck it, why not thank him, just for being a good friend? It's my book, I can do what I want.

Thank you to **Johnson H.**

But the most special of thank yous go to the **1,800 people** who shared their stories with me, just because I asked. If I had the time, I would have emailed every single one of you personally to tell you how brave you are, how strong you are, how you deserve the best things that life can offer. Fuck, I'm still blown away. Your stories shaped this book and my entire writing process. I wish I could have shared all the stories but this book is already *way too long*. Thank you, from the bottom of my heart, for trusting me.

FURTHER RESOURCES

You can find more information about **Chantal Gautier** on her website: www.chantalgautiertherapy.com

Find **Miranda Kane** and all of her projects, including Club Indulge and her podcast Smut Drop on: mirandakane.co.uk.

For more on **Jodie Mitchell,** follow them on social media on @jodiemitchetc or go see their drag king shows via pecsdragkings.com.

Justin Hancock lives on justinhancock.co.uk – go get his books and follow him on social media.

WILL I EVER HAVE SEX AGAIN?

Juno Roche has no website or social media (legendary behaviour), but please read their books *Queer Sex, Trans Power and A Working Class Family Ages Badly.*

You can find more information about the lovely **Jean Smith** on jean-smith.com.

Go have fun with **Ersties** at ersties.com.

You can find **French Brutus'** sexy stuff (!) on OnlyFans and PornHub and he is @thefrenchie_1 on Instagram.

I highly recommend these books about/related to sex: *Rough* by Rachel Thompson, *Sex Ed* by Ruby Rare, *Sex Up Your Life* by Julie Archambault, *Tomorrow Sex Will Be Good Again* by Katherine Angel, *The Sexual Healing Journey* by Wendy Maltz, *The Art of Receiving and Giving: The Wheel of Consent* by Betty Martis, *The Right to Sex* by Amia Srinivasan, *The Incel Rebellion* by Lisa Sugiura and *The Sex Lives of African Women* by Nana Darkoa Sekyiamah.

If you like books and me, Sofie Hagen, you can listen to my podcast **Help Hole** wherever you get your podcast. I talk self-help books with my friend comedian Abby Wambaugh. It is a lot of fun.

REFERENCES

INTRODUCTION
Emily Nagoski (2015). *Come As You Are*. London: Scribe
Publications.

SEXUAL MISEDUCATION
Meg John-Barker and Justin Hancock (2017). *A Practical
Guide to Sex: Finally, Helpful Sex Advice*! London: Icon
Books Ltd.

Justin Hancock (2021). *Can We Talk About Consent?*
Beverly, Massachusetts: Frances Lincoln Children's Books.

WILL I EVER HAVE SEX AGAIN?

Nick J. Fox and Pam Alldred (2013). 'The Sexuality-Assemblage: Desire, Affect, Anti-humanism'. *The Sociological Review*. https://journals.sagepub.com/doi/10.1111/1467-954X.12075 (Accessed 15.01.2024.)

SEXUAL TRAUMA

Georgina Lee (2018). 'Men are more likely to be raped than be falsely accused of rape'. *Channel 4 News*. https://www.channel4.com/news/factcheck/factcheck-men-are-more-likely-to-be-raped-than-be-falsely-accused-of-rape (Accessed 15.01.2024.)

Home Office news team (2019). 'Violence against Women and Girls and Male Position Factsheets'. *Gov.UK*. https://homeofficemedia.blog.gov.uk/2019/03/07/violence-against-women-and-girls-and-male-position-factsheets/ (Accessed 15.01.2024.)

Pamela J. Sawyer PhD, Brenda Major PhD, et al. (2012). 'Discrimination and the Stress Response: Psychological and Physiological Consequences of Anticipating Prejudice in Interethnic Interactions'. *American Journal of Public Health*. Volume 102. pp. 1020-1026. https://ajph.aphapublications.org/doi/full/10.2105/AJPH.2011.300620?role=tab (Accessed 15.01.2024.)

Rachel Thompson (2021). *Rough: How violence has found its way into the bedroom and what we can do about it*. London: Square Peg.

Liv Moloney. 'Off Limits: Is Rape the Perfect Crime?' *Sky News*. https://news.sky.com/story/99-of-rapes-reported-to-police-in-england-and-wales-do-not-result-in-legal-proceedings-why-12104130 (Accessed 15.01.2024.)

EVAW (2018). 'Major new YouGov survey for EVAW: Many people still unclear what rape is'. *End Violence Against Women*. https://www.endviolenceagainstwomen.org.uk/major-new-survey-many-still-unclear-what-rape-is/ (Accessed 15.01.2024.)

Radhouane Achour, Marianne Koch, et al. (2019). 'Vaginismus and pregnancy: epidemiological profile and management difficulties'. *Psychology Research and Behaviour Management*. Volume 12. pp. 137-143. https://www.ncbi.nlm.nih.gov/pmc/articles/PMC6419599/# (Accessed 15.01.2024.)

Peter T. Pacik and Simon Geletta (2017). 'Vaginismus Treatment: Clinical Trials Follow Up 241 Patients'. *Sexual Medicine*. Volume 5(2). https://www.ncbi.nlm.nih.gov/pmc/articles/PMC5440634/ (Accessed 15.01.2024.)

GENDER

Amrou Al-Kadhi (2019). *Life as a Unicorn: A Journey from Shame to Pride and Everything in Between*. London: 4th Estate.

Chaka L. Bachmann and Becca Gooch (2018). 'LGBT in Britain: Trans Report'. *Stonewall*. https://www.stonewall.org.uk/system/files/lgbt_in_britain_-_trans_report_final.pdf (Accessed 15.01.2024.)

Jay McNeil, Louis Bailey, Sonja Ellis, James Morton and Maeve Regan (2012). 'Trans Mental Health Study 2012'. *Equality Network*. https://www.scottishtrans.org/wp-content/uploads/2013/03/trans_mh_study.pdf (Accessed 15.01.2024.)

Juno Roche (2018). *Queer Sex: A Trans and Non-Binary Guide to Intimacy*. London: Jessica Kingsley Publishers.

BODIES

Naomi I Eisenberger (2003). 'Does Rejection Hurt? An FMRI study of social exclusion'. *Science*. Volume 302(5643). pp 290-292. https://pubmed.ncbi.nlm.nih.gov/14551436/ (Accessed 16.01.2024.)

Allyson Chiu (2022). 'How to make self-affirmation work, based on science'. *The Washington Post*. https://www.washingtonpost.com/wellness/2022/05/02/do-self-affirmations-work/ (Accessed 16.01.2024.)

Janine Dutcher et al. (2016). 'Self-Affirmation Activates the Ventral Striatum: A Possible Reward-Related Mechanism for Self-Affirmation'. *Association for Psychological Science*. Volume 27(4). pp 455-466. https://www.janinedutcher.com/uploads/4/1/3/8/41383683/dutcher_et_al_2016_psychosci.pdf (Accessed 16.01.202.)

David A Frederick, et al. (2017). 'Differences in Orgasm Frequency Among Gay, Lesbian, Bisexual, and Heterosexual Men and Women in a U.S. National Sample'. *Archives of Sexual Behaviour*. Volume 47(1). pp. 273-288. https://pubmed.ncbi.nlm.nih.gov/28213723/ (Accessed 16.01.2024.)

Ana Carvalheira and Isabel Leal (2013). 'Masturbation Among Women: Associated Factors and Sexual Response in a Portuguese Community Sample'. *Journal of Sex and Marital Therapy*. Volume 39(4). pp. 347-367. https://www.tandfonline.com/doi/full/10.1080/009262 3X.2011.628440 (Accessed 16.01.2024.)

Laurie Mintz (2018). *Becoming Cliterate: Why Orgasm Matters*. New York: HarperOne.

Laurie Mintz (2023). 'The Orgasm Gap and Why Women Climax Less than Men'. The Conversation. https://theconversation.com/the-orgasm-gap-and-why-women-climax-less-than-men-208614#:~:text=This%20is%20called%20the%20orgasm,heterosexual%20women%20said%20the%20same (Accessed 16.01.2024.)

Jevan Hutson et al. (2018). 'Debiasing Desire: Addressing Bias and Discrimination on Intimate Platforms'. *Proceedings of the ACM on Human-Computer Interaction*. Volume 2(73). https://www.karen-levy.net/wp-content/uploads/2018/09/Debiasing_Desire_published.pdf (Accessed 16.01.2024.)

Lynette Rice (2017). 'Shonda Rhimes opens up about weight loss… begrudgingly'. *Entertainment Weekly*. https://ew.com/tv/2017/06/26/shonda-rhimes-weight-loss-newsletter/ (Accessed 16.01.2024.)

Ronald Alsop (2016). 'Fat people earn less and have a harder time finding work'. *BBC Worklife*. https://www.bbc.com/worklife/article/20161130-fat-people-earn-less-and-have-a-harder-time-finding-work. (Accessed 16.01.2024.)

SM Phelan et al (2015). 'Impact of weight bias and stigma on quality of care and outcomes for patients with obesity'. *Obesity Reviews: An official journal of the International Association for the Study of Obesity*. Volume 16(4). pp. 319-326. https://www.ncbi.nlm.nih.gov/pmc/articles/ PMC4381543/ (Accessed 16.01.2024.)

Kim Wong-Shing (2023). 'Fatphobia is killing us. What will it take to end it?' *CNET*. https://www.cnet.com/ health/fatphobia-is-killing-us-what-will-it-take-to-end-it/ (Accessed 16.01.2024.)

SEXUALITY

'Am I a Lesbian? Masterdoc'. *Tumblr*. https://heystacks. com/doc/308/copy-of-am-i-a-lesbian-masterdoc (Accessed 16.01.2024.) – This has seven tumblr urls at the bottom, here they are just in case:
https://veganscully.tumblr.com/
http://thatdiabolicalfeminist.tumblr.com/
http://cyberlesbian.tumblr.com/
https://closet-keys.tumblr.com
http://positive-lesbian-vibes.tumblr.com/
https://adviceforwlw.tumblr.com
https://butch-kira.tumblr.com

NEURODIVERSITY

Jean Smith (2012). *The Flirt Interpreter: Flirting Signs from Around the World*. Lucidus Publishing.

Dr Neff (2023). 'PTSD and Autism'. *Neurodivergent Insights*. https://neurodivergentinsights.com/misdiagnosis-monday/ptsd-and-autism (Accessed 16.01.2024.)

'Can childhood PTSD be mistaken for autism?' *PTSD UK*.https://www.ptsduk.org/can-childhood-ptsd-be-mistaken-for-autism/ (Accessed 16.01.2024.)